THE ILLUSTRATED GUIDE TO BETTER FISHING

By Bob Zwirz

DBI BOOKS INC., NORTHFIELD, ILLINOIS

Publisher
SHELDON FACTOR

Editorial Director
JACK LEWIS

Production Director
SONYA KAISER

Art Director
DENISE HEGERT

Art Associate
DANA SILZLE

Production Coordinator
BETTY BURRIS

Copy Editor
DORINE IMBACH

Contributing Editor
MARK THIFFAULT

Produced By:

Arms and Armour Press, London, G.B., exclusive licensees and distributors in Britain and Europe; Australasia; Nigeria, So. Africa and Zimbabwe; India and Pakistan; Singapore, Hong Kong and Japan.

ISBN 0-910676-38-0

Library of Congress Catalog Card Number 81-70997

CONTENTS

ACKNOWLEDGEMENTS

I wish to thank all of our loyal friends in the tackle industry, plus the vast fraternity of anglers with whom we've fished, worldwide, for these many years. It is from such sportsmen and the free-giving spirit with which they shared long-held fishing secrets that my own knowledge and success in the sporting field has evolved.

Our personal gratitude goes to the exceptionally helpful people at Zebco, and to Berkley and Company, makers of Trilene monofilament. Both of these organizations granted permission for our use of line art and data that had been researched by their staffs as well as field-testers of their product line.

It also must be acknowledged that over the past several years a number of states and foreign governments have sent their own photographs along so that appropriate photos would be available to illustrate the articles and books I've produced on both freshwater and saltwater fishing. Without their assistance, there would have been far more time spent behind my own cameras than behind a rod.

And last but certainly not least, I wish to thank my wife, Glad, who so often shares dawn and dusk, sun and rain to be at my side, be it on a wild river, impoundment or an uncomfortably rough ocean. It is all too often this lady who rewires boat trailers, washes decks after a frenzy of fishing activity – and gets to pull up a reluctant anchor. It is also this same lady who for twenty-seven years had wielded every type of fishing tackle and taken a lion's share of trophy fish. Even more important, to me, is the amazing fact that this same Glad has clearly shown that a wanderer who fishes, hunts and works with firearms for a living is exactly the kind of guy with whom she'd share the hearth.

Bob Zwirz

INTRODUCTION

ANY PERSON can be a successful angler if he stops occasionally to observe the natural way of life in fish-inhabited waters, then learns to use the knowledge he has gleaned to best advantage.

At one time or another we all have met those misguided novice fishermen who, striving for some sort of answer to the proper artificial lures, flies or baits, have accumulated several hundred pieces of assorted hardware and literally pounds of neatly tied fur-and-feathers.

Then there is the king-size closet-and-a-half crammed full of rods and reels that cleverly worded advertisements have sworn must be possessed if we harbor any hopes of fishing success. The sportsman who gives way to this glossy fantasy practices not the art of a discerning fisherman, but has instead become a collector.

Culling through such a bewildering collection while floating aimlessly atop some massive freshwater impoundments, or by the side of what has turned out to be an unproductive streamside pool, has caused most of us to feel frustrated and complain, "If I only could operate with a few truly productive lures and baits in a sensible number of winning colors what a different game this could be."

When you add saltwater fishing to our agenda while realizing that spinning, bait-casting, fly fishing and the presentation of natural baits are all part of the widely knowledgeable fisherman's far-reaching domain, then you clearly realize that oversimplification of tackle and methods will never be in the cards. Not unless you limit yourself to either fresh or salt water, then go a step further and lock yourself into a pattern of fishing for only a very few of the game fish available.

A sunfish is one critter, a tarpon something else, just as a snapper blue can be held in your fingers, while some great marlin are so massive as to be a problem for some anglers to put aboard a smaller craft.

In this book, we shall attempt to reduce to the basics all that is possible. And without neglecting the popular game fish that have long remained all-time favorites. Further, we shall carefully examine the new tackle, baits and allied equipment that have brought almost unbelievable sophistication to a sport that uses electronics and all manner of wizardry to produce record catches for those who learn their lessons and take fishing seriously.

The chapters that follow will be kept as basic and simple as possible; will take you through the world of knots and lines, modern and long-proven lures and baits, the fishing methods that produce heavy stringers and even a few techniques not all that familiar to a great number of knowledgeable fishermen.

However, a sense of responsibility forces me to bring certain facts to your attention. These facts demand examination, as they endanger one of the oldest sports.

Simply explained, the same breed of non-realists that wish to ban all forms of hunting, now have talked to God concerning fishing. They wish to teach our children that you and I are sadistic murderers that kill fish wantonly and almost entirely for kicks.

One of the lovely ladies behind a group called The Kindness Club (KIND), Hope Sawyer Buyukmihci, has prepared anti-fishing propaganda that has been widely circulated to grammar-school children throughout America.

Are sportsfishermen perverts? Is sportfishing evil? Ask some of the school children brainwashed by these and other groups that preach to our youngsters while they are a captive audience beyond parental control. The pamphlet, interspersed with Bambi-like "little fishy" cartoons, urges young readers to press adults to stop fishing! The following are several paragraphs that will give you an idea of the type of psychology used in such campaigns:

A FISH is a little animal like you except that to him water is like air to us.

Once two Chinese men were watching some fish. "Look how happily the fish are jumping in the water," said Chuang Tse. "That is the fish's joy." Hui Tse said, "How can you know the fish's joy?" "I know the fish's joy from my joy when I watch them from the bridge," said Chuang Tse.

When we see someone riding a new bicycle, we know just how he feels. When we see a person stub his toe or cut his finger, we know how that feels too. If we put ourselves in the place of any living creature, and use our imagination, we know how he feels, even if he doesn't look just like us!

When a fish is caught on a cruel hook, he tries desperately to get away. He is fighting for his life. Is it sporting for a big human being to laugh and call that fun? When they've begun to THINK, many grown-ups who used to fish, have given it up, and now instead of killing, they find fun in studying fish just as Chuang Tse did.

In clear water much can be learned by watching fish from above. Those who swim under water are able to look through a window in their headgear and study them in their homes, disturbing them as little as possible of course.

If you know people who just won't give up fishing even when you tell them, it's not right to kill anything "just for fun," ask them to use artificial flies instead of living worms, who have feelings too. And beg them to put the fish back in the water, or at the very least, to kill it AT ONCE.

To kill a fish strike it on the head with a stick or a beach rock to put it out of its misery as quickly as possible. Or, put your thumb in its mouth and bend its head backwards, thus breaking its neck.

It's hard, isn't it, to call such killing "kind" – but it's better than allowing the poor creature to flop up and down until it finally gasps out its life.

When we find ways of having fun that do not cause pain and death to any other living beings, we'll all be happier! In the meantime –

HOW WOULD YOU LIKE TO BE A FISH?

In the area of fishing, we may have some responsible people looking out for our interests. Congress is currently considering bills S.546 and H.R.2250 that would help crush any anti-fishing movement directed at U.S. school children. The most outspoken advocate of the proposed legislation is Ray Scott, president of the Bass Anglers Sportsman Society, a national fishing organization with more than 385,000 members.

"Until now, fishermen haven't had an effective way to combat the fanatics who seek to destroy sportfishing," says Scott. "As a result, many of our youngsters, especially those in lower grades, have been brainwashed into believing that fishing is wrong, even sinful. We adults should be ashamed we have permitted that to happen. It won't continue happening, though, if Congress acts favorably on the Dingell-Johnson expansion bills. But I hate to think of the image that schoolchildren will have of sportfishing if the bills don't pass."

Since 1950, Scott explains, fishermen have been paying a ten percent excise tax on purchases of rods, reels, lures and creels. Under the expansion, anglers would pay ten percent on virtually all tackle items, and three percent on depthfinders, certain boats, outboard motors and boat trailers. The tax money collected by the federal government – an estimated $80 to $100 million – would be channeled to the states and used exclusively for much-needed fisheries and improvement projects: stocking, reservoir construction, boat ramp construction and maintenance, research and pollution control.

"The list of taxable items must be enlarged," says Scott. "Otherwise, we won't be able to adequately sustain our fisheries resource or provide safe boating access to our waters. The fishermen – the guys who will foot the bill – are for the expansion, and so are President Reagan, Vice President Bush and Interior Secretary Watt."

One of the bills' most important provisions allows states to allocate up to ten percent of their D-J money for youth-oriented aquatic education programs, to include species identification, water conservation, preservation of the fisheries resource and basic fishing techniques.

"Children then will be exposed to the truth about fishing," says Scott. "They will learn to appreciate its joys; they will learn that fishing isn't sinful; that it isn't cruel; that people who fish aren't perverts. Passage of the D-J expansion bills would mean defeat for the anti-fishing crowd who are on record as being against the propagation of a specie for what they call sporting slaughter."

Besides the anti-fishermen, other opponents of the D-J expansion include the National Marine Manufacturers Association and the American Fishing Tackle Manufacturers Association. The latter two groups are fighting passage of the bills, says Scott, "because they're more interested in short-term profits than in the future welfare of fishing or the long-term recreational pleasures of fishermen. They're so shortsighted that they're willing to sacrifice fishing merely to gain a few immediate dollars. They're simply greedy."

As far as I'm concerned, these two groups have jumped – perhaps unknowingly – right into bed with the anti-fishermen, the same people who are trying to poison our children's minds against the sport, and the same people who have been successful in hampering dove hunting and deer hunting in several states. Can you imagine that: the boating and the fishing industry aligned with the anti-fishermen? It's sad. Actually, it's criminal.

"But I'm convinced," continues Scott, "that the D-J expansion will pass if America's fishermen and boaters write their congressmen and express their strong support of the measure. That's something we owe to ourselves and our children."

To this I say, Amen!

Bob Zwirz,
Ridgefield, Connecticut

CONNECTION WITH SUCCESS

The Correct Line, The Right Knots Will Contribute To Your Take Of Fish

IF YOU could ask an Egyptian fisherman from 2000 B.C. what kind of fishing line he was using, he'd probably reply, "braided Arabian horsehair!"

I can remember my grandfather complaining bitterly about the problems associated even then with the early braided natural-fiber lines, recalling the nuisance of having to pre-soak those old silkworm gut leaders and post-dry their natural silk braided lines.

Today's fishermen wouldn't mind swapping the quality of fishing available in pre-World War II, but how many would be willing to trade their present tackle for what was available forty years ago? Maybe the good ol' days were not that great.

The first major indication of better fishing lines surfaced in the late 1930s with a totally new class of synthetic fiber-forming materials known as polyamides. Another word for polyamide is nylon.

Nylon monofilament fishing lines have been around for nearly thirty years. At first most of the nylon came from one company, but by the mid-Fifties, many firms were making general-purpose nylon. During this time, a northwest Iowa tackle manufacturer began secret research, both above water and underwater, to perfect the next breakthrough in nylon chemistry. Their work focused on specialty fishing lines from unique systems called "nylon alloys."

To take something as good as nylon line and make it better for the fisherman, the most important advancement would be to make it stronger. Those good old nylon monos

On the bank of the Rio Parana separating Argentina from Paraguay, author hooked, played and landed savage dorado with Penn reel, Berkley line and big spoon.

Opposite page: Chris Houston, 1980 Angler of the Year Trilene/Bass 'N Gal Award, demonstrates winning form to her daughter, Sherri. You can bet that Chris knows line selection and knots.

Fishing with author in Florida, this vivacious lass shows she knows her bait-casting tackle, line and terminal knots (above). While pup doesn't seem impressed, Zwirz was!

were twenty-five percent or more weaker than the general-purpose nylon available today.

Compare that early line against the nylon alloys used to make the premium line of today. Modern alloy lines have one hundred percent higher break strength. That's twice as strong as the line your father used when new Chevrolets were selling for $1200.

"Just how strong can you make a nylon fishing line?" The Trilene fishing scientists, where the patented alloy lines were developed, are asked that question often. In theory, they should be able to make new nylons that, size-for-size, would be twice as strong as the strongest alloy lines known today. If that were achieved, our grandchildren might look back on the lines of the early 1980s and smile.

Fishermen aren't usually polymer chemists, but they sure understand the benefits of having stronger, yet thinner lines. They know stronger, thinner lines catch more fish, but will the tackle industry be able to meet this demand?

The Trilene chemists remind us that, while there are many different kinds of nylon being made by numerous companies, the majority use chemical building blocks which are derived from crude oil. Once these molecular Tinker Toys are depleted, where will our fishing lines of the future come from? What will these lines be like? Are we living in the golden years of sportfishing? Will the day come when we wished we had saved a spool of today's line?

Research by serious sportfishermen, coupled with the fantastic strides within fishing tackle companies have brought us products, proven research data and the latest in how-to facts that help improve our angling skills and knowledge of equipment, its care and use.

Industry cooperation brings about a trade of research data that goes beyond helping the corporate entities. The

The little things often make difference between success or failure on the water. For example, below are shown two wire leaders, swivels and snaps. Top one, of chrome, is visible even to depths of 40 feet. Compare it with Black Cross-Lok snaps, black wire and black swivels held in bottom hand.

facts and pro-tips they discover make our fishing forays that much more rewarding.

These two companies have joined hands in what has turned out to be the fishing tackle industry's largest promotion. When a giant reel manufacturer such as Zebco is filling those reels with Berkley's Trilene line, you've got front page news in any industry.

Both companies view this relationship as having all the right ingredients for success. They look toward increased sales that Trilene's brand acceptance and quality image will generate for their reels. A company spokesman relates, "Of all the premium monofilaments tested, only one stood out in all the important performance categories. That was one Berkley's Trilene. Its thin diameter means increased line capacity and less water drag. Extra strength assures the

Again in South America, Zwirz successfully tries fly rod on dorado. He made custom tapered leaders from varying pound-test Trilene monofilament when he ran short on trip.

angler of maximum fish fighting control. That's why this line is so popular among tournament fishermen."

There are a number of reasons why such a marriage as this took place. It is, however, logical that a 1981 comparative analysis of the break strength properties of eight premium monofilament fishing lines – and the end-result – would cause any fishing reel manufacturer to take notice.

Watch your line for abraded spots caused by contact with coral, sand, rocks or stickups. A weakend line will not get a big snook like this guy into the boat and deep-freeze.

Material Tested

Five spools each of eight different brands of 10-pound-labeled nylon monofilament fishing line were evaluated. The spools of line were identified as follows:

1. Trilene XL
2. Trilene XT
3. Stren
4. Sigma
5. Gladiator
6. Royal Bonnyl II
7. Maxima
8. Ande

These spools of line, purchased by Berkley from different geographical areas across the United States, were supplied to Springborn Testing Institute, Incorporated, in unopened, original packages with the purchase date, price and area of purchase on each package of lines.

Testing and Sampling Procedures

The packages were opened at Springborn Testing Institute and sampled as follows:

From each spool, a total of ten samples, each one yard in length, was removed at ten-yard intervals. Each one-yard sample was cut into two one-half-yard test specimens. The remaining nine yards were retained. The two one-half-yard specimens were identified and collected for subsequent

Fishing smallmouth bass and landlocked salmon on Palfrey Lake, New Brunswick, author shows that a "connection with success" is both important — and fun! Others seem to agree.

testing. In this manner, twenty one-half-yard test specimens were removed from the outer one hundred yards of each of the forty spools of line.

The tensile break strength tests were run on an Instron tensile testing machine. All test results were recorded on a strip chart so that a permanent record could be kept of the tests.

The Instrom was calibrated, throughout testing, with a five-pound weight approved by the National Bureau of Standards. The minimum diameter of each test specimen was determined after the specimen was clamped into the test apparatus. This diameter measurement was made using a machinist micrometer calibrated with measurement blocks also traceable to the National Bureau of Standards.

The tensile break load in pounds divided by the cross-sectional area of the fishing line in square inches ($in.^2$) gives the tensile strength in pounds per square inch (psi) of the fishing line. This value gives a true measurement of the line strength. The higher the psi tensile strength number, the stronger the line.

SUMMARY OF TEST RESULTS
TENSILE TESTS

Sample ID	Average Diameter (in.)	Average Dry Break Load (lb.)	Average Tensile Strength (psi)
Trilene XL	0.0113	13.1	130,600
Trilene XT	0.0124	15.0	124,200
Stren	0.0118	12.1	110,600
Sigma	0.0120	12.3	108,800
Gladiator	0.0120	12.2	107,900
Royal Bonnyl II	0.0122	12.2	104,400
Maxima	0.0139	15.7	103,500
Ande	0.0111	9.7	100,200

Samples were tested after storing a minimum of 40 hours at 23 ± 2°C and 50% ± 2% relative humidity.

Conclusion

On a size for size basis, it was concluded that Trilene XL is: 18% stronger than Stren, 20% stronger than Sigma, 21% stronger than Gladiator, 25% stronger than Royal Bonnyl, 26% stronger than Maxima, and 30% stronger than Ande.

As you read this chapter, we'll discuss such subjects as selecting mono line, spooling it, setting of drags, fishing knots and how to make them work for you. Much of this information has been the result of more than twenty years of study and testing by Berkley fishing scientists and their research team. Paul Johnson, vice-president for Berkley and Company, Incorporated, has been responsible for much of the information in this chapter.

Selecting Monofilament Line

Dozens of firms manufacture various types of nylon, each type specially formulated for a specific use. But only a handful of companies make monofilament fishing line, each utilizing a process that involves extruding nylon material.

With standardized procedures, most line manufacturers produce a fishing line that offers similar performance benefits. Anglers find it difficult to distinguish between various lines, because they are so similar. And even though each manufacturer's label claims his line contains some or all of the same properties, fishermen have no way of knowing how these properties have been balanced or how they will affect the line's performance.

At Berkley, the Trilene research team has discovered new nylon alloys that produce a superior fishing line. Testing of the new alloys has showed that fishing line performance depends on more than a dozen different physical properties, seven of which are critical. Researchers found that every angler must rely on break strength, stretch, knot strength, uniformity, stiffness, abrasion resistance and color. Varying fishing conditions put different demands on the line.

To select a premium monofilament fishing line, you have to know the conditions you'll be facing, what species of fish you're after and the equipment you'll be using. Then you can determine which of the seven critical line properties – or what combination – will be most beneficial to your fishing needs. To help make that decision, here's a rundown of the seven critical properties:

Break Strength – What you see isn't always what you get. Lines are sold by break strength and the label might read 6, 8 or 10-pound test and so forth, but that's not the actual break strength of the line. Nationally known brands usually break above the label rating. This is because nylon monofilaments lose strength when they are immersed in water. Depending on the nylon, some line will be ten percent weaker or more.

The label designation for premium monofilaments is based on *wet* strength rather than dry strength. Some manufacturers take advantage of this by "underrating" their lines. They do this by selling line of larger diameter and heavier break strength with a label that lists it as a lower pound test than it really is. The result: a fisherman may think he's getting a much stronger line, but he's not. Underrated lines typically have larger diameters and excessive stiffness.

Stretch – When a fish hits and runs on a nylon monofilament line, the line's break strength is put to the test; so is its ability to stretch. Strength and stretch go hand-in-hand under actual fishing conditions. The stretch serves as a shock absorber to keep the line from breaking, but once stretched to capacity, the line will break.

Fishing line with too much stretch may appear to be really tough when dry. Put it in water and it will stretch like a rubberband, making it difficult for the fisherman to set the hook. A line with little stretch is just as bad. This type may have a high break strength compared to its

It may be "Chinese Fire Drill" when two anglers' lines tangle, but that wasn't the case here. These three heavy bluefish hit author's multiple sand eel rig, often called an umbrella rig. Hand-tied of monofilament the umbrella rig took brutal beating from battlers, but knot failed not.

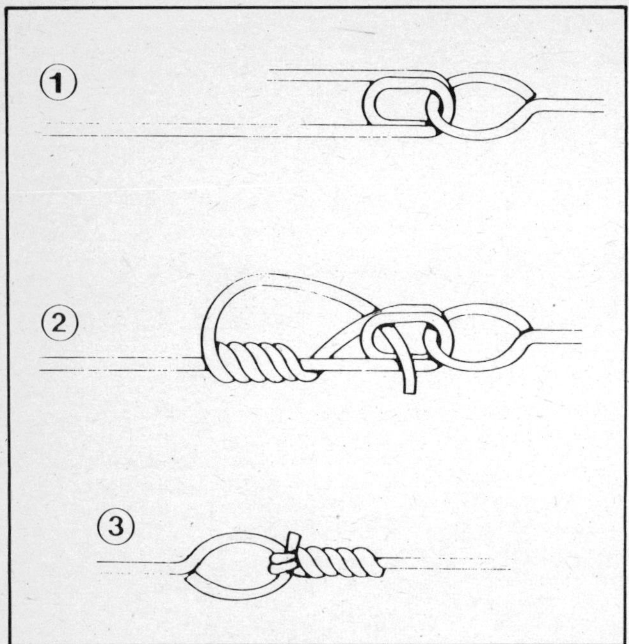

The Trilene knot is recommended when using Trilene line, and it provides a dependable general-purpose knot with 85-90 percent of the original line strength. It's easily tied.

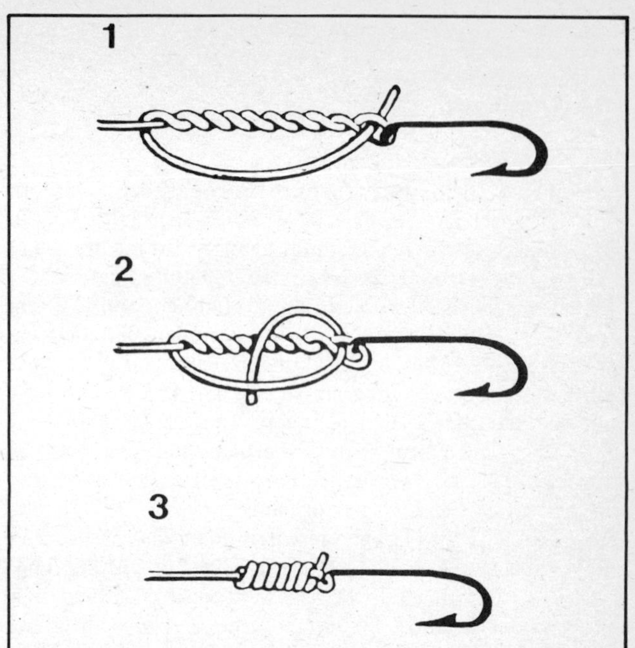

The improved clinch knot is an all-time favorite, though not as strong as today's newer knots. Seven wraps with a line under 17-pound-test, five with higher test, are best.

diameter, but it will lack shock absorption and prove to be brittle. A good premium fishing line should have a proper balance of strength and stretch, with neither property exaggerated. When one property is increased to the extreme, problems occur.

Knot strength poses a more complex problem. You can find lines that have excessive stretch coupled with good knot strength, but they perform poorly under fishing conditions. If you want maximum knot strength, you must begin the manufacturing process with the right nylon molecules.

King sling knot creates an end-loop knot used primarily with stickbaits or crankbaits. Knot enables angler to get optimum action from lure by letting it work freely in water.

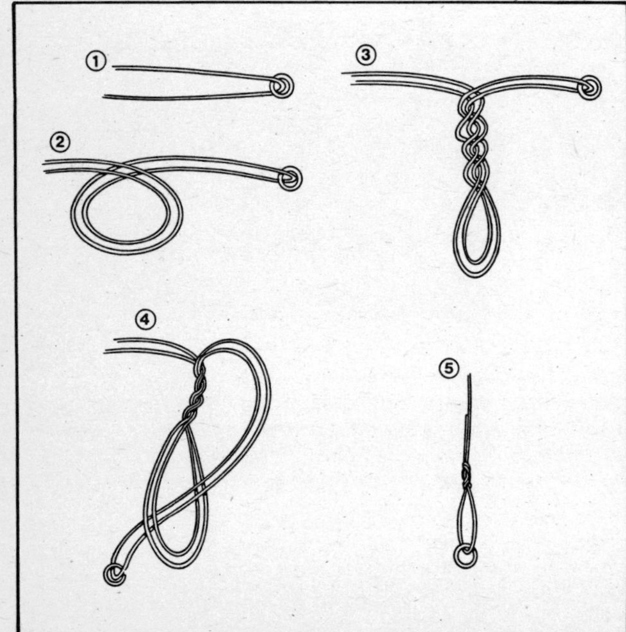

These nylon alloys provide exceptional knot strength. The unusually tough, abrasion-resistant surface layer on these alloys (visible under an electron microscope) helps prevent knots from slipping. That's why maximum knot strength starts with the brand of line you buy and ends with the kind of knot you tie. Even the best lines can be severely damaged by a poor knot. Learning to tie a consistently strong fishing knot will be time well spent, but exercise a little caution when dealing with knot strength. A line's *wet* strength should be the determining factor when you're getting ready to tie on your favorite lure.

Uniformity – If you could test a hundred-yard length of any nylon monofilament inch by inch, you would discover that some areas are stronger, others weaker. That's one reason why a ninety-nine-cent spool of mono may not be the bargain you think it is. Economy-grade line is much less uniform than premium monofilament. Even among the premium grades, there is a difference. Like a chain, monofilament line is only as strong as its weakest section.

Uniformity varies from brand to brand. If you measured the diameter of two different brands of line at frequent intervals, you would find variations. It takes great skill in the manufacturing process to produce a nylon monofilament line with consistent uniformity.

Stiffness – Under actual fishing conditions, especially in cold water, you can recognize the effects of stiffness easily. Wiry lines coil and spring off the reel in loops and snarls even among fishermen using the best rods and reels.

Suppleness and lack of "memory" or "curliness" are two significant features of the Trilene nylon alloys. Fishing lines of these alloys are meant to provide greater casting performance and more natural lure presentation.

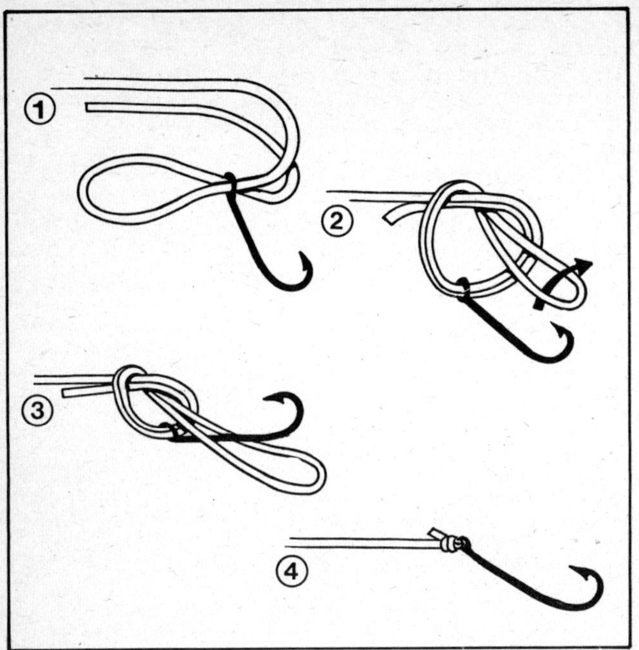

Double wrap of monofilament through eyelet of Palomar knot – as with Trilene knot – provides protective cushion and added safety factor. Palomar gives 85-90 percent strength.

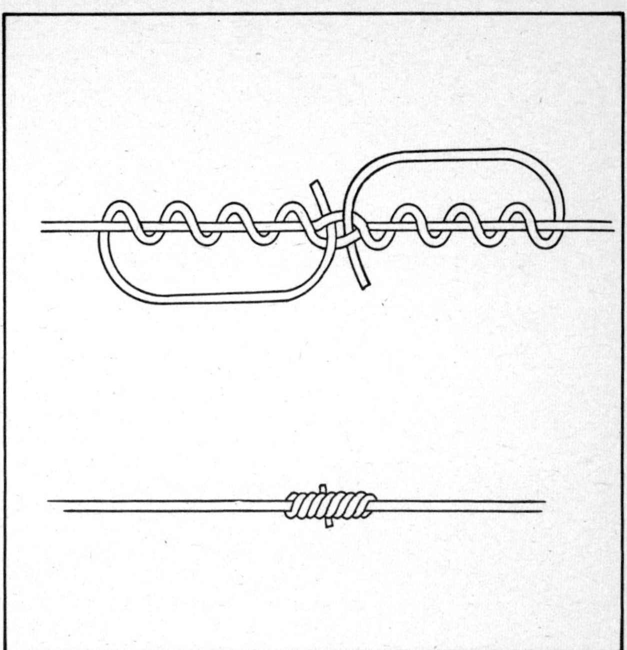

Connect lines of similar or differing diameters with the improved blood knot. It's been around for years. Knowing how to tie it can save your fishing day if you need joint.

Abrasion Resistance – This property protects the line from nicks, cuts and scrapes that can be inflicted by rocks, logs, fish teeth, gills and other underwater abrasive surfaces. Simply, abrasion resistance helps keep the line from becoming weak.

Measuring abrasion resistance in a fishing line can be misleading. Laboratory tests cannot come close to simulating actual fishing conditions.

Color – This is one property in fishing lines one can see and measure. Some fishermen believe a line should be invisible underwater. Others think they should be able to see the line at all times. No matter which you prefer, one aspect is obvious: regardless of color, there is no such thing as an invisible nylon monofilament line. Fish are capable of seeing any fishing line. That's why it's wise to remember that a line's appearance is important above and below the water's surface.

Another aspect is the color of the water. Water colors vary greatly, from the transparency of a window pane to blue, green and even chocolate.

Lines can be colored three ways. The cheapest is simply to dip the monofilament in a dye solution, making sure the dye penetrates the surface of the material. This method is fast, but the color fades quickly when the line is exposed to natural sunlight. Since most anglers fish during daylight hours, this type of coloring isn't practical.

Powdered colorants can be added to the nylon pellets prior to melting. This gives the line a uniform, rich-looking appearance and resistance to fading. In a third method, chemicals are made to react with the nylon molecules. Thus, the color becomes chemically incorporated into the nylon, producing high-visibility colors that are long-lasting and fade resistant.

The human eye sees some colors better than others. Look at a range of colors going from dark blue through green, yellow, orange and red and your eye responds best to colors in the yellow/green spectrum.

When fluorescence is added to a fishing line, it makes it easier to see. The line soaks up light from the sun, then discharges it, making the line brighter and more visible. A fluorescent fishing line seems to glow above the water's surface, but fluorescent lines continue to glow underwater, too. Some line colors actually will spook fish.

If you've wondered about the type of knot to use to attach reel to line, try easy-to-tie arbor knot. It's a quick and easy method for attaching line. Follow diagram directions.

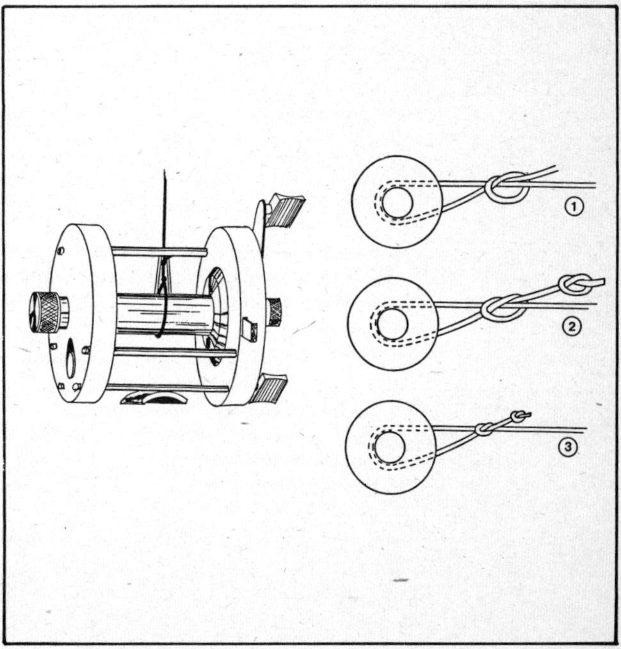

The reasons for using, and how to tie the Albright knot, are given at right.

Albright Knot

The Albright Knot is most commonly used for joining monofilament lines of unequal diameters, for creating shock leaders and when a Bimini Twist is tied in the end of the lighter casting line. It is also used for connecting monofilament to wire.

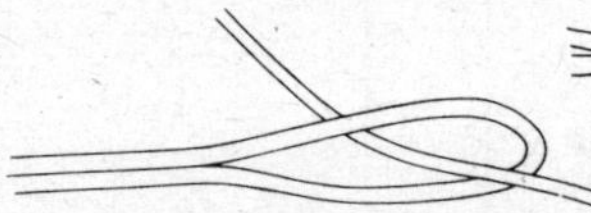

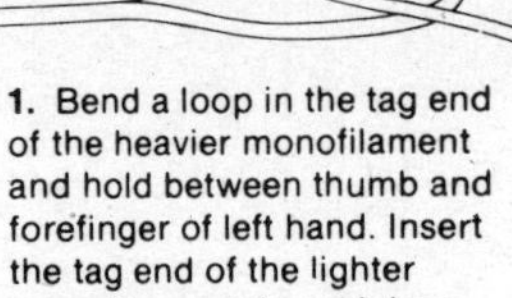

1. Bend a loop in the tag end of the heavier monofilament and hold between thumb and forefinger of left hand. Insert the tag end of the lighter monofilament through loop from the top.

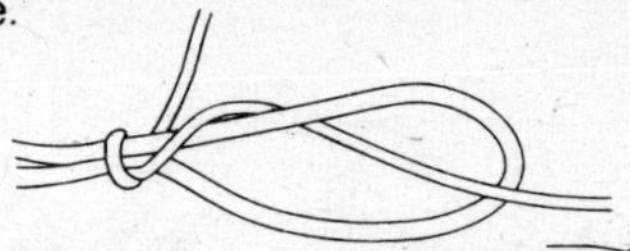

2. Slip tag end of lighter monofilament under your left thumb and pinch it tightly against the heavier strands of the loop. Wrap the first turn of the lighter monofilament over itself and continue wrapping toward the round end of the loop. Take at least 12 turns with the lighter monofilament around all three strands.

3. Insert tag end of the lighter monofilament through end of the loop from the bottom. It must enter and leave the loop on the same side.

4. With the thumb and forefinger of the left hand, slide the coils of the lighter monofilament toward the end of the loop, stop 1/8" from end of loop. Using pliers, pull the tag end of the lighter mono tight to keep the coils from slipping off the loop.

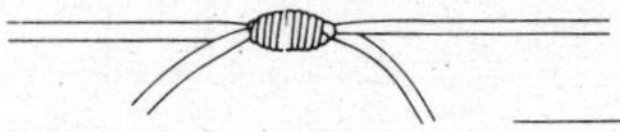

5. With your left hand still holding the heavier mono, pull on the standing part of the lighter mono. Pull the tag end of the lighter mono and the standing part a second time. Pull the standing part of the heavy mono and the standing part of the light mono.

6. Trim both tag ends.

Useful with a leader is the snell knot. Easily tied as shown here.

Snell Knot

The Snell Knot provides a strong connection when fishing with bait and using a separate length of leader. (You can only use a Snell Knot with a leader.)

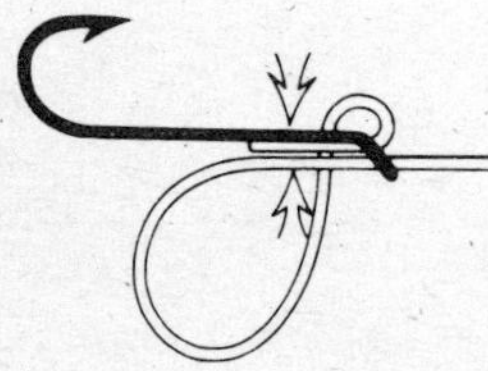

1. Insert one end of the leader through the hook's eye extending one to two inches past the eye. Insert the other end of the leader through the eye in the opposite direction pointing toward the barb of the hook. Hold the hook and leader ends between thumb and forefinger of your left hand. Leader will hang below the hook in a large loop.

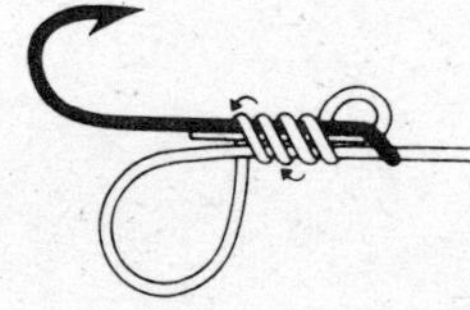

2. Take the part of this loop that is closest to the eye and wrap it over the hook shank and both ends of the leader toward the hook's barb.

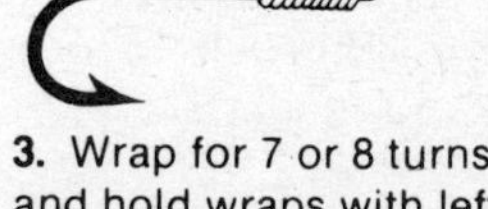

3. Wrap for 7 or 8 turns and hold wraps with left hand. Grip the end of the leader that is through the eyelet with your right hand and pull it slowly and steadily. Hold the turns with your left hand or the knot will unravel. When knot is almost tight, slide it up against the eye of the hook. Grip the short end lying along the shank of the hook with a pair of pliers. Pull this end and the standing line at the same time to completely tighten the knot.

4. Trim the tag end.

For that reason, choose fluorescent lines carefully. While a fluorescent lure might attract fish, a glowing fluorescent line can have the opposite effect. Fluorescent colors range from bright gaudy yellows and oranges to more subdued blue shades. Research indicates that fluorescent blue/green lines work better, even though they may glow underwater.

In waters where bass feed on shad minnows and other bait fish, studies show that fluorescent blue/greens can attract fish. The same research demonstrates that bright yellow lines appear to alarm bass, contributing to lower catch rates when used.

Underwater Trilene research indicates that clear monofilament works best in clear water where fish have a tendency to spook easily. The same nylon alloys with a high-visibility blue/green fluorescent coloration seem the appropriate choice when you have to watch your line for signs of a subtle strike.

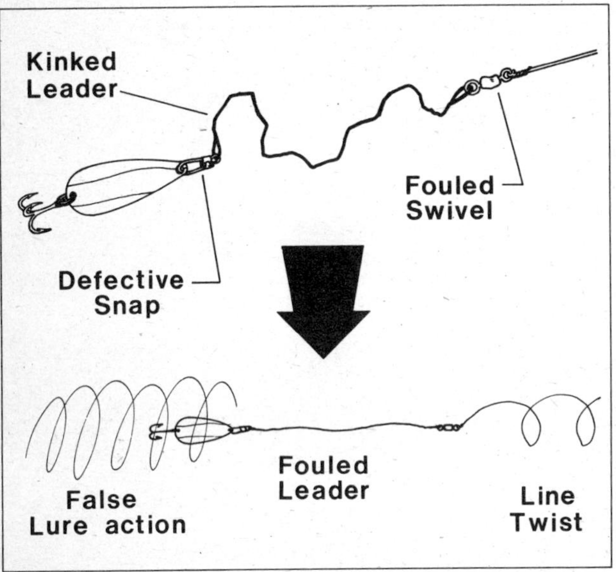

Problems you can encounter with leaders and swivels.

No one has written the final word on line colors yet. But natural, uncolored nylon monofilament has become more popular. The only drawback is that most uncolored lines are milky. The new Trilene nylon alloys, however, offer unusual underwater clarity in a natural, uncolored monofilament. A clear line is always a wise selection when in doubt about water conditions and colors.

The Line That's Right – Now that you're better acquainted with the seven critical properties, you're ready to choose a premium fishing line. But before you do, consider all the factors involved: type of fish; location – lake, river or salt water; water conditions – clear, open, muddy, heavy vegetation, submerged trees, rocks, etc.; equipment – tackle, lures, reel, rod. Which combination of the seven critical line properties would prove to be the most beneficial?

One line can't match every fishing condition you might face. A line that claims to possess just the right balance of all seven properties isn't practical. A compromise is necessary. Some conditions require a line with high abrasion resistance; for others, castability is more important. But the one element that every good premium line should have is overall strength, the most important performance feature of any fishing line.

Refer to the seven critical properties. Keep in mind that a line with a smaller diameter is less visible to the fish and offers more spool capacity and better total performance.

Spooling Up – Engineers design reels to be fished with a full spool of line. A properly filled spool will afford longer, more accurate casts, better drag performance, a wider range of drag settings and more line to successfully play a fish. Even the best reels misbehave when spools are less than half full.

There are advantages in having the dealer fill your reel using a line-metering machine, because it spools line evenly and under the proper tension. But you also have the option of buying bulk spools or filler spools and filling your own reels.

Deciding on the proper pound-test line is easy if you consider the type of fishing you plan and the size of the reel you will be using. If you are going to fish where there are obstructions or for big fish, you'll need heavier line. Line diameter also must be matched to the reel spool. Ultra-light and mini reels use small-diameter monofilament (6-pound test and under). Spin-cast or push-button reels work best with medium-break-strength lines (6- to 14-pound test). Bait-casting reels perform well with monofilament in the 10- to 30-pound range. Remember that the new nylon alloys can be used at slightly higher pound tests because of their smaller diameter.

If you fill your own reels, the simplest way is to slip a pencil through the center of the bulk spool and have someone hold it while you crank the line on the reel, allowing the bulk spool to rotate freely.

Overfilling can be as troublesome as underfilling. Put too much line on the spool and it will balloon off and tangle. To prevent overfilling, here are a couple of tips: On bait-casting reels and other conventional models, fill them until the line reaches the point where the top of the spool begins to flare outward. The line on a correctly filled spinning reel should stop within one-eighth-inch of the lip. Spin-casting reels never should be filled above the level of the spool.

Reel spools should always be filled under uniform minimum line tension. Applying excess tension has the same effect on a spool as wrapping a rubberband around your finger. Each succeeding wrap causes increasing compression on those underneath. Too much build up can burst or permanently warp a metal reel spool.

Some reel spools with large capacities can be expensive to fill completely with line. Advanced anglers have a remedy for this situation. They wrap a core of heavier braided line around the reel, tie it off, then put the monofilament on top of it. The braid acts as a cushion and reduces the pressure on the hub of the spool. When you change the line on your reel, jot down the date and the line's pound test on a piece of tape and stick it on the reel foot. It'll serve as a handy reminder just as the sticker in your car tells you when the oil was changed last.

Setting The Drag On Your Reel – Some fishermen always seem to catch big fish on small diameter lines. One reason is that they use the best, most uniform monofilament they can find. But the basic reason for such success is that they have mastered the art of using the drag on their reels. Advanced anglers know the right drag control can help put them in command of any fishing situation; mastering drag control should be just as important to you.

To keep the line from breaking, the drag assembly on your reel must yield line while still allowing you to maintain control. Once you know how to set the drag correctly, you should be able to play a strong fish on a light line successfully.

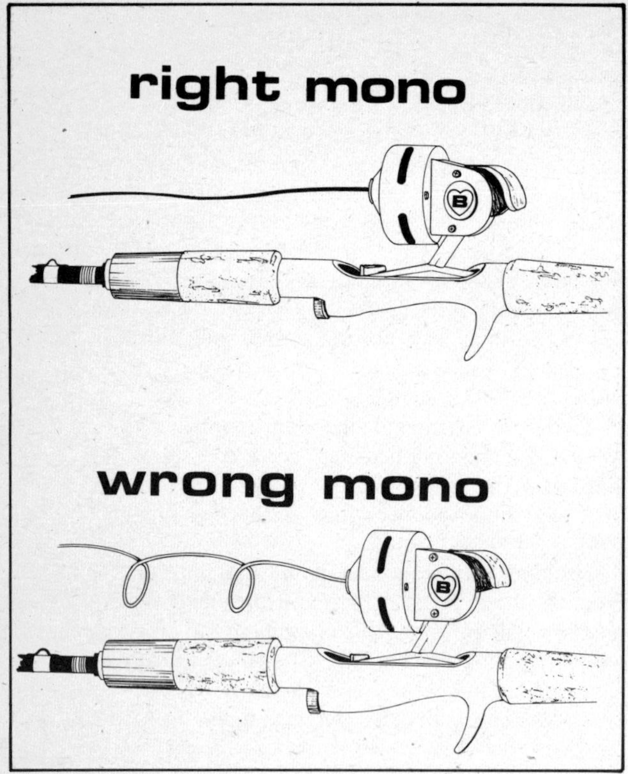

This shows how mono should – and shouldn't – come off.

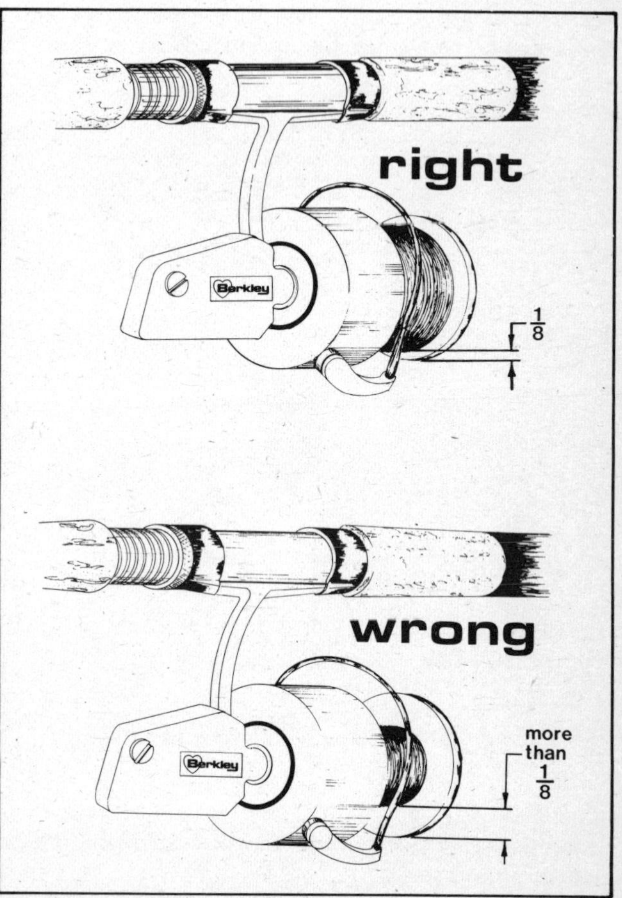

Too little or too much line on spool can influence casts.

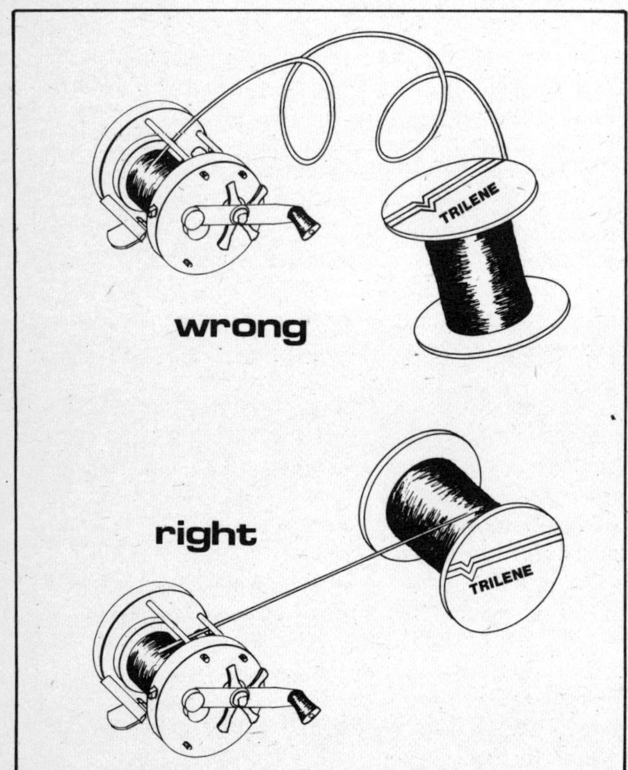

Correct spooling determines how line will come off reel.

The key is to set the drag properly before you start fishing. Here's how to do just that:

Put the reel on the rod and run the line through the guides. While holding the rod at a forty-five-degree angle, as if fighting a fish, have a friend pull on the line. As the line is pulled, adjust the drag-setting knob or wheel until the line flows a moderate line tension. If you need additional drag while fishing, place your hand against the reel spool.

If you have a scale, hang the end of the line on it and measure the amount of tension, with the rod *pointing directly at the scale.* The Trilene research team recommends the drag be set at twenty-five percent of the rated break strength of the line.

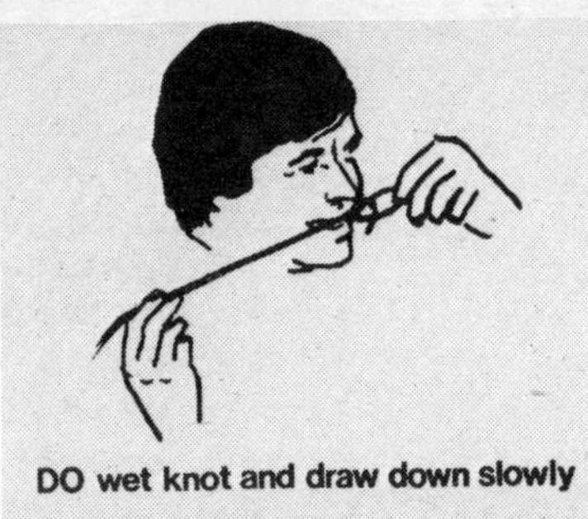

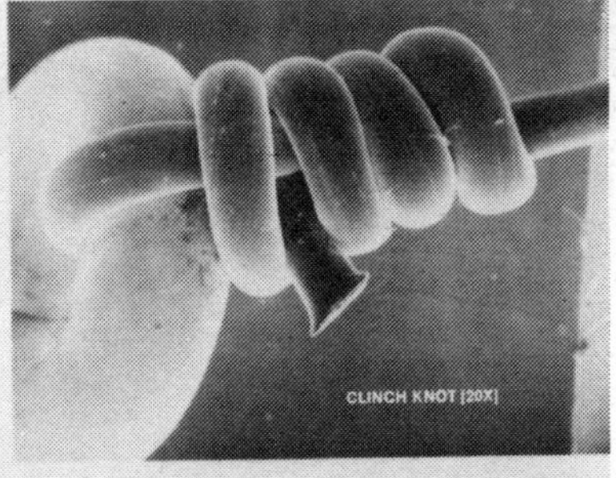

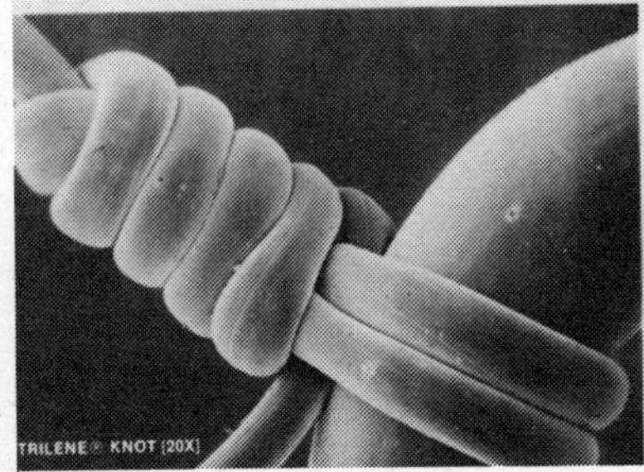

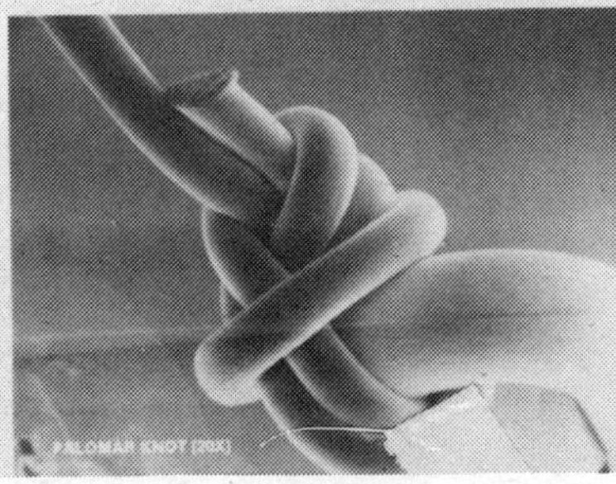

Closeups of knots discussed, magnified twenty times by Berkley lab technicians.

It takes more force to start the drag slipping than to keep it slipping. When you first set the hook, you'll have maximum drag resistance, but as the fish runs, drag resistance drops. Test your reel's drag design to become familiar with it. Know how much knob adjustment to make and how to decrease drag on a strong, running fish.

Many people are surprised to learn that a reel's drag resistance increases as a long-running fish empties the reel. The common mistake is to tighten the drag in an attempt to stop the fish. Usually, the line breaks before the fish stops.

What one should do is to loosen the drag as the fish takes more line. This reduces tension on the line and will also extend the life of your reel's drag control. And it's another reason why it's important to start with a full spool of line.

Spotting a faulty drag is easy. Watch the rod tip top, while a friend pulls the line. If it bounces up and down, the drag assembly is either defective, needs lubrication or is improperly set and poor for fishing. With a well-lubricated, properly set drag control, the rod tip should dip in the direction of the pull and remain almost stationary as additional line is pulled off.

To expect top performance from your reel's drag, you must take care of it. Inspect it after each trip and clean the drag assembly frequently. (Silicone spray can work wonders in smoothing out sticky reel drag.) Grit and dirt can destroy smoothness and a faulty reel drag control can undermine the best line and tackle.

Tight Knots Work Best – Good knots will fail if they are not tied right. The Trilene research team has discovered that a knot in monofilament will begin to slip just before it fails. Knowing this, it makes sense to draw a knot up as tightly as you can. The drawing process should be slow and steady, using water as a lubricant to reduce friction and help the turns in the knot slide easily.

Experiments have shown that human saliva can weaken knots in monofilament line. If you cinch up a knot too fast, you can generate enough heat to weaken the knot. Speaking of heat, some fishermen insist on burning the tag end of the monofilament with a cigarette or a lighter. They reason that a "knob" on the end will help prevent slippage. This practice actually causes more harm than good. The flame frequently burns the knot or heats it, reducing the break strength of the line.

After you have tied a knot, examine it closely. If it doesn't look right, cut it off and retie it. If you think it might be weak, pull on it. It's better have a knot break or slip in your hands than when depending on it to hold a fish. When trimming the tag end, use a pair of cutting pliers or nail clippers. But be careful; anglers sometimes nick the knot or adjacent line while trimming, weakening the knot or line.

A *tag end* is the part of the line in which the knot is tied. Think of it as the shorter end of the line. It also refers to the excess line that remains after a knot is tied. Distinguished from the tag end, the *standing part* is another name for the main length of line or the longer piece. A *turn* or *wrap* is one revolution of line around another. It simply means passing the tag end around the standing part.

Knot-Tying Checklist – Before you start practicing your knots, here are some helpful tips to keep in mind:

1. Clip off any damaged section of line before you make a new tie, usually about two feet.
2. Check the hook or lure eye for barbs or rough spots.
3. Use plenty of working line when tying a knot.
4. Tie your knot wet. This allows the knot to cinch up smoothly without kinking or weakening the line.
5. Tighten the knot with a steady, even motion without hesitation.
6. Pull your knot up tight.
7. Don't trim too close. Leave at least one-eighth-inch of line at the knot.

The illustrated knots are relatively simple to tie, are reliable and provide good knot strength. With a little practice, you'll tie them with confidence.

Line must be checked continually for abrasion, weakness due to snagging, exposure to sunlight over long periods, even improper storage habits. Faulty rod guides or burred reel surfaces are all contributing problems. A cracked carbide or ceramic guide cuts running or stressed mono like a razor.

MODERN LURES AND BAITS

Artificials Are Nearly As Old As Civilization, But Even Today's Products Can Be Improved Upon By The Knowing Angler

WHETHER THE lure you decide to tie onto your line is one of those tested and proved over the years or one of the constantly changing, excellent designs introduced during the late Seventies or early Eighties, one basic requirement will remain: The big trick is in choosing the best lure from among the six or so basic types available to both freshwater and saltwater anglers.

Your fishing success certainly will not be improved if you are presenting surface lures/baits when the species you seek are feeding or lying suspended at a depth far below. Certainly as much of a time-waster is to discover you are presenting a bait down among the bottom cover while spring water temperatures have brought game fish species into relatively shallow waters where a lure only a foot below the surface could bring savage strikes from fish on the feed after a hard winter and a reduced diet.

Over the many years since plugs and lures became serious business among fishing tackle manufacturers, general requirements for artificials were pretty well agreed upon – they must be either highly convincing imitations of the natural food eaten by the various species or of a design referred to as a disturber. An imitation of natural food is simple for anyone to understand, but what is this disturber-type lure?

Simply explained, most game fish can be pushed into striking at an artificial lure out of pure, unadulterated anger. Chosen correctly and presented wisely, your lure brings out the aggressive side of the fish; he wants it out of his domain, or he may simply want to kill the obtrusive critter. There are times when a species' need to feed takes a back seat to their psychological necessity to take and hold the advantage.

Opposite page: The wobbling spoon, sized according to the quarry sought, imitates a fleeing bait fish upon which fat, predatory lunkers like steelhead here feed.

Canadian guides call this artificial "The Beaver," and it's intended to resemble a baby beaver or perhaps small muskrat. It's fooled many a wary muskie into striking savagely.

By and large the majority of long-famous lures were, and the newer ones still are, designed to appear as life-like as a natural item upon which that species normally feeds. To go a step further, you'll find that great care is taken by makers of artificial baits in order to come up with the closest color combos, plus an act-alike resemblance in such areas as natural action, movement through or on the water, transmission of realistic sound to the fish's senses. Of late, built-in odors trigger an acceptable response on the part of fish you seek.

This is a hawg bass that was fooled by surface plug the angler presented in natural manner, then manipulated just right. It takes practice, but that's all part of fishing!

This matter of fooling fish into striking a hook is no recent innovation. As far back as the Third Century A.D. some imaginative angler had the ingenuity to fashion an artificial fly made of feathers and a hook that produced the desired result: It caught fish! In fact, methods of casting a line by hand were known during the days of the pharaohs of Egypt.

Ultimately lure makers began to find that lures did not have to represent aquatic or terrestrials in order to fill a stringer. Largemouth and smallmouth bass, northern pike, muskie, tarpon and snook strike or seize an item for other reasons than to feed on an object which they positively can identify as a common and natural item in their list of favorites. This is why a flashing spoon, weird-appearing plug or the numerous types of spinners take such a sizable share of fish.

Today's line-up of crank-baits is nothing more than an assortment of hardware, rubber-band-like fluttering tails, weighted heads, all meant to put a hook within reach of some good ol' hawg-bass, but they work miracles!

As for the hooks normally used on a lure, they range from a single hook to a double, a weedless single to a weedless treble. Just plain treble hooks must be produced

Night fishing off the North Carolina coast for blues and stripers netted one angler good results, while the other grabs a gill to get his hefty charge ashore. The right lure is the key to fishing action, so read text.

Author used a dressed fly tied by wife, Glad, to get this fat, fighting Atlantic salmon within tailing range.

by the millions, since so many of our modern plugs sport as many as three sets of trebles; that adds up to nine chances that you'll sink a barb into the fish at which you are casting.

The artificials and rod/reel combos employed by Hank Parker to win the BASS Master's Classic are displayed. The angler spent the requisite time to learn use of each.

Whether a typical European-style spinning lure or one of American design and manufacture, with a little experimentation, it can be fished at almost any strata from surface all the way down to an area of cover far below you. Success is all in your patience and your retrieve. The same is true of plugs, spinner-baits and weighted worm rigs. Most modern plugs are designed so that angle and length of the lip, plus lure balance, takes it to depths where the fish are

As the crucial moment approaches, Michigan lady angler brings to net steelhead displayed proudly back on page 20. The flashing spoon she used is clearly distinguishable here.

For certain species, such as the landlocked striper, certain lures have earned reputations as consistent producers. Author fooled the game fish with these five artificials. Perhaps you might try them down South?

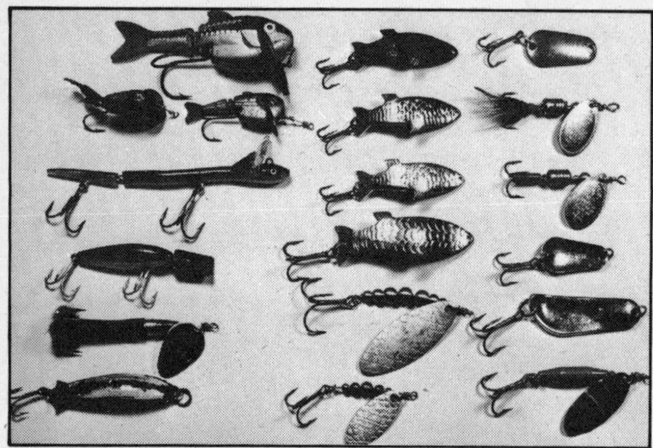

These lures are twenty years old — and still effective! That's because they were designed to imitate natural food.

Spinners have endured decades of angling tests, and have produced tons of bass, trout, northern pike, and others.

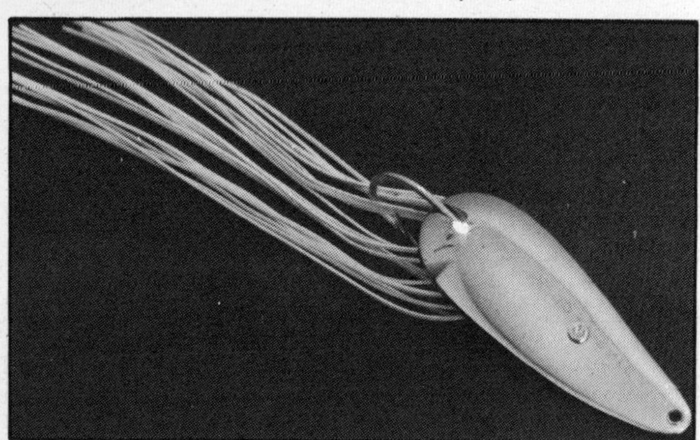

Plastic wiggly tails of today's jig lures may produce a little better than these old-timers that sported feathers.

Left: A skirted Bass Devle is practically weedless and a great lure for bass or pike in weedbeds or tight cover. Above: They now come in many shapes, sizes and tail configurations, but this lure is still a grub-jig.

apt to be lurking. Some of these plugs go deep without addition of extra weight, and super-deep if you use a drail system, a Gapen Bait-Walker or one of the sophisticated downrigger setups.

Back in early spring, I was talking with Joe Hughes, who is with Arkansas' famous lure maker, Cotton Cordell. He had just sent me testing samples of their two newest fish-getters: a Spot that floats and a floater/deep-diver Super-C. Both had a bit of that special magic built into their designs. The maker had tested them out and believed they were winners. Naturally he admitted to being curious as to the results I might have had when I got around to thrashing them on and about my favorite bass waters.

Cotton Cordell's Spot floats; plunk it down by the side of your bass boat and you'll notice that it floats at a kind of strange angle. On a good cast, with your rod held high and using a medium-slow, erratic retrieve, the floating Spot's tail will break the surface intermittently, creating what to a bass seems an attractive wake. During a medium-to-fast retrieve, it wiggles just below the surface.

I found this test lure to have more than enough built-in vibration to agitate the rattles inside and the way it's hooked allows it to be fished in and around relatively heavy cover. If we had any doubts concerning its hooking effectiveness, four keepers plus a 4¾-pounder dispelled fears. The color combos are a turn-on for fish. The Chrome/Black Back; Smokey Joe; Chartreuse Crawfish; and Natural Bluegill all are delightful to a bass.

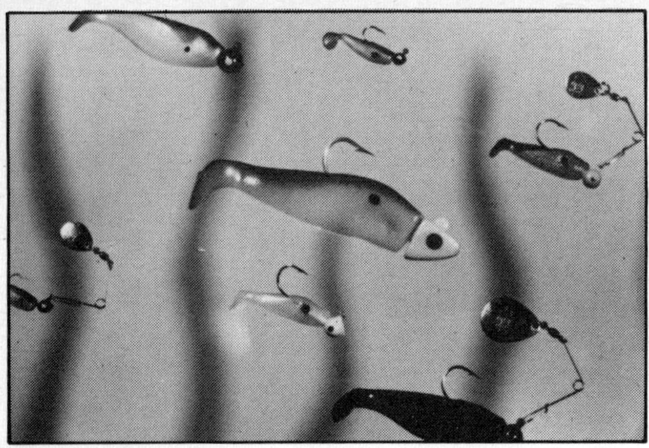

Plastic jigs are marketed with or without spinner-type attractors. Sometimes the extra flash is required.

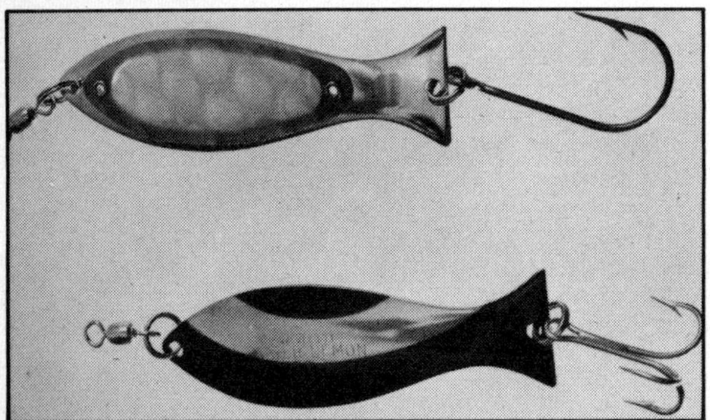

Worth lures have earned their reputation for taking fish and this style is available in many color combinations.

Cotton Cordell, as mentioned in the text, is one of the greatest lure innovators. These samples show paint detail.

Tom Mann, the noted angler and lure maker, has produced the Craw George with tail spinner. It's a sinking lure.

Mepps is practically synonymous with spinners, and the firm offers a fantastic variety from which to stock up.

A day's test session with Cordell's Super-C showed it to be one of the most complete new artificial baits to come along in the past couple of seasons. There is a chart unofficially known as the High Acceptance Range. This artificial passed in every major category, including depth, size, vibration, adaptability to different rates of retrieve, finish and the ability to swim true right out of the box. Here's the score on the Super-C:

Depth: This is the most critical area for any artificial and the factor an angler should consider when evaluating a lure. During recent years, the most productive/popular lures attained depths of between seven and nine feet. The Super-C made all of 8½ feet using 12-pound-test mono. It should go deeper on lighter test line.

Size: It's small enough to catch numbers of fish, yet large enough to tempt a trophy bass.

Vibration: This relates to the way it wiggles and the noise created by the built-in rattle. You can feel one and hear the other!

Speed Adaption: Retrieve slow to fast or rapidly troll

A knowledgeable angler and the "accepted lure of the day" adds up to a solidly hooked striper from a Southern lake.

and the balance design kept our Super-C down.

Finish: The quality of the finish, after kissing a few rocks and deadfalls, reflects the above-average care used to develop the lure. The color patterns represent a veritable feast to any hard-feeding hawg-bass – like: Pearl/Red Eye; Natural Crawfish/Red Eye; Green Crawfish/Red Eye; Chartreuse Crawfish/Red Eye; and Chrome/Black Back/Red Eye.

For every Cotton Cordell, there is a Tom Mann and his super-fine lures; manufacturers like Mepps, Creek Chub, Panther, Arbogast, Worth, Lindy Joe, Heddon, Creme, Bagley, Rapala and Rebel, plus dozens more, keep working to design and produce every type of lure an angler could possibly desire.

Always keep it clearly in mind that rod, reel and the

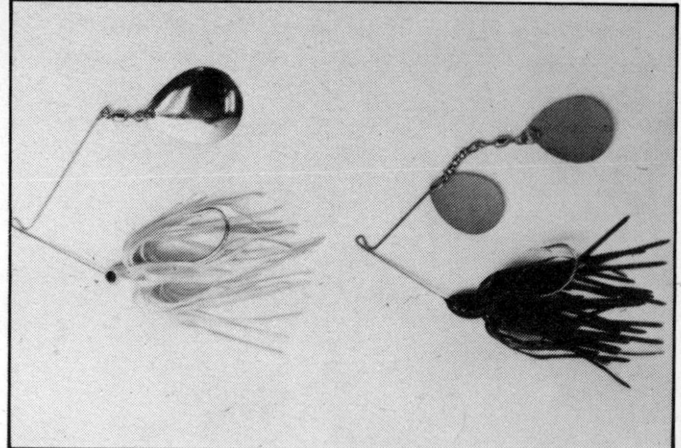

Lindy's Little Joe and its original spinner-bait are both excellent producers, especially when buzzed by big bass!

strength of your line must to some degree be considered when you choose any of the basic types of lures referred to in this chapter. I'm not stating that spinning tackle won't handle all types, but I am pointing out that a particular rod, reel and line combo is designed to handle lures that fall into weight classes that lend themselves to that rig. Even a weightless fly can be cast with spinning tackle when attached to a casting bubble with the capacity to vary its weight by the amount of liquid placed inside.

To say it somewhat differently, you can't cast a 2-ounce jig with an ultra-light outfit and the lightest mono – nor can you cast a one-eighth-ounce spinning lure with a conventional saltwater rod and reel spooled with 80-pound-test line.

I don't think it's unreasonable to estimate that – in this world of spoons, spinners, plugs, flies and plastic artificials, plus the enormous variety of lures that are a combination of one or more of the above-mentioned basic types – there are actually thousands of varying designs and colors from which to choose. And as you might imagine there is often an amazing difference between the productivity of one design/action/color, as opposed to that of another maker.

Something new and downright deadly are the Fish Caller trio made by Action Lures. Sounds, commotion attracts.

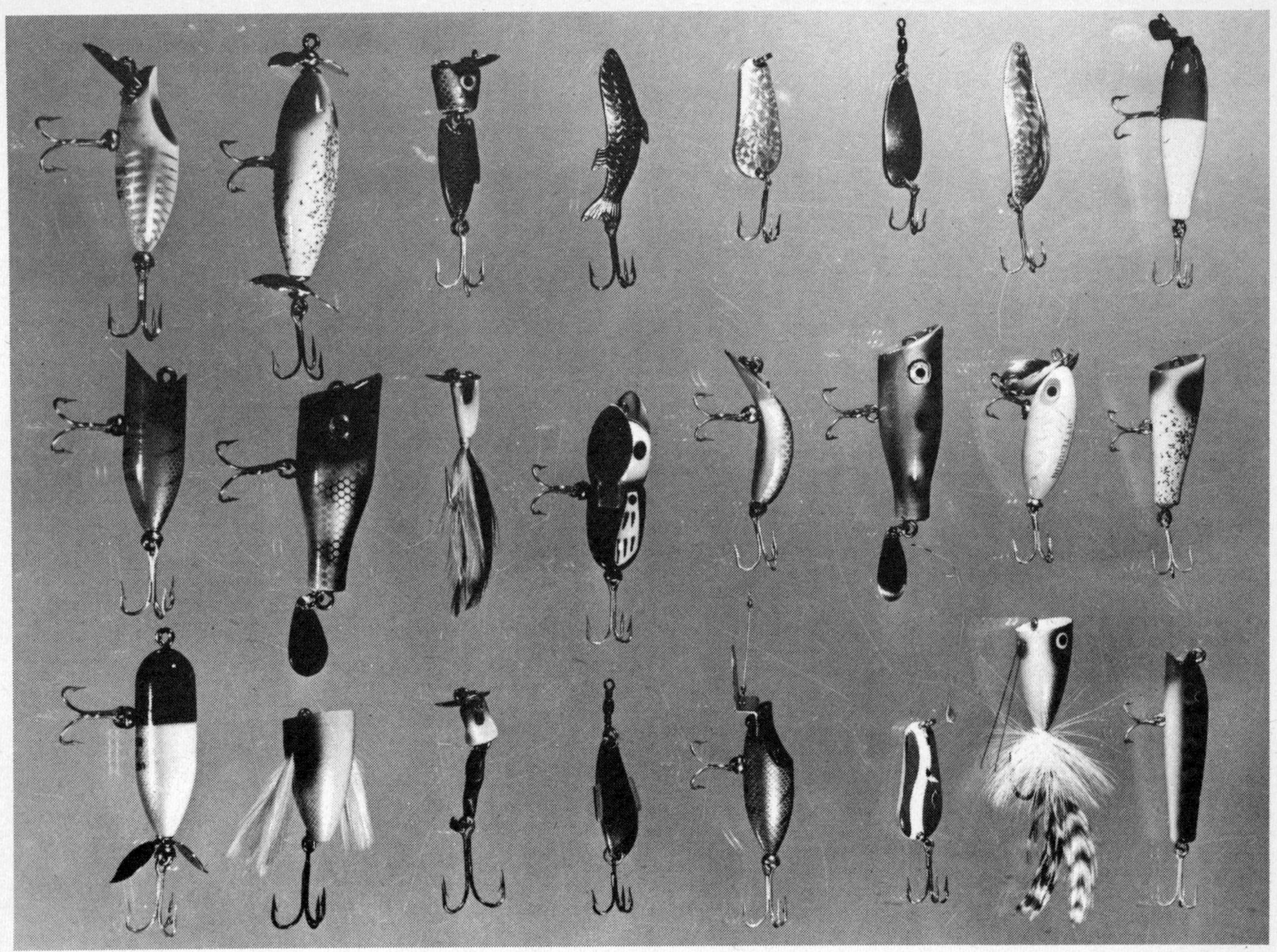

These plugs of the past can, when presented properly and cranked in carefully, produce as well as today's modern lures.

It also should be pointed out that a plug that is a great success on southern largemouth bass may be a wipe-out north of the Mason-Dixon line, and as an added negative, practically useless on cold-water smallmouth bass. Just a few plausable reasons for such failure could include factors as simple as too large a bait, colors uncommon to the water you will fish, or a plug that just doesn't run effectively at a depth the local fish tend to prefer.

Rather than choose from the modern fisherman's arsenal of lures and baits in a haphazard manner – making only the tackle dealer happy – I suggest reading some of the how-to data constantly appearing in today's outdoor periodicals. In such articles, well known fishermen not only are aware of which lures hang the big one, but they tell all!

Many of the already great lures and baits can be gussied-up to be made even more effective than the designer may have thought originally. A good example of innovations would be combining Uncle Josh pork rind on lures that work as designed with a pork leech on a Lindy-rig; a Twin-Tail on a marabou jig; a ripple rind on a Lindy Single Spin; a Spin-Tail on a Swedish Pimple; a Fly-Strip on a Countdown Rapala; a Ripple-Rind on a jig or a Twin-Tail on an Arbogast Hawaiian Wiggler.

Many game fish can be finessed into a decisive strike by such extra adornment. Sulky, deep-water largemouth bass are just as susceptible to combo lure setups. Try a Bass Strip on a Johnson Silver Minnow; a Black Widow Eel on a Weedless Bucktail Jig; a Ripple-Rind on Harrison's Weed-Wing; a Spring Lizard Pup on Roger's Vinyl Skirted Jig. The possibilities go on and on, adding potency to solo lures already having powerful medicine going for them.

One piece of advice: don't *ever* neglect to carry an assortment of jigs such as the type made famous by Tom Mann, one of those who promoted the plastic worm to the peak of the Ten Top Lures list. Mann's stubby Jelly Worm looks and acts like a grub and takes endless sea trout! Anglers also have learned that it drives largemouth bass wild.

In time, swimming tails, wiggling tails and cork-screwing tails came on the scene; nearly every fish in a stream, river or lake will clout such lures. Once upon a time, these lures were for saltwater fishing use, dressed with animal hair, synthetic fibers or feathers. Today, they are used for a greater variety of species with more success than dreamed possible.

EVINRUDE

BASICS OF BAIT-CASTING

Big Bass Favor This Technique, But Don't Count Out Other Species

DUE TO A continuing spotlight on the country's bass pros, plus a clear view of the trophy bass they bring to the boat, day in day out, tackle manufacturers have come to realize bait-casting rods, reels and baits are the current route to higher sales volume.

Bait-casting is really the only fishing method of strictly American origin. *Plugging* is the term by which our fishermen know the method, since a plug or a fairly heavy spoon – seldom a bait, in the natural sense – is used as a lure.

In the United States, bait casting is still the most popular method of taking fish on artificials. There is, of course, plenty of competition from fly casters, spin fishermen and trollers, but the pluggers still outnumber each of the others. In Canada, where the fish are bigger and more numerous per angler, bait-casting has little competition from other fishing methods. Big bass, giant northern pike and muskie are best fished with the powerful bait casting gear.

In the recent trend toward smaller lures and lighter gear, the bait-caster hasn't been left out in the cold. Casting a

Opposite page: Dick Kotis, famed angler who heads up Arbogast Tackle Company, fooled this whopper barracuda using a bait-casting rig and one of his personally designed plugs. Bait-casting tackle has long been employed in the angler's quest for black bass. It's rugged enough to haul in lunkers from beneath lily pads and weed beds, and in the hands of the knowledgeable practitioner, can be cast accurately. A good presentation is vitally important.

Youngsters and bait-casting outfits have been standard fixtures across America, including the Salt Creek waterway in Oregon's Willamette National Forest. His form is perfect for using natural bait with the plugging rig!

A surface popper delicately presented to the edge of a shady mangrove brought this hair-raising action with a school of tarpon. This is top sport on a medium-action plugging rod and bait-casting reel spooled with 17-pound-test monofilament.

plug holds such fascination in itself that few of these fishermen are going to give it up in favor of spinning, where skill and control of the reel are negligible factors. So the modern bait caster who feels the need to use lighter and smaller lures simply gets a light lure casting outfit – longer, more flexible rod, free-spool reel and extra-light line – with which he can toss the quarter-ounce and three-eighths-ounce plugs and spoons. By no means is the bait-caster handicapped when it comes to fishing – he will be in there pitching for many years to come.

Just what is plugging? The basic function of plug casting gear, however, has always been to put a big meal before a big fish, hook him solidly when he strikes, then be able to control his frantic struggle to escape. It takes a fairly stiff rod and heavy line to put this kind of pressure on a lunker fish. And, since big game fish are seldom found far from natural cover of some sort, your biggest problem in landing one will be to keep him from tangling your tackle in weeds, logs, tree roots or other obstacles.

In bait-casting, the lure must be heavy enough to start the reel spool turning at the instant of release, as well as to carry the line through the friction of the guides out to a desirable fishing distance. With standard equipment – a medium-stiff rod five or 5½ feet long, conventional level-winding reel with 4X or 5X multiplying ratio and 15 or 18-pound-test line – you'll need a lure weighing not less than a half-ounce. A lure just a bit heavier will be found to cast even better, so many of the regular plug lures are in the five-eighths-ounce class.

Most of the lures used in plugging are based on the fact that large game fish usually eat smaller fish, either their own kind or smaller members of the panfish or minnow family. Virtually all underwater and diving plugs imitate (or are supposed to imitate) a small fish that game fish include in their diet. Many of the surface lures do, too, especially the wounded minnow or crippled minnow designs. Surface lures, of course, are also designed to suggest other forms of fish food — frogs, mice, bats, large moths, even small birds.

Lures designed for casting with the plug rod come in an endless variety of form and color, rivaling in number only the fly fisherman's artificials. Any of them will take fish occasionally; a few of the time-tested lures will take fish when any plug is accepted. Every bait-caster has his pet colors in lures, as well as a few favorite designs in the surface, subsurface and diving models.

For plug fishing in any one area, a great variety of lures isn't at all necessary. But, if you're fishing over a wide area in different waters, you'll be forced to add baits as you go along. Species of food fish vary from one body of water to another, and you have to use a lure with appropriate shape and action. Since visibility of the fish is affected by the tint of the water, the color of your lure is important, too. Dark water demands lighter-colored lures; clear water calls for a more neutral shade, approximating the true colors of the food fish.

Underwater plug lures wiggle or wobble to suggest the swimming movement of a frightened bait fish. In general, these lures give proper action at only one speed of retrieve, limiting what you can do to attract a fish with any one lure. Your success in fishing these depends on finding the exact speed of retrieve that gives the most action, then on putting your lure in the right place at the right time.

In thinking about the importance of the right speed in

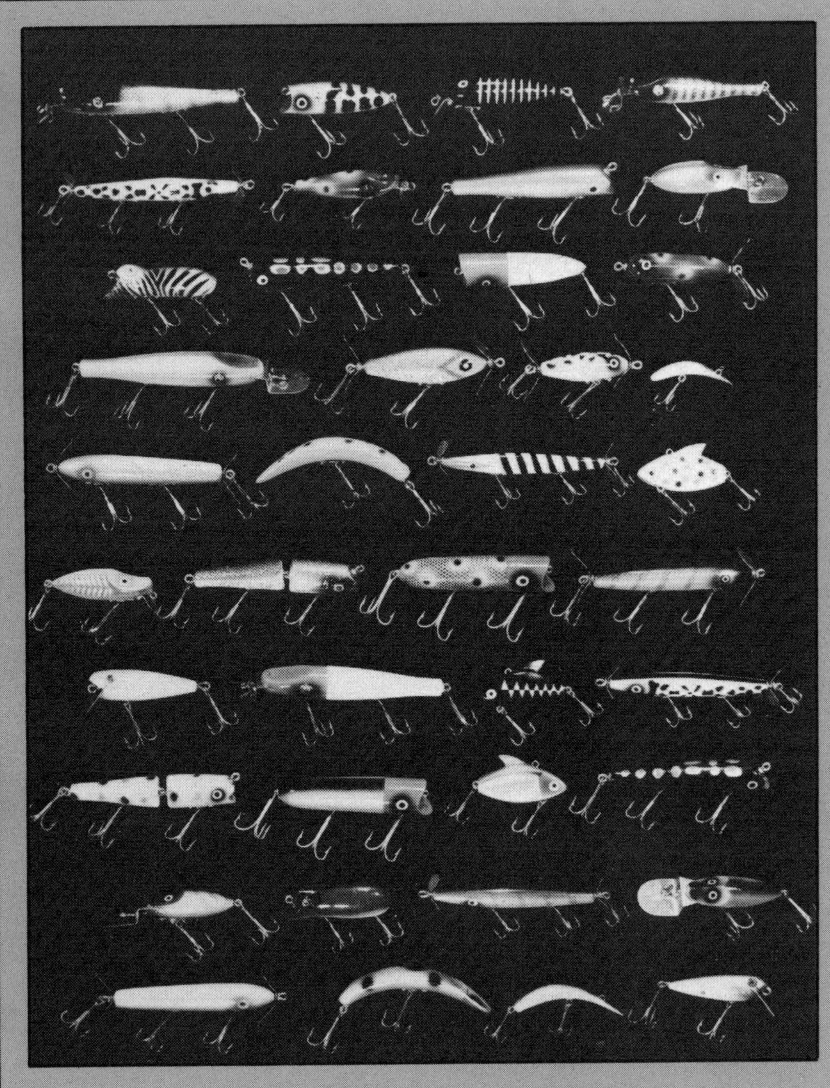

A dizzying array of plugs is available to the modern bait-caster, and each will produce action — if it's what the quarry is seeking at that particular moment, and if it's cast properly.

A plugging rod bent double in shirt-sleeve weather can mean only one thing: tarpon fishing in Florida's flats. In this case, the angling action is taking place after dark, and the fish seems just as feisty as in daylight.

any one lure, I'm reminded of a morning on a well-known bass lake in the Catskills. I'd spent a number of seasons on this lake and had learned enough about it to know that good fishing was limited to the hours between the crack of dawn and sunrise, and from sundown to complete darkness. Surface lures, for some odd reason, did not interest the bass in the morning, although they rose well to these after sundown. The best lure for morning fishing was the old Heddon Vamp in what's called the pike scale – a dark or dirty yellow that looks like no pike I've ever seen, but which the bass liked better than any other color in this lure.

This little lake was filled with logs, stumps, pads and weeds – all ideal bass water – but, although the bass hit well in the stumps and weeds in the evening, it was no-go there in the morning. In the middle of the lake, away from shorelines and most of the natural hazards, a couple of cranberry bog islands floated in the deeper water, anchored by a few trees that apparently were rooted in the bottom of the lake. Many bass hid under these islands, lying in wait just under the edges of the bog to dash out for unsuspecting bait fish swimming by.

The technique was to paddle close to one of the islands and cast the plug at the edge of the bog, making the retrieve so that the lure traveled almost parallel to the island's edge. Surface lures got little attention from the bass. They obviously were so far under the bog that the lure had to get down to their line of vision.

The ideal retrieve here was just as fast as it was possible to move the lure without killing its provocative wiggle. Experience gave me the clue, but apparently I was the only fisherman on the lake who knew it. One early July morning I took a friend along. He was a good fisherman and plugger, but never had seen this lake before. We worked from the same boat, taking turns at rowing and casting. Each of us was equipped with the same pattern of lure, the pike-finish Vamp.

In the beginning, I had a definite advantage over my partner, since I knew the better hiding spots for bass, but actually we fished the same water and in almost the same way. For some reason, my friend couldn't get the right speed of retrieve. He would retrieve either too slowly, which didn't make the lure dive deeply enough, or he would retrieve so rapidly that the plug didn't work the way it was intended.

Within an hour's fishing I had taken sixteen bass, several over three pounds. My partner had come up with only two in this same time, even though he was making almost two casts to my one. The morning's take amounted to twenty-three fish, twenty for me, three for him – and for no other reason than that his speed of retrieve was wrong.

Effective bait casting isn't easy. Many of our best all-around anglers agree that it's more difficult to do a good job with the plug and the short rod than to perform properly with fly tackle. Whatever the degree of skill involved, it's certain that you won't become a skilled plug caster in a week of fishing.

As in any effort requiring good coordination, the selection of equipment is important. Your rod must be of the correct action to suit the weight of your bait. The reel must be exceedingly free-running and the line should not be heavy enough to develop excessive friction on the guides. Ideal for casting the half to five-eighths-ounce lures are: a good make of modern day rod, 5¾ to six feet long, in medium action; a good reel, with level-wind device and adjustable end bearings; and a braided nylon casting line, dacron, monofilament, not over fifteen-pound-test.

An excessively stiff rod tip will not flex properly under the weight of the lure; thus you'll get little spring action to drive it out. In casting, the work is done by the wrist and

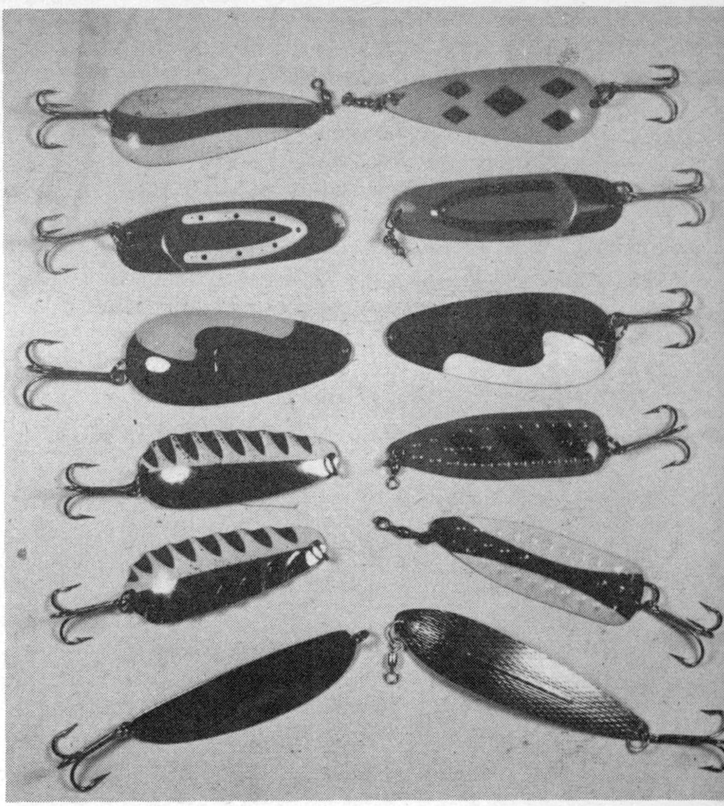

Heavy spoons that are good on both fresh and salt water fish are made to order for a powerful casting rod, bait-casting reel and monofilament that will stand a smashing strike!

North Carolina's Currituck Sound gave up this heavy stringer of bass. Happy angler used bait-casting rig.

Ricky Clunn, a professional who's won some of the biggest bassin' competitions around, checks plug's performance in his swimming pool before casting it upon the waters.

Cold, clear Finnish waters gave up these trout, taken by author using a finely adjusted Ambassadeur bait-casting outfit and relatively lightweight Mepps spinners. Try it!

forearm alone. Your arm power flexes the rod against the weight of the lure, and the rod, in turn, tosses out the bait.

It's best to learn how to cast your plug before you attempt to do any fishing. Use a regular tournament casting weight, or remove the hooks from an old plug so that you can cast over a lawn or any pond without hanging up on every cast.

Accuracy is of major importance in fishing with the plug. You'll be called on to drop the lure into small pockets in the weeds, close against overhanging banks, right next to a stump or a log – situations in which your bait must land within a foot or two of the spot where you want it.

This isn't as difficult as it sounds, if you first learn the overhead cast and good control of the reel spool. The overhead cast permits you to line up accurately on your target and you control the distance to the exact spot by putting pressure on the reel spool with your thumb. All good casters deliberately overshoot the mark so that the lure, if unchecked in flight, will drop beyond the target. Your thumb checks the overshoot, dropping the lure just where you want it. Once you've mastered the overhead cast, the sidearm – which you won't often use – is a cinch.

Your tackle box for plugging should hold a variety of different lures: top-water, diving and sinking. Mostly, these plug lures are for bass, both smallmouth and largemouth, but many will be effective on northern pike, muskie, walleyes, and, on occasion, big trout. They also are becoming increasingly popular for saltwater anglers.

If you're a pike and muskie fisherman, you'll need to add a good assortment of spoons and big spinners equipped with feathered trebles. Nothing attracts big pike as well as big, flashy, wobbling spoons, which come in an assortment

Joel Arrington, one of North Carolina's finest fishermen and frequent angling compadre of author, strains while hauling in a striper that was fooled by his surface plug presented with a bait-casting rig. This is top action.

Among the dazzling array of plugs and spinnerbaits usable with bait-casting tackle is this "Bullcat," which resembles either a bullhead or small catfish. Either of these minnows are hungrily sought by larger game fish.

of finishes. Red and white, gold and silver (or brass and nickel), and in some waters copper, black and white, and green and white wobblers are tops.

Surface baits are used mostly in taking both species of bass, though in shallow water, muskie and northern pike also will belt these. Unlike the diving and spinning plugs – which have a more-or-less fixed speed of retrieve – surface lures demand considerable fishing skill. Such baits can be fished with little movement. Allow them to lie motionless on the surface for some moments before giving them a slight twitch to stir them into life.

In most bass fishing, you'll find that the slower you fish the lure, giving it plenty of action on the retrieve, the more bass you'll arouse. A steady swimming movement can be effective, too, in certain waters and for certain species of fish – particularly muskie – but most pluggers bring their lures back much too quickly. Watching these anglers in action suggests they're interested only in getting the lure back as fast as possible in order to make the next cast. If it's casting practice you're after, that's all right; but if it's fish you want, slow down the retrieve. Work and actually fish the lure carefully. An exception, relating to speed would be a buzz-bait worked across surface/near surface growth. Here the ticket is rod high and a fast retrieve. If a bass hits it, he smashes it!

Your choice of lure will have some bearing on how you'll fish it. If it's a frog, bring it back in a series of little jerks, pausing every yard or two to let it come to rest. Crippled minnows should be moved slowly, with many pauses in the movement. The straight plunker and popping plugs depend on violent surface action to attract fish. These are the baits you'll use for fishing after dark or over fairly deep water, where it takes real surface agitation to get some attention from the fish.

Continued on page 41

Deadly by themselves or on the tail hook of a flashing spoon – Uncle Josh's "Big Daddy" pork frogs. Note colors.

Kentucky bass smashes surface plug, visible in the fish's mouth, as bait-caster slurps a red-and-white close to his boat. Many subsurface baits are employed with plugging rods and the cranking reels, also, when need arises. Opposite page: Two light-fingered bait-casters show what you can do with this tackle/method in Nebraska river.

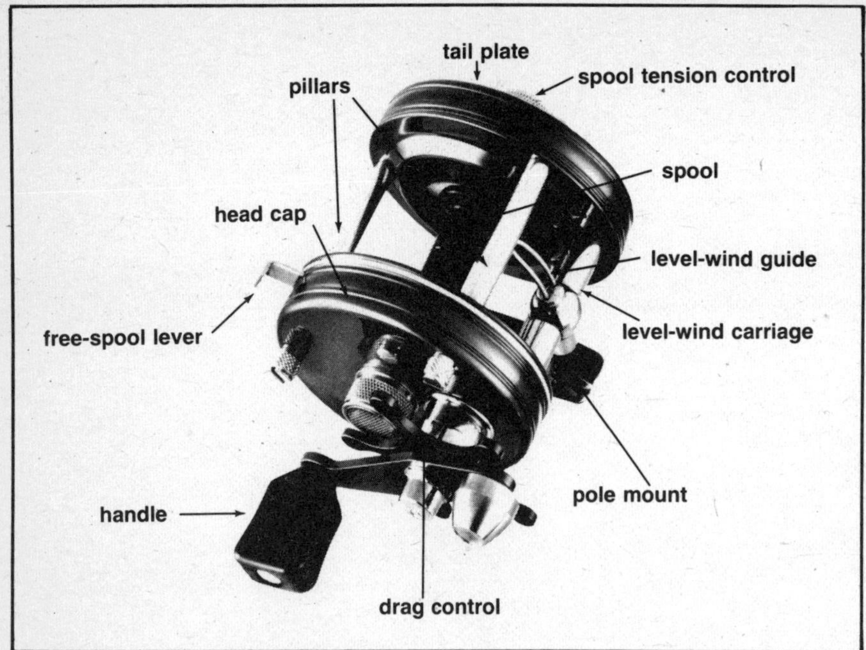

Selecting Your Equipment

Bait-Casting Level-Wind Reel — A free-spool, medium-priced, level-wind reel is recommended for beginning bait-casters. Its features will include independent tension-control systems for the spool and for the line, plus a free-spool device which disengages the handle from the spool gears during the cast.

Bait-Casting Rod — The only difference between a bait-casting rod and a spin-casting rod is the title the particular manufacturer chooses to give it. Again, the rule of balanced tackle should apply. Preferable for beginners is a fairly flexible five to six-foot rod using bait or lures weighing three-eighths to five-eighths ounce.

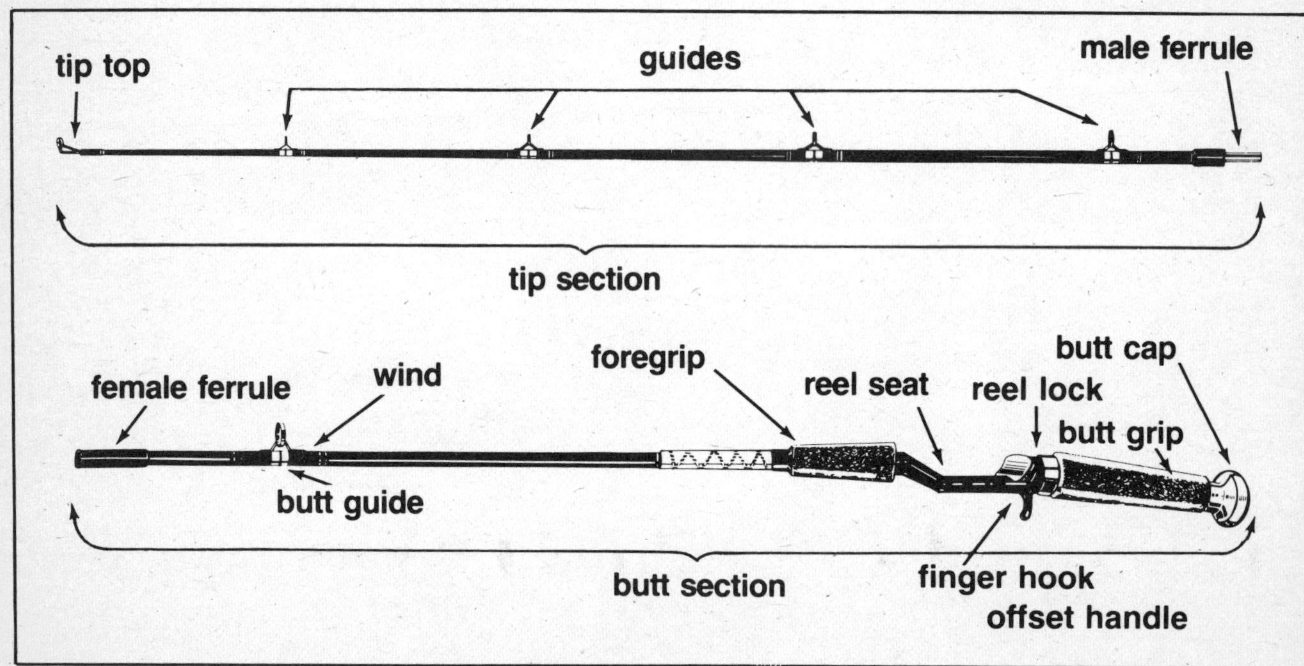

Bait-Casting Lures — Should you be confused by the variety, remember that lures fall into three basic categories; surface, floating-diving, and sinking. To start out, choose a few varied-color samples of each — no more than a dozen in all — and learn to use them well. Be sure to include a barbless plug for practice casting.

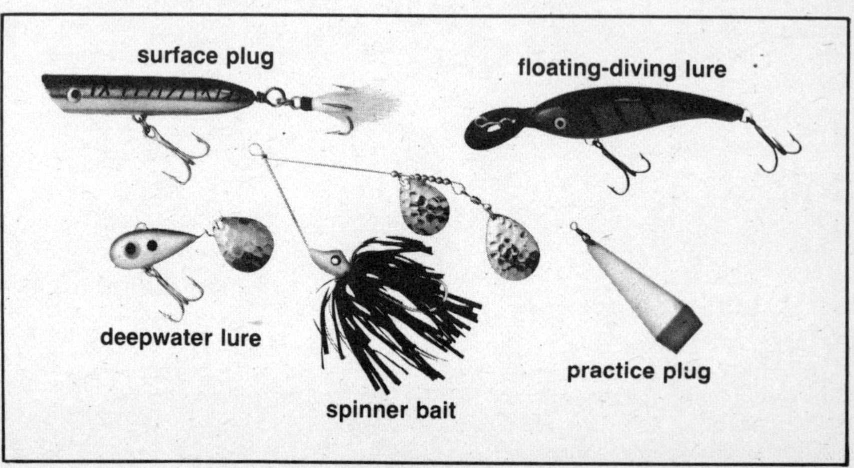

The Overhead Cast

Making Your Play

An important note: backlash, and how to prevent it. Backlash refers to line-entanglement on the spool and is a common "pitfall" in bait-casting. When a lure is first cast, both line and lure are traveling at about the same speed. The lure encounters wind-resistance, however, and almost immediately begins to slow up. The spool, meanwhile, is still obeying the command of the initial thrust and is not so quick to lose its momentum. Its line peels off with nowhere to go and begins to counter-wrap itself.

Backlash can be avoided by use of the "great equalizer" – your thumb. Placed lightly against the spool from the outset of the cast, its pressure can be gradually increased to keep lure, line and spool in time with each other. When the moment arrives, you can supply the thumb pressure necessary to stop the flow of line altogether, hitting the target right on the nose.

It takes practice, true. But there's no mystery to preventing backlash.

The overhead cast. Prepare for the cast by putting your reel in free-spool and tightening the spool tension knob all the way. Now hold the rod level and gradually lessen the tension until your practice plug slowly pulls the line to the ground. Make this adjustment each time you cast with a different weight lure. Add extra tension when casting into the wind.

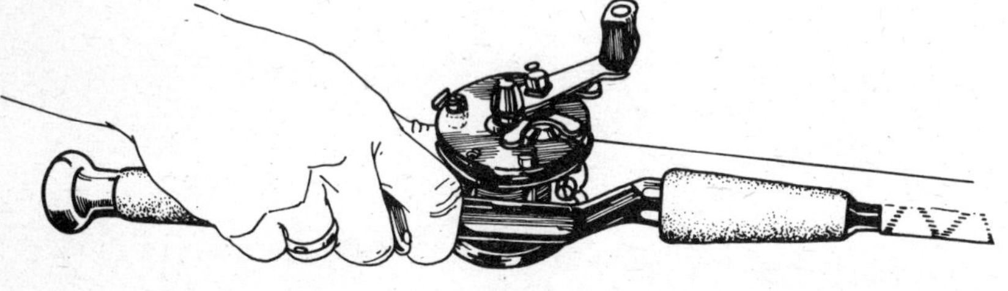

Hold the rod as shown with the reel handles pointed up. With the reel in free-spool, rest your thumb on the line.

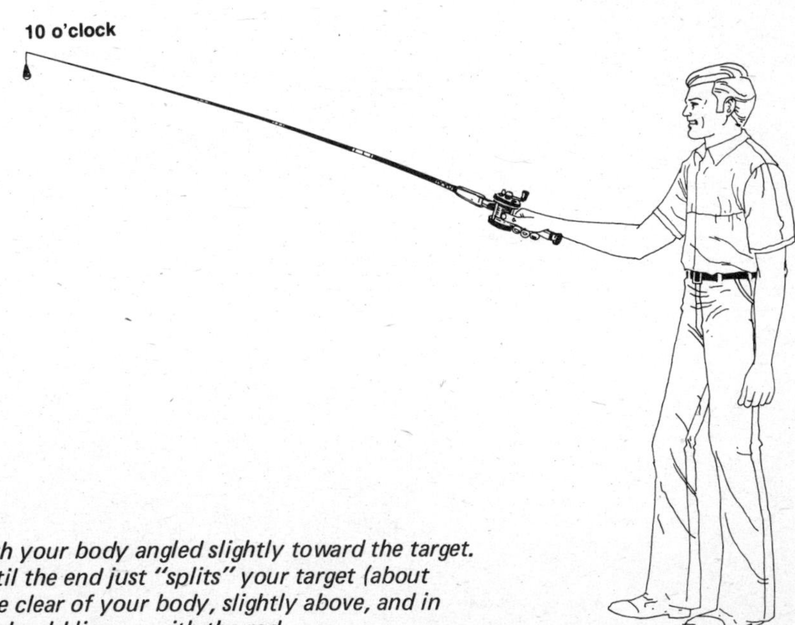

Stand firmly and comfortably with your body angled slightly toward the target. Cocking your arm, lift the rod until the end just "splits" your target (about 10 o'clock). Your elbow should be clear of your body, slightly above, and in front of your hips. Your forearm should line up with the rod.

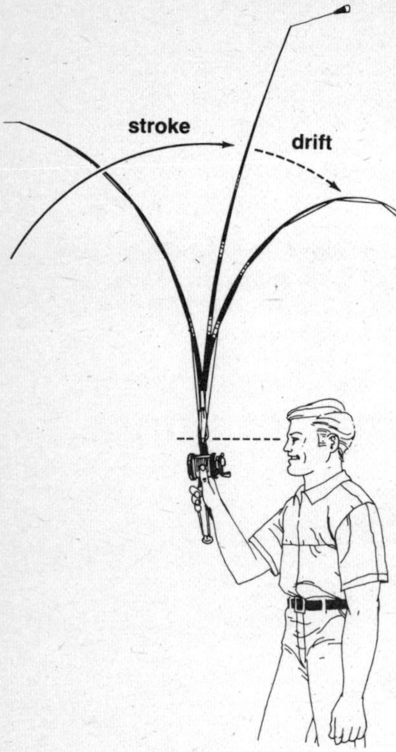

stroke

drift

Start the overhead cast with a swift movement that brings the rod to the vertical position — the reel handle still toward you and just below eye level. At this point the rod will develop a casting bend due to the weight of the lure.

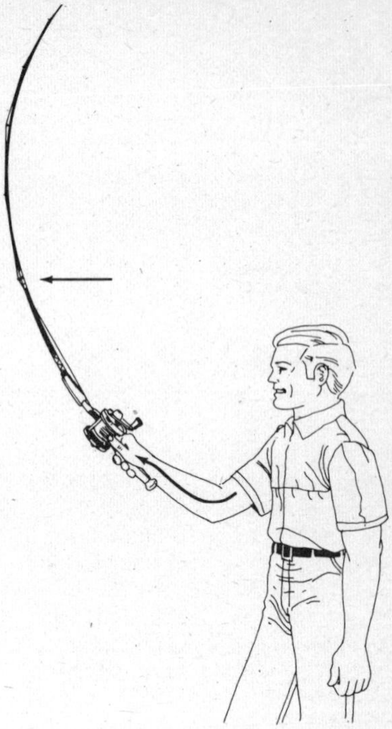

Without hesitation, begin the downstroke, using a slight wrist-twist for added power. As the rod reaches the 11 o'clock position, ease off on thumb pressure. The lure is soon in flight, with your thumb gently braking the unwinding spool.

Follow through by lowering the rod tip to follow the flight of the lure. As the lure nears the target, begin to increase thumb pressure. Brake the spool to a complete stop the instant lure reaches its destination. Practice will reduce the arc of the outgoing line, and with it, the effect of the wind upon your aim.

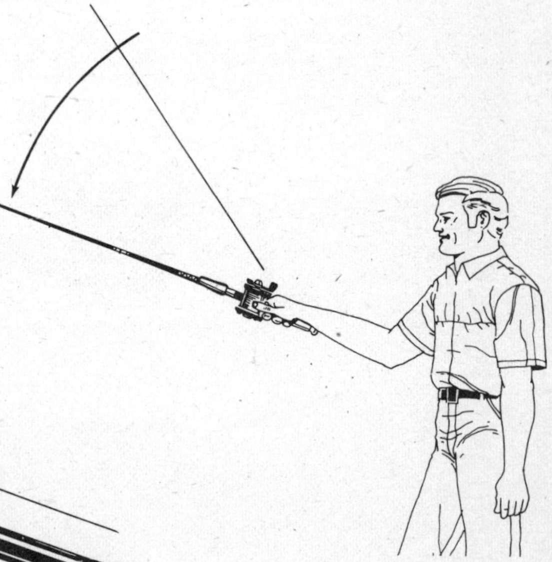

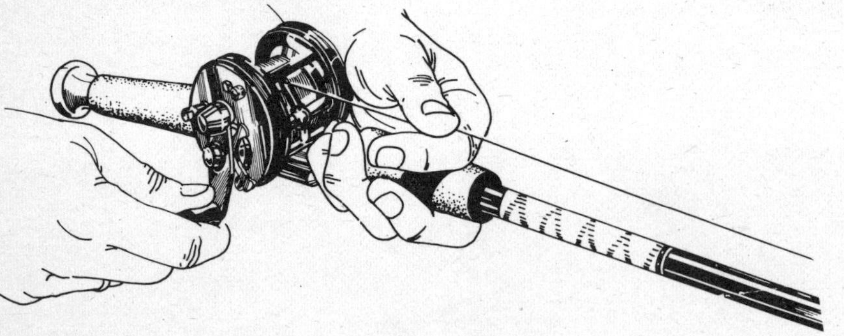

As with spin-casting, we are again "palming" the reel on the retrieve. One hand takes a combination hold on the reel, forward grip and line while the other hand turns the handle.

Only experience can teach you how fast to retrieve. By rule of thumb, it should be only so fast as necessary for your lure to achieve its designed action. If that happens to be wobbling along the bottom, then let it wobble along the bottom; if popping along the surface, then make it pop along the surface. One approach is to vary the rate of retrieve until you find the right lure action. If a fish follows but does not strike, for instance, try slowing down your retrieve on the next cast. If still nothing — speed things up.

Many of the diving plugs can be fished as surface lures. They're doubly effective used this way, since you're forced to fish them slowly to prevent their diving under. Many skilled pluggers deliberately dive the plug quickly, then allow it to float slowly to the surface on a slack line to develop an appealing crippled minnow action.

Most game fish, once they achieve fairly large size, are rather lazy in their movements. A big bass or pike will lie under a log or pad bed well protected from prying eyes, waiting for some unsuspecting minnow to move within reach. Schools of minnows often scurry but not more than a couple of yards from one of these hiding predators without any action. But let one of these little fishes show any desire to lag behind the school, either from laziness or

Shakespeare's line of fine-quality spin-casting reels can be matched with the plugging rods to produce for you.

SKP-4 Lightweight

SKP-7 Lightweight

SKP-9 Deluxe

SKP-12 Deluxe

SKP-15 Deluxe

EVINRUDE 85
PowerCat
BULL-A-GATOR

because of injury, and he'll be gobbled in a flashing rush of water. Big game fish seem too lazy for a long chase after a healthy bait minnow, biding their time until easier prey comes along. Since this goes for almost any big freshwater game fish, from trout to muskie, remember this when you fish those surface lures.

This won't apply to the same degree when you're fishing a diving plug, yet some of the same hesitant action can be imparted to the lure by stopping the retrieve over hot-looking spots, then permitting the bait to struggle up toward the surface before you put it under way again.

When using the sinking plugs or the big spoons and wobblers, there's not much you can do to vary the speed of retrieve. With the sinking plug, you'll be working in deep water for fish that are lying deep because of hot weather. When your plug hits, allow it to sink to the right depth before making the retrieve. And if you're trying to keep it well down throughout its travel, you'll also need to make pauses in the retrieve to allow it to sink again. The pull of the line tends to work the lure up to the surface, so slack off every few yards to let it get down to the desired depth.

Wobbling spoons obviously demand a fixed, minimum speed of retrieve so they won't tangle with the bottom or with the underwater weeds. The optimum speed is that which allows the lure to swing freely from side to side while maintaining an even depth in the water. Speeding up this type of lure simply causes it to revolve, which defeats its purpose as a lure. Occasionally, when working over shallow weed beds, you'll find it necessary to bring the lure to the surface, retrieving rapidly and holding the rod tip high so the lure skates over the water. This is effective on pike and pickerel in shallows.

The superiority of bait-casting to other methods really shows up in fishing the big lakes for northern pike. There's no lure you can handle on a freshwater rod that's so large a big pike can't take it. Their mouths are filled with sharp, curved teeth and the gaping jaws demands a big hook.

Fishing for big pike with a fly rod or light spinning lures is asking for trouble. Neither fly rod nor spinning rod normally has the stiffness it takes to sink the big hooks in a pike's jaw. As for holding one of these freshwater leopards in water filled with brush and weeds, you'll have trouble enough with a rugged plug rod and eighteen- or twenty-four-pound-test line. When a twenty-pound northern starts for his den under a tree stump, no slip-clutch spinning reel and light monofilament is going to stop him, but you'll have a chance with bait-casting tackle.

On the other hand, if you're a light-tackle fanatic and prefer to take your bass and smaller pike on the lightest equipment, get rigged for the smaller lures. You'll also find these necessary in many of the spots where fishing pressure is heavy and the fly casters and spin fishermen have been educating the fish.

Pick a rod about six feet long with a fast tip action, fit it with a light free-spool reel and fill this with a six- or eight-pound-test braided casting line. With a barrel knot, tie a short length of monofilament to the end of the line, and you're ready to compete on equal terms with the light-tackle boys. With this outfit you'll have little trouble in getting good fishing distances with quarter-ounce baits, both plugs and spoons; in most cases, you'll get more accuracy and have better control of the hooked fish.

Opposite page: Plug casting in and around deadfalls close to a dropoff produced this fine result. Great day's sport!

No matter what your casting gear, your terminal tackle is important. For bass fishing, particularly with surface baits, tie in a five- or six-foot length of monofilament line for a leader. This is only if you still are addicted to using braided nylon, as some old-timers will – not if you spool top-quality monofilament on the reel. Attach your small snap swivel to this, if you like, though many anglers feel the

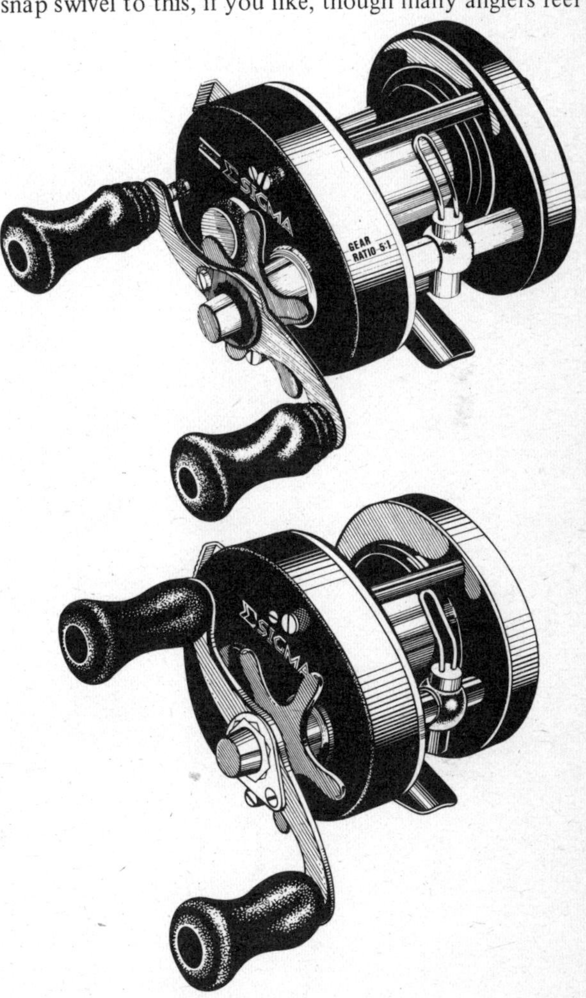

Shakespeare's Sigma series of bait-casting reels have been afforded popular acclaim by serious angling fraternity.

snap swivel interferes with the best action of surface lures (and also some underwater lures) unless tiny and light. This monofilament makes the connection between line and lure less visible and prevents the rod tip from fraying the line as the result of continual casting.

For pike and muskie fishing, a short wire leader next to the lure is essential; the same is true in saltwater fishing for bluefish. The sharp teeth of these fish will fray a line quickly, no matter how strong, and you'll lose both fish and lure. These days you can buy light, twisted-wire leaders as invisible as a monofilament line, so there's no need to take chances with these multi-toothed fish.

Author shows powerful "double haul" technique for driving large flies into the wind. A member of International Fishing Hall of Fame, he won group's highest honor, Dolphin Award, in 1964. He's won distance/accuracy casting titles in U.S., South America, Europe.

FLY IT!

Fly Fishing Has Become As Popular In Salt Water As On The Trout Stream

FLY FISHING, both on fresh and saltwater, has reached a popularity never dreamed possible a few years ago. It now is recognized as the pinnacle of sophistication for the skilled freshwater angler, whether he fishes for trout or other challenging game fish. Not surprising, the saltwater scene also continues to see more masters of the long rod conquering powerful species. The anglers' success is due to a combination of polished skills, highly perfected tackle and terminal gear, with flies and poppers that work strong magic on even the wisest of popular game fish.

Spinning has possibly reached its peak of growth and popularity. Today, there's no evidence of anything less than continually growing interest in long rods, fly lines and miniscule, weightless lures. But maybe the reason is simple: no other method of fishing can match it for fun, excitement and challenge.

No angler can consider himself an all-around fisherman until he's fairly proficient in working a stretch of water, whether a lake or saltwater, with fly tackle. Admittedly, it takes time and effort to pick up the rhythm of casting the heavy line and light leader carefully and accurately. But there's no facet of angling that affords quite the same thrill as hooking and fighting a good fish on such delicate tackle.

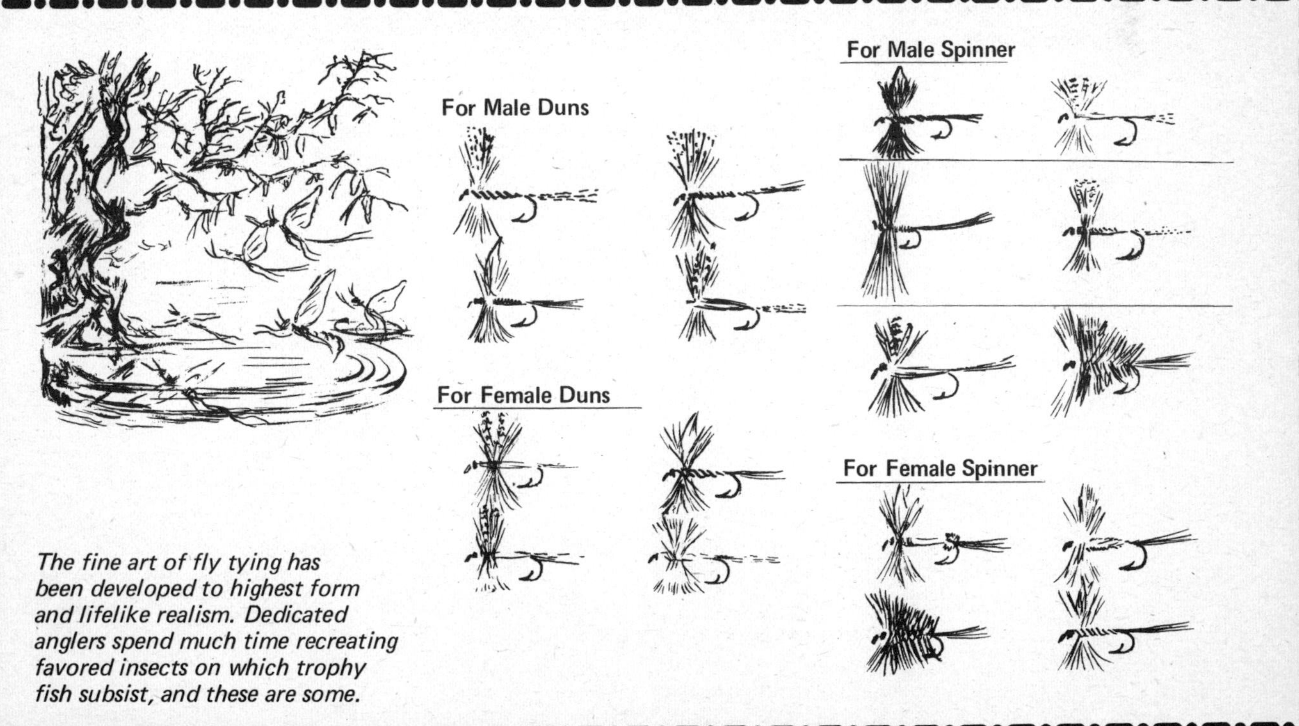

The fine art of fly tying has been developed to highest form and lifelike realism. Dedicated anglers spend much time recreating favored insects on which trophy fish subsist, and these are some.

Fast and deep Canadian water gives up a fresh-from-the-sea Atlantic salmon to fly rod and a "guide pattern" fly.

The fly rod and light terminal gear impose the least restraints of any tackle on a fighting fish. They give him not only the opportunity to do his stuff in the air and underwater, but to take every possible advantage of natural hazards to make a clean getaway.

Aside from the unique thrill, it's also the best practical means for taking those game and panfish that thrive on flies, nymphs and other tiny forms of aquatic life found everywhere in our waters. It's true, after a fashion, that you can fish flies with a spinning rod and bubble, but why do it unless necessary? The fly rod was and still is the best tool for the job.

The fly rod shows to best advantage on the trout stream for which it was created. With it, you'll cast the tiny surface dries, the wet flies that imitate immature insects, the artificial nymph itself and a host of different patterns of streamers and bucktails which, it is hoped, look like small food-fish big trout find to their liking.

You can imitate any of an aquatic insect's transformations, from larvae to imago (adult spinner), merely by changing terminal gear and artificials to suit your need. You may find it necessary to carry such a wide variety of fly patterns every day you fish that you can spend all your time just making changes. This isn't the right approach to fly fishing, but it illustrates how suited to a great variety of methods and techniques the fly rod can be, if you learn to use and develop the methods. You'll find, too, that methods vary as the season progresses and you'll

Using 4X tapered leader, Zwirz creeled and released fourteen native trout from this stretch of water in New York State. This trout liked a stone fly nymph cast accurately.

vary your technique often during a single day on the stream.

Insect life follows a regular pattern from early spring through the summer and into fall. Nymphs begin to stir as soon as the water begins to warm up; however, they stay well down at this time. Hatching doesn't start until the air temperature and bright rays of sunshine bring the water temperature to the correct degree for nymphs to break out of their shucks and prepare to take to the air. But you'll find nymphs swimming and drifting days before hatching time. Some crawl out onto rocks or tree roots prior to hatching, returning to the stream as adults to drop their own eggs. There's almost always some sort of insect activity going on in the stream every day of the season and you can imitate it with the fly rod artificials.

The wet fly method probably demands more skill and knowledge of the habits of fish than any other type of fly fishing. The dry fly is fished exclusively on the surface and is given no movement other than that imparted by the

This half-dozen of author's favorite salmon flies also are employed occasionally to take bass and other species. It's his feeling that using these same patterns show how presentation and finesse are as important as imitation.

A dry fly with wide appeal to trout on both sides of the Mississippi is called the "Christmas Caddis." It's a great multi-purpose pattern (right).

The St. Mary River in Nova Scotia is known as one of the fine spots for taking heavy, hard-fighting salmon. This smaller guy was netted after he hammered a deep-worked wet pattern.

varying currents, while the wet fly can be fished near the bottom, in mid-water, close to the surface or it can be skipped over the surface. You can present it either upstream, across the stream or downstream. Conditions determine the approach and method.

The basic method is to cast your fly across the stream, dropping it well above the spot you expect to find the fish; in other words, a good lie or feeding station. Once the fly is in the current, tighten up on the line and allow the fly to swing down in a long arc until it passes over the fish, the current doing the work.

A variation of this method is to use the same casting technique, then strip off line quickly, following the progress of the fly downstream by pointing the rod tip directly as it moves. The idea is to allow the fly to drift freely without drag as it passes over the fish. Nymphs that are almost ready to come to the surface and hatch drift along in this manner.

When trout aren't feeding visibly, the fast fly method often will arouse their interest to the point that one will make a pass at your fly. In this method, the cast is made exactly the same way, but as soon as the fly hits the surface, the rod tip is raised quickly and the line stripped in, bringing the fly dancing across the surface just above the trout.

It often helps to give the fly even more kick in the retrieve by pumping the rod tip rapidly in small jerks. This system often will do the trick in fast pocket water, where the trout has little time to look over the fly. It's the skipping movement that attracts the attention. It works best in fast water with two or more flies on the leader. The tail fly will offer just enough drag so that the dropper can be kicked up and down on the surface in a real effort to lure a fish.

Deep fishing the wet fly can be a problem in studying currents. You have to get the fly precisely where it's wanted, yet keep it at an attractive depth. Fishing the fly directly upstream and allowing it to sink at will gets it down to the trout at their feeding depth, and often they'll grab it. However, movement often is essential in fishing a deep fly to attract attention.

An alternate method is to cast upstream after first taking

There's little the author likes better than to flip a saltwater streamer before a wary giant tarpon that's feeding in the shallow waters along the West Coast of Florida. The open rear of a charter boat makes an excellent casting platform; on windless days Zwirz can float artificial to quarry without spooking him.

a stand directly opposite the fish, calculating the speed of the current so the flies will sink properly just as they come to the fish. You'll often need to throw loops and mend the cast as the flies come downstream to prevent drag from lifting them to the surface. Then, as the flies come to the fish, the rod tip is pumped up and line stripped in to give the flies an upward swimming movement, as though they are struggling upward toward the surface.

The conventional and easier method of fishing the wet fly is, facing across the stream, simply to cast it downstream at about a forty-five degree angle and allow it to hang in the current for a moment. All methods work at times; you may have to try them all as the day goes on.

Your versatile fly rod is well adapted to handling large bucktail and streamer flies for luring the largest trout in the stream. Big fish like a big bait. In fact, many trout actually disdain small insect food when they achieve truly large size, preferring to feed less often but taking a bigger meal, either minnows, crawfish, frogs or whatever happens to attract their notice. But the minnow is top attraction for big trout almost anywhere, almost any time. The bucktail fly, properly fished, will take many of these minnow-feeding fish.

These artificials are fast-water flies. They are big enough to attract attention in the heavy current and they are meant to be fished fast so a trout doesn't have a chance to get too long a look. Obviously, if a big fish gets a good look at such a large fly, he'll know it isn't the real thing and usually will refuse it even though he'll come back to have another look. You can fish them across stream, just like a regular wet fly, retrieving them in short jerks, either by manipulating the rod tip, stripping line quickly or both. Make your casts a bit

Joel Arrington of the North Carolina Tourism Bureau plays a good trout taken on a dry fly in the mountain areas of that state. Zwirz says the fish normally grow larger in the low areas, where food washes downstream and collects.

The author feels that these are the really deadly ones. At top is the Whitlock's Sculpin, and in middle row from left are: Marabou Muddler, Muddler Minnow, Spuddler, Black & White Marabou Muddler, Whitlock's Multi-Marabou Muddler. The bottom row from left is: Fulsher's Black Nose Dace, Whitlock's Matuka and always popular Yellow Muddler fly.

Using a light trout fly rod, Zwirz hooked and landed six Atlantic salmon in one day in Labrador River. This is some feat in the enormous body of water that was running at near flood stage! This is angling sport at its best!

End of the battle shown on page 49: Zwirz prepares to release 110-pound giant tarpon taken on 12-pound-test leader material. Playing a fish of this caliber is an arm-aching challenge!

upstream, allow the fly to sink, then work it across the stream over the good lies as it swings down. Most of your rises will come as the fly approaches a forty-five degree downstream angle.

If you find a trout rising to your bucktail and consistently refusing it, either by rolling under or jumping over it, this is a signal to change either to a different pattern or to a smaller size. If you're fishing a bright pattern, say, a yellow and white, change to an all brown or other dark fly. In clear water you often can get a trout to come to a bright fly, but he'll flash at it and refuse to take it when he gets close enough to look it over. He may feel it's too big a mouthful to handle, although this is seldom the case, if the fish is good-sized.

Another stunt is to fish two bucktails or streamers, one on a dropper about four feet above the tail fly. The dropper often will attract attention, and the trout usually will follow and take the darker fly on the tail.

Another old but effective trick with these big flies is to add a strip of skin from a trout's belly for added flutter and, perhaps, meat flavor. Cut a strip from the white belly of a trout, about two inches long, a quarter-inch wide at one end and tapering to a point. Scrape off the flesh and pierce the wide end with your knife point. Run your leader through this, then tie on the fly. The skin will slide down to the eye of thy hook, giving added action in the water. Little things like this often make the difference.

The nymph is one artificial that isn't used generally by

A worthwhile technique for quick change from one wet fly to second is to use Orvis Kwik-Klip, which allows eye to be slipped right into spring holder without retying clinch knot. Use improved clinch knot to attach device to leader or dropper.

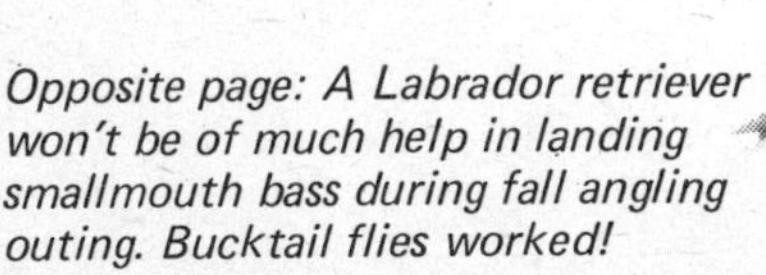

Opposite page: A Labrador retriever won't be of much help in landing smallmouth bass during fall angling outing. Bucktail flies worked!

Several of author's favorite-of-all-time saltwater streamers are shown here. He uses them for all big game fish, such as tarpon, big stripers, snook, etc. Large brown trout will also take them. Author caught 24-pound sea-run brown trout with streamer at top left during a too-short stay in Tierra del Fuego.

Standby patterns that produce huge catches year-in and year-out are shown below, tied and painted by Glad Zwirz. From left are: White Marabou, Gray Ghost, Black Nose Dace and Koller's Brook Chub.

A huge rainbow smashes through surface of a Michigan river as he slashes at delicately presented fly (above). The angler who doesn't know top fish-holding areas and likely lunker spots may come home with empty creel, though.

stream trout fishermen to the degree that it should be and this is a mistake. Nymphs make up at least eighty percent of the insect life a trout eats. They are in the stream all the time and fish will feed on them throughout the entire year. Good nymph fishermen are scarce, but there is no need for this to be so in this day and age. Nymphs aren't difficult to fish successfully; you simply need patience to acquire the slow technique that is most effective in this type of fishing.

The artificial nymph does its best work in fairly slow water, where the rising and feeding trout have unlimited opportunity to look over all food before deciding whether it's good to eat. This is the type of water where trout will consistently refuse to take conventional wet flies, purely because they don't look enough like a live nymph. Unless the trout are surface feeding, you had better turn to nymphs if you want to take fish.

These flies are best fished on long, fine leaders – the same type used with a dry fly – and you can fish them upstream as you do a dry fly. This is a bit touchy, since you won't be able to feel a taking fish on the slack line of an upstream cast. The best solution is to tie in a bushy dry fly a few feet above the nymph to act as a bobber. When the fly pops under, it's time to set your hook. However, you'll probably find that the nymph does its job best when cast across and downstream, giving it the natural look outlined in wet fly fishing.

Taking bass and other popular game fish on the fly rod really goes a step farther when it comes to proving fly fishing versatility. Originally, bass fishing, for both large and smallmouth, was done only with a plug rod and casting reel. But that's all in the past. Fly casters have been finding out that the long rod and small top-water bugs will attract bass when they positively refuse to look at a plug, spoon or bait. This is particularly true in well-fished waters where bass can identify every known kind of plug and lure. These small, delicate lures look more natural to the bass, they create less fuss on the surface and can be handled in a much more subtle manner than the big, ungainly artificial baits.

The biggest plus in this fishing is the extra sport you will find. No bass can give you the same battle on the plug or spinning rod that he hands you on fly fishing tackle. And, you can handle a big one on light gear, if you can steer him clear of weeds, stumps and logs.

Because the bass bug features greater size than the fly

Continued on page 60

Selecting Your Equipment

Manual Fly Reel – Since the fly fisherman strips the line from his reel before casting, the fly-cast reel spends most of its time serving only as a line storage unit. When it is called into action, however, it is rigorous action, and that's why the right reel is important. In selecting your fly reel, look for one which has the capacity for holding thirty to thirty-five yards of fly line, plus at least 150 yards of braided back-up line; a consistent, adjustable drag; and a handy, interchangeable spool.

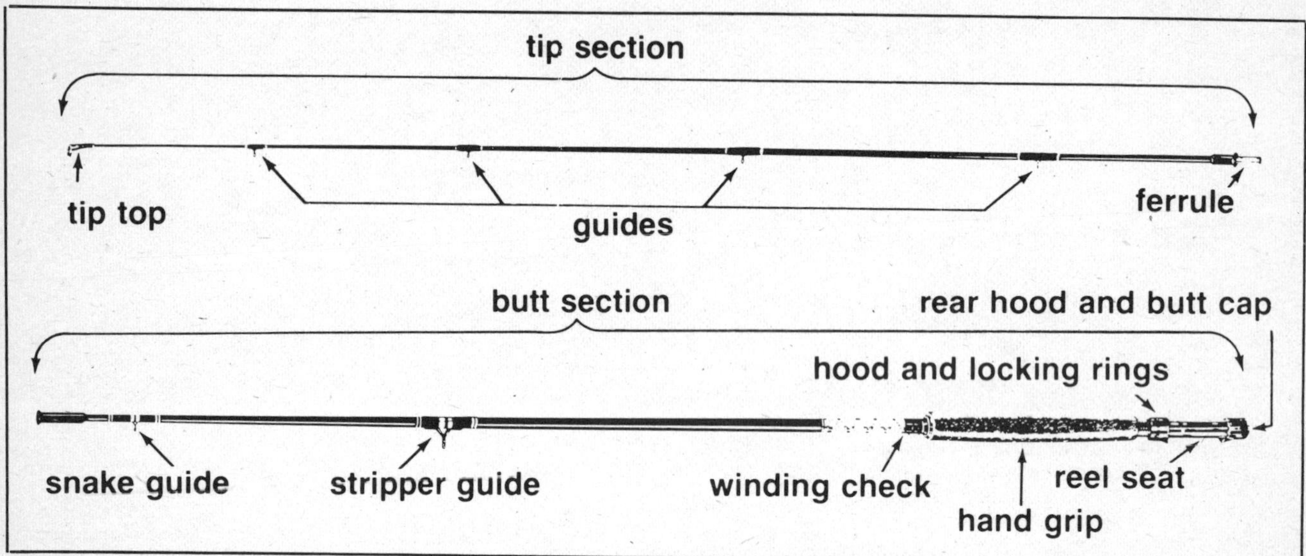

Fly Rod – An eight-foot rod matched to a No. 7 or No. 8 line is a wise investment for the first-time fly fisherman. In buying, "switch" the rod crisply to test for medium play. Check to see that the top of the rod is not too "soft." The ideal fly rod will combine strength and flexibility in both the butt and tip sections, and have a smooth, even bend.

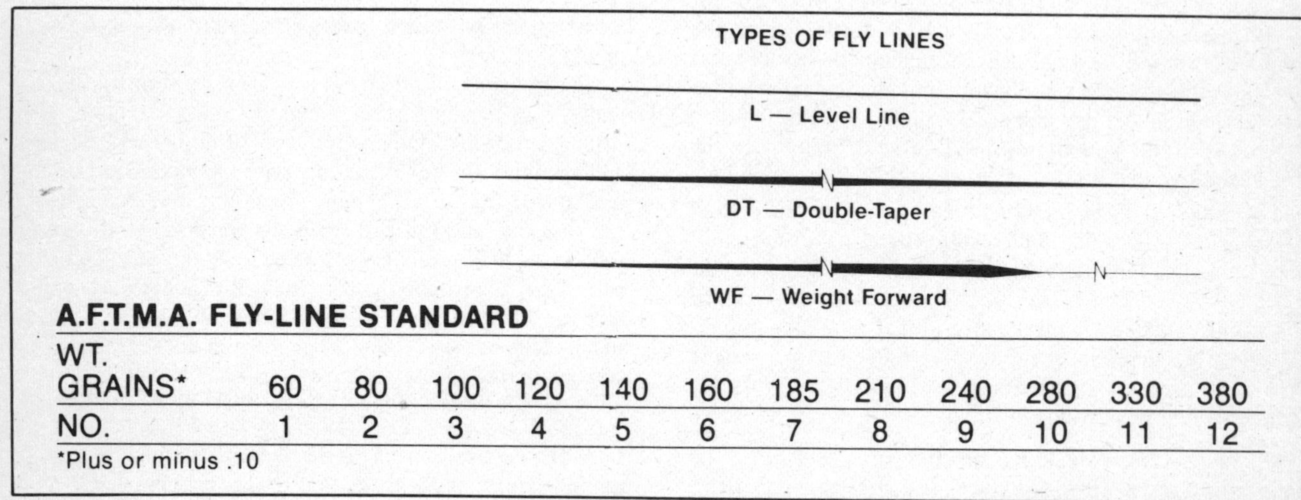

A.F.T.M.A. FLY-LINE STANDARD

WT. GRAINS*	60	80	100	120	140	160	185	210	240	280	330	380
NO.	1	2	3	4	5	6	7	8	9	10	11	12

*Plus or minus .10

The American Fishing Tackle Manufacturers' Association has developed standards for rating fly lines, as shown.

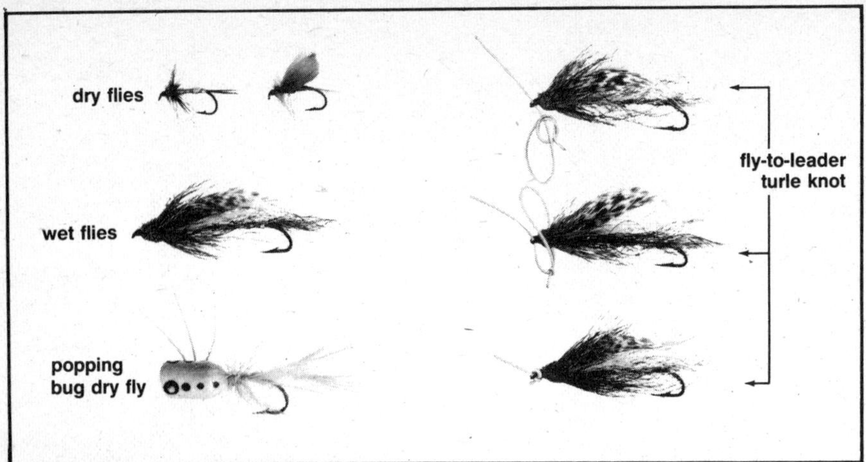

Leader and Fly — Depending on what they're taking, you'll fish with one or two types of flies: wet flies, fished below the surface, or dry flies, fished on top. A 7½-foot leader line allows the fly to drift insect-like while forming an invisible bond to your fly line. Use a bright yellow or white fly. Cut the hook from the fly and use only the hair portion for practice purposes.

Making Your Play
A. The Overhead Cast

The fly rod must be held as shown in order to perform correctly. With your fingers, take a "suitcase" grip on the handle. Line your thumb up with the rod and place it as near the top as you comfortably can. It is in this position that the thumb will brake the rod in the back cast; apply pressure for the forward cast. Bend your wrist until the rod becomes a parallel extension of your forearm.

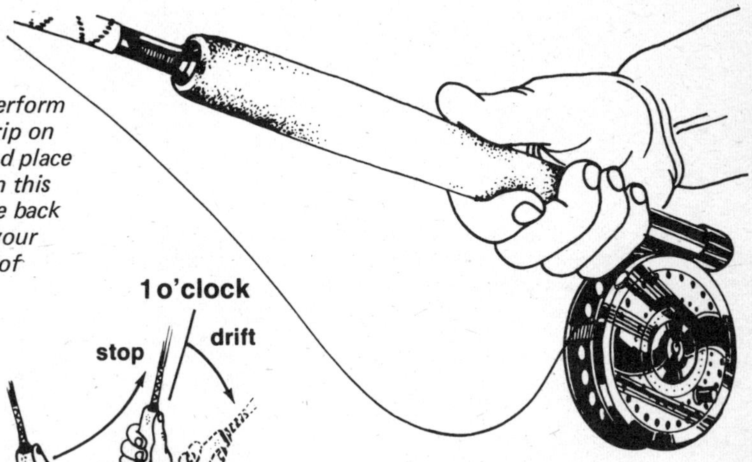

The perfect casting stroke takes place between 11 o'clock and 1 o'clock. Since the angle of the cast is a relatively small 30 degrees, there may be a temptation to let the wrist do all the work. Resist it, or suffer an exaggerated, crooked arc. Instead, study the relationship of the wrist to the rod in these illustrations. Note that the entire hand must travel in a nearly straight line, with a slight upward lift through the back cast; a slight overhand on the forward cast.

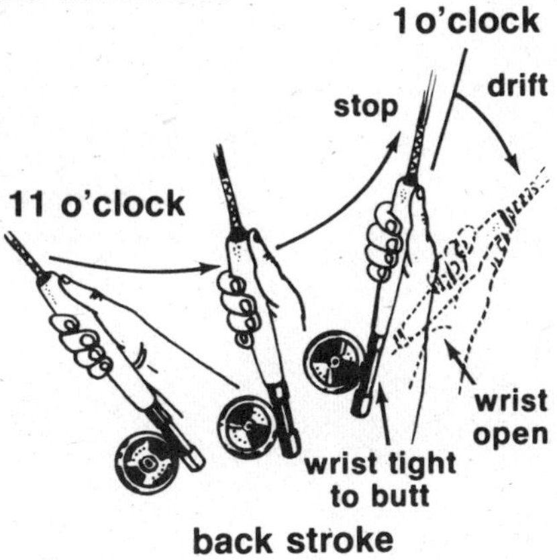

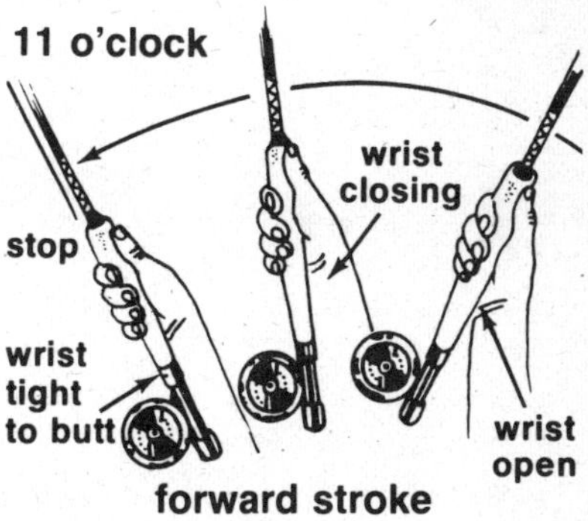

11 o'clock
stop
1 o'clock
drift
wrist tight to butt
wrist open
back stroke

11 o'clock
stop
wrist closing
wrist tight to butt
wrist open
forward stroke

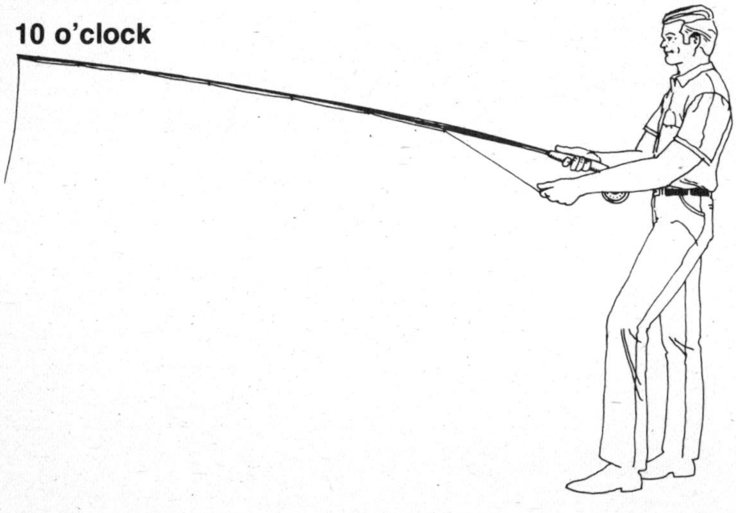

10 o'clock

By way of practice, pull some twenty feet of line from the top of your rod and let it lie on the ground. Leave a little slack between the reel and the stripper guide, and take it in your free hand. This will serve to "anchor" one end of the line while the rest is in the air. Now stand easy, with your body weight on the casting-arm side.

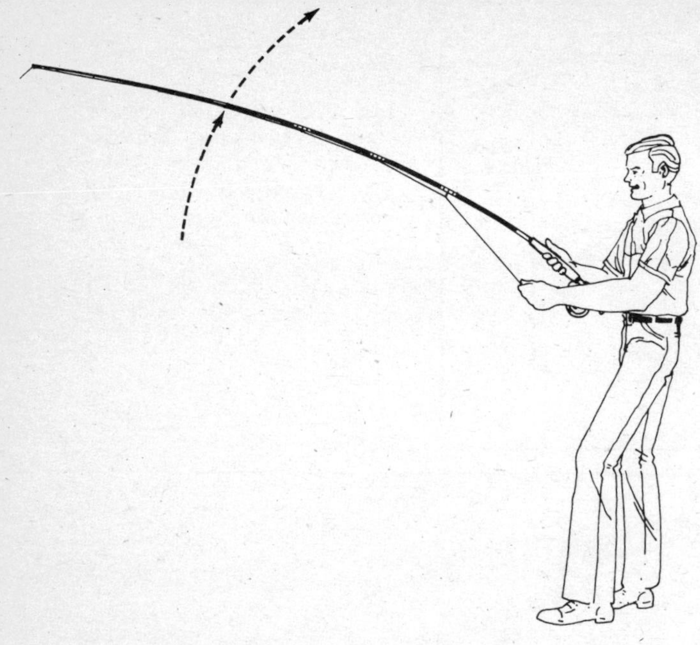

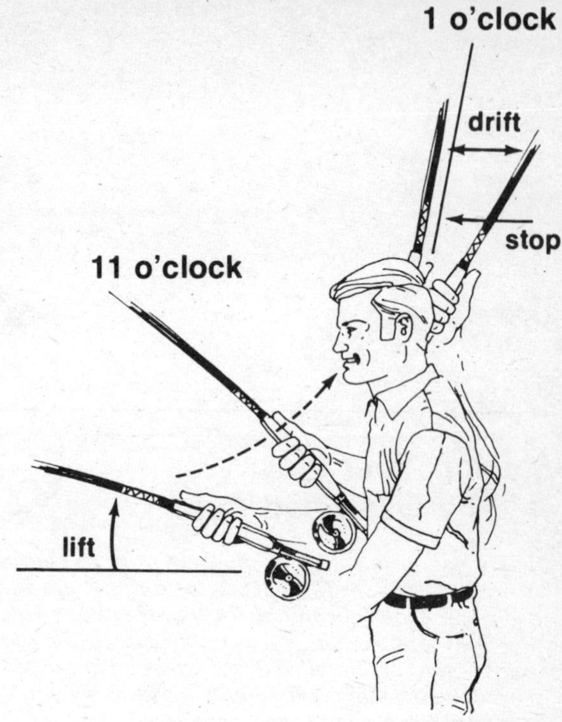

Begin your back cast with a smooth, even lift-off. Don't jerk. A hard, ripping pull not only scares fish, but improperly sets the line in motion. Raise the rod until the leader is almost clear of the ground. A slow-starting, rapidly accelerating movement will smoothly pick up the line.

As the rod passes the 11 o'clock point, speed up the backward motion and flip the line up and back, stopping the rod hard at 1 o'clock. Immediately open your wrist enough to allow the rod to drift back with the weight of the line.

The back cast rolled almost out to its end, begin the forward cast. Move the rod smoothly, closing the gap between the rod and wrist as you do so. Stop the action hard at 11 o'clock. Give it that final little flip that results in extra footage, and let your hand follow through with the casting stroke.

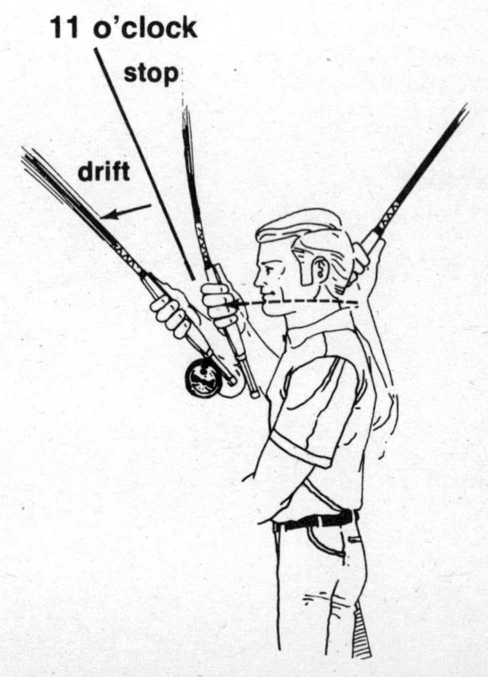

B. The Line Hand

As your casting skills develop, the line hand will play an increasingly important role. It serves as part of your line retrieval system. It helps to maintain tension during the strike. It holds the slack line with which you will "shoot" for longer casts.

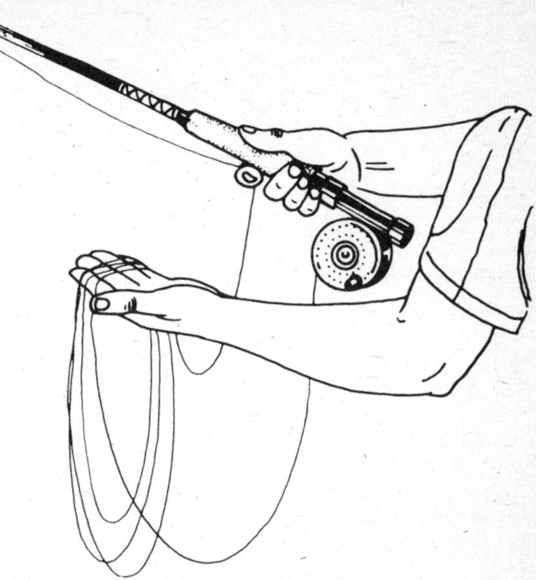

To prepare to shoot the line, pull the twenty or thirty feet you have been used to from the tip of the rod. Now increase the length of your "anchor loop" between the reel and stripper guide by another ten to fifteen feet. Take this additional line across the palm of your line hand in long, loose loops. Keep the loops separate and in order, the last one lying nearest the tips of the fingers.

Keeping the line taut with your line hand, commence your cast. Raise the rod smoothly to 11 o'clock; speed up; stop at 1 o'clock; let your wrist drift open with the flex of the rod; turn and watch the loop roll out behind you. Start forward.

Stop hard at 11 o'clock. And just as you make that final flip of the rod, open the line hand. The momentum will pick up the slack and shoot it through the guides for that extra 10 or 15 feet.

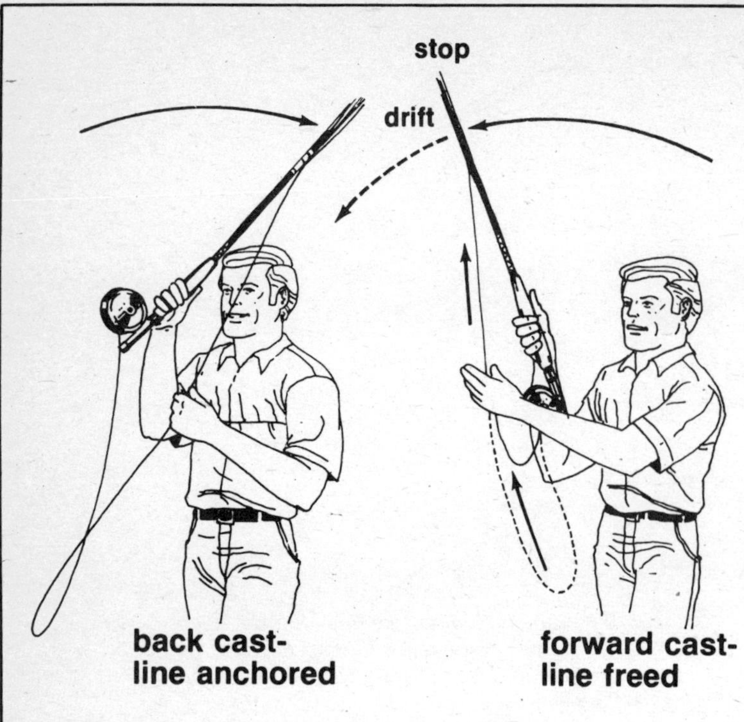

The line hand also comes into play during the "false cast." The false cast is an incomplete cast that is repeated again and again – either to dry out a water-logged fly or to extend the reach of the line. In the latter instance, the line hand's work is coordinated with the back-and-forth strokes, continuing to free-up additional line until the target is reached.

Each time the 11 o'clock position is reached on the forward cast the line hand lets a few feet of line shoot out; then tightens up again. A new back cast is started as soon as the forward loop is rolled out and before it has a chance to fall to the water. When you have reached your target, or have as much line in the air as you can handle, go ahead and complete the cast.

without material increase in weight, there is considerably more air resistance in pushing them out. Usually, this means that you'll want a stiffer rod if you plan to do a fair amount of bugging, plus a heavier line in one of the weight-forward tapers. This latter design of fly line, incidentally, is tops for bugging or casting any heavy fly under both fresh and salt water conditions.

Casting the bug calls for much slower motion than traditional fly fishing. You'll need to regulate your timing to the slower movement of the larger lure as it whips through the air. But, in all other respects, bugging is the same as casting a dry fly. The bugs, of course, are all surface lures usually designed to imitate the big moths or millers that bass favor. However, so-called bass bugs also are made in many other designs to imitate natural food such as frogs, mice, minnows, dragon flies, dobson flies and the like. All of them will take fish quite well throughout the season.

Bugging for bass is at its best early in the season, when the fish are still near the shorelines. June is a great month for bugging if you are fortunate enough to have the bass season in your area open that early. Once the weather settles down to steady heat, however, you'll find the bass staying well down in the cool depths, although a good proportion of these fish will move into shallower water near shore when the sun leaves the water. In shallow lakes, home of the largemouth bass, you'll find them hiding under the lily pads, stumps or any cover that shields them from the hot sun. In the real deep impoundments, bass bugging becomes more of a problem.

Fishing the dry fly probably is the easiest of all ways to take trout on fly rod artificials. The top-water purist probably won't agree with this estimate of his favorite method, but the logic is there. All that's required to make the method effective is to keep your fly over the fish without drag. You have no problem of fishing at different depths, no need for tricky manipulations of the fly.

The trick in dry fly fishing is to study the currents so you can avoid having your fly pulled under by heavy drag on the line. In dry fly fishing, you'll seldom try to drop a straight line on the water. The so-called perfect cast, whereby the line and leader make a straight line as the fly drops, is not for dry fly fishing, except in quiet water or over stretches that have a uniform flow of the current. The varying current speeds within a typical pool or run continually affect the line as it drifts, pulling on the fly.

Good dry fly fishermen throw loops in the line, allowing the fly a reasonable float before drag occurs. Even with a straight upstream cast, it's advisable to throw a wrinkle in the line, causing it to lie on the water in a snake-like path. By the time the currents have straightened out the wrinkles, your fly will have had a fair time to float over the fish.

Your line should float well and you should use a leader

These nymph patterns have fooled even the wisest old fish, when realistically manipulated along the bottom by the skilled angler. Many techniques come only from practice and observation.

with as fine a tapered end as will handle the fish you are seeking. The lighter the leader, the less drag on the fly, minimizing the tendency of the leader to weigh down the fly and thus drown it.

The standard advice on dry fly fishing always has been to fish upstream. This is good in a general sense, because you'll be out of sight of the fish and both line and fly can float back toward you with minimum drag. However, it's never smart to put your line over the fish before he can see the fly. If your rising fish is directly upstream from your position, a cast above him will put the line, or at least the leader, over him before the fly floats down to his position. This will probably put him down, possibly for keeps.

A good cast is one that's made about a forty-five degree angle, up and across stream, aimed so that the fly will drift by the fish on your side. Do it this way and he won't have much chance to be frightened by the leader before seeing the fly.

Your fly rod also is the ideal instrument for getting the most fun out of panfish. These scrappy little members of the perch and sunfish families feed on insect life for a great part of their lives. Bluegills, white and yellow perch, crappie, rock bass, bream and many others are great fly fish, and you'll find them almost anywhere.

Use your lightest trout rod or buy a little seven-footer of inexpensive hollow glass just for this purpose. Fit it with a medium-weight fly line of appropriate number and use a six-foot leader, four-pound monofilament for a leader. A supply of bright flies, both wet and dry, a few tiny floating bugs with either hair or cork bodies and you're in business for these species.

Almost all of the panfish species run in schools. Crappie, bluegills and rock bass are the real surface feeders and

Just wisps of feathers and the finest hook obtainable comprise these delicate experimental flies Glad Zwirz tied for a museum display. Wonder if they'd work?

Forty years of fishing all over the globe were employed successfully against this hard-fighting Atlantic salmon. Author isn't always lucky!

you'll take dozens of them in an evening on a dry fly or the little bug. Fish for them just as you'd bug for bass. You'll very likely find schools of them traveling near the surface, out in deep water right at sundown and often early in the morning. Fish the edges of lily pads and weedbeds and along shorelines where there is protective cover. Allow your dry fly or bug to lie motionless on the water for a time, half a minute or more, before you move it or pick it up for the next cast.

Both white perch and crappie are fond of a small streamer fly, trolled slowly. If you locate a school bubbling

Shakespeare has produced the Beaulite fly reel for the fly-casting fraternity, one of the better models around.

on the surface, row or paddle in a wide circle around the school, dragging the fly along its edge; a number six or eight white bucktail or streamer fly works well here. For those who have access to an electric trolling motor, you'll find that these do not usually spook your fish.

Yellow perch usually feed in deeper water than other members of the panfish family, so you'll need to get your lure down to them to do business. Rig three bright patterns on your leader and nip a split-shot on the leader between them. After making your cast, allow time for the fly to sink ten or even fifteen feet before you begin your slow retrieve. A few gentle wiggles of the rod tip as you strip line will usually add an appealing motion and get some extra strikes.

Anglers only recently have begun to appreciate the versatility of fly fishing in both fresh and salt water. Although trout and salmon still are the favorites, fly casters

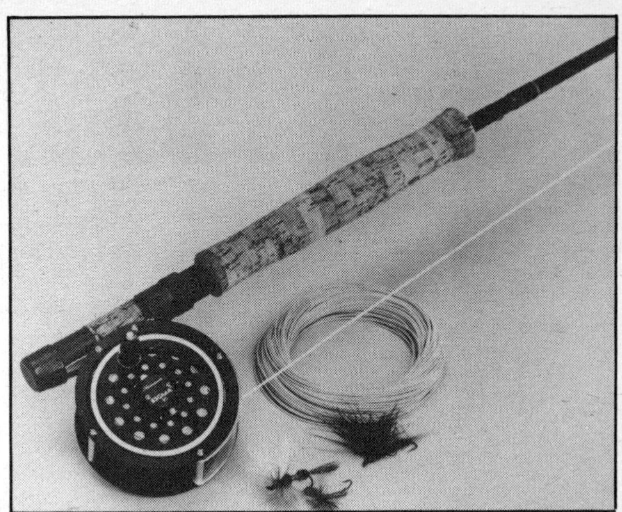

Much touted Sigma Fly Fishing System incorporates Sigma 95 single-action reel, Supra 1000 graphite rod and Sigma brand fluorescent floating fly line. It's matched and balanced.

are catching literally every kind of fish known to take artificial lures. Bass, pike, muskie, king and silver salmon as well as the true saltwater fish, stripers, blues, sailfish, tarpon and many others are being taken on the long rod.

The fly fishing outfit need not be expensive. The hollow glass rods are great in performance and durability and one can get a good one for a fraction of the cost of a fine bamboo or graphite model. These glass rods need little or no care and usually will outlast the lifetime of the average fisherman. A lost winding and guide is about the only thing that can go wrong, and these are replaced easily or repaired.

A fly fisherman really needs two rods. First, a light eight-footer will take trout and panfish with small flies or bugs. A stiffer-action nine-footer will handle heavy trout on streamers and big wet flies, bass on the bug, salmon on the streamer, either trolled or cast. Obviously, for larger saltwater fish a more powerful rod will be required, but this is a special field of angling that I am not getting into in this particular chapter. Two rods will cover ninety percent of the fly caster's needs in any given season.

If your fishing won't involve any species heavier than five or six pounds and you want to limit yourself to one rod, a medium-action 8½-foot rod will do the job for everything from dry-fly fishing to bugging. You won't get quite the delicacy and good fight from your trout fishing or have quite the stopping power for bass that you would if you had the two rods, but it's not a bad compromise for a one-rod angler who doesn't get out on the water all that often.

Two reels are a must, unless, for economy's sake, you get one that features an extra spool. The single actions are best all-around. Make sure the reel you select has ample line capacity and a rugged click device. It's not a bad idea to pick a reel that will handle one of the torpedo tapers – weight forward – with at least fifty yards of light backing line. Such a reel shouldn't weigh more than six ounces, which is about right for average rods.

Lines should be fitted to the rod to bring out the best action as indicated. Follow your dealer's recommendations or check with the manufacturer's specifications.

THE HOWS & WHYS OF SPIN-CASTING

Just Because You Can Lay That Lure Where You Want It Doesn't Make You A Fisherman!

DURING THE early days of spinning, as this new-to-behold tackle began to show up on U.S. waters, a staunch phalanx of old-school fishermen looked on while forecasting that "it'll never last!"

As some traditionalists were wrong about Ford's car, the airplane and dozens of other items that are now part of all our lives, they were wrong about spinning!

It doesn't matter a mite how you view the scene, spinning continues to offer something for everyone. Stating a case no longer requiring defense, spin-casting has and still does, represent the greatest single incentive for new fishermen of all ages to take up fishing as a sport and as pure fun-recreation.

With no previous experience in handling any kind of tackle, a novice can pick up spinning gear and make presentable casts with no more than fifteen minutes of

Opposite page: Pacific anglers looking for heavyweight salmon or steelhead often show preference for stout, top-quality spinning gear. This Sacramento River fisherman, however, is using tackle that's as light as you could want. Above: An Orvis 300 reel was well-used to crank in these saltwater gamefish from Florida Keys area.

North American anglers must use fly rods and flies to take Atlantic salmon, but Europeans may use spin-casting outfits. This Finnish angler prepares to net a fine fish that's fresh from Lapland waters (right).

coaching and practice. With little more than an hour, he is almost in the expert class, as far as casting for distance is concerned. It's a fact that such a novice will be getting all the distance required to take a share of fish in more places and under most circumstances.

As a method, spinning probably has more advantages for stream fishing than any other freshwater use. It's about perfect for early-season work when the weather and water are cold and the fish, particularly trout, are lying deep. The natural weight of the spinning lure, whether wobbler type or spinner, tends to keep it down where the fish are lying.

This is a marked advantage over fly fishing, where considerable effort and knowledge of stream currents are needed even to bring a fly to the notice of the fish. I am taking into consideration the use of modern intermediate and fast-sinking fly lines. Fast currents coupled with deep channels and pockets can do much to foul-up even the built-in sophistication of such lines; further, the fly's swing is difficult to control. The lack of control usually is related to the speed of the fly in such water. Usually it is far too rapid to be realistic.

The constant goal of fishermen is to take larger fish – no matter what some anglers tend to tell you – so the spinning method is made to order for the stream/river trout fisherman. It's a realistic concept that most big fish like a big bait and, compared with the average fly, any spinning lure can be considered a big bait. Another advantage shows up when streams are above normal or a bit cloudy from rain.

The constant goal of fishermen is to take larger fish – no matter what some anglers tend to tell you – so the spinning method is made to order for the stream/river trout fisherman. It's a realistic concept that most big fish like a big bait and, compared with the average fly, any spinning lure can be considered a big bait. Another advantage shows up when streams are above normal or a bit cloudy from rain.

Just because you now can lay that lure out where you want it, however, doesn't automatically make you a fisherman. There's more to the game than that.

Still, when spinning, or spin-casting, there are some solid advantages. For one thing, your line is light – and if using monofilament, it's almost invisible to the fish. Also, you have almost no line-drag worries. Best of all, if you're inexperienced in handling fish, the spinning gear's slip-clutch reel automatically helps overcome that deficiency.

The flash and glitter of most spinning lures is a big help in visibility. Big fish tend to be timid, retiring in nature, reluctant to show themselves in any situation in which they might become easy prey. Thus, when water is slightly high and cloudy, it's a fine feeding time for the bigger trout. It also becomes a fine time for spinning.

Choosing Lures: As in all stream fishing, you'll continually encounter different types of water as you work a stream. Fast riffles, deep runs, quiet pools, rapids and pocket water all can be fished successfully with spinning tackle provided you have enough foresight to include a variety of lures in your kit. By variety, I don't mean just different shapes and colors. You'll find, as you experiment with different lures, that just as there are many shapes, there's also a wide difference in the ways lures act when you retrieve them.

For example, a host of small wobblers is on the market, all suited to spinning. One of the most representative, certainly one of the most effective, is the Wob-L-Rite. This lure, which casts easily, is designed to wobble from side to

A nice-sized gray trout mouthed a cast lure for this sportsman fishing in Quebec's Parc Mistassine impoundment.

Zwirz snapped this photo from inside a streamside sauna while lovely Finnish lass displays hefty brown fooled with spinning outfit. What a way to relax and admire nature.

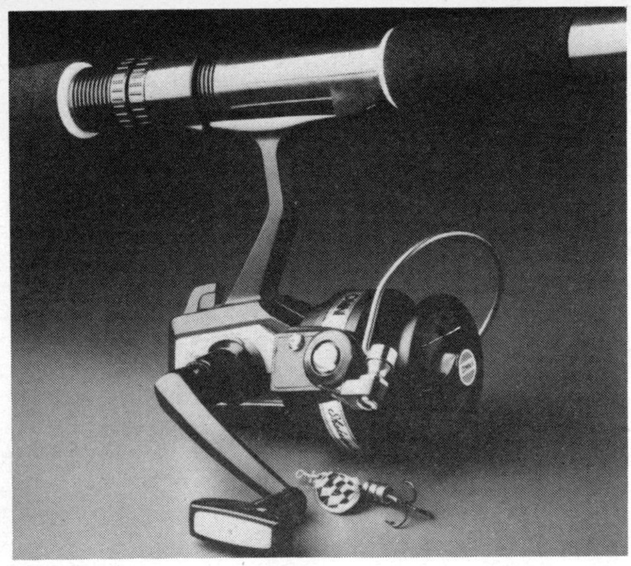

Shakespeare's Omni series of open-faced spinning reels have been exhaustively tested by author on waters all over the globe, and have earned his stamp of approval. Below: Florida fisherman was out for bonefish, but a small shark liked his spin-cast bait instead. His belt knife will surely be used to retrieve his feathered jig in this case!

side, not revolve in the water. Aside from its fish-taking qualities, it is not a line-twister, which can't be said of many other spinning lures. This particular lure is made in sizes ranging from one-sixth-ounce to one-half-ounce for freshwater use. All are good lures for trout, as well as for large and smallmouth bass and any other game fish.

As good as the Wob-L-Rite sounds, it's certainly no final answer. Its best effect is obtained with a medium-speed retrieve, which makes it best suited to fishing deep pools and deep, medium-fast runs. It's not terribly effective in fast water and for fishing rapids and fast riffles it's practically useless, since it sinks rapidly and fishes deep. Every water condition calls for its own particular answer. That's where experience in spinning comes in.

Lures For Fast Water: Another wobbling lure is the Sidewinder, definitely a fast-water lure working best at a fast retrieve. In fact, it's almost impossible to retrieve this lure fast enough to make it spin. This little wobbler can be fished in the fastest water and even over shallow riffles with no danger of snagging on the bottom and no loss of effective action. In general, when you're looking for a fast-water lure, choose one that isn't deeply cupped in the bowl. Heavy cupping in the design makes a good wobbler for slow or medium speeds of water.

The spinners, of which there are multitudes, are mostly for use in slow to medium water. All of these inflict a heavy pull on the rod under a fast retrieve. The faster the water, the heavier the pull, and if you make any attempt to hold them to a slow pace as they spin over a fish, they most

A closed-face reel and spinning rod in the hands of author brought to creel a nice stringer of Colorado rainbow trout.

often come right up to the top. This pretty well destroys their function as a lure.

I've found that the most effective use of spinners in fast water is on an upstream cast, retrieving them just a bit faster than the speed of the current. But that's a matter each angler has to work out for himself on his particular stream.

Your selection of lures for stream fishing must be varied enough to suit each different stretch of water you'll encounter, keeping in mind the cardinal rule of spinning: for any given body of water, the correct lure is the one that will ride well down in the water without digging to the bottom or surging to the top.

As an important tip, don't forget the line-up of new and deadly smaller-size bait fish plugs.

Colors: The best colors in lures for stream spinning depend on the clarity of the water being fished, the kind of local fish food and just the sheer cussedness of the trout. Brass or gold-plate is universally good, although nickel is productive on some streams, especially those having a dark-brown cast to the water. Copper is favored in some areas; it's tops in Alaskan waters, perhaps because the trout and grayling are accustomed to feeding on the reddish-orange salmon eggs. Color is pretty much a local matter – a good one to study and a good one to argue about with other fishermen. Everyone is an expert.

Sizes In Spinning Lures: For stream fishing, the accepted standard in lure weight for spinning has been the one-quarter-ounce sizes. However, the trout fisherman, always trying for more delicacy, has been going to lighter lures until now when it's not unusual to find spin-fishermen using one-sixteenth-ounce lures. This makes sense in most waters, since the trout, on the average, isn't a large fish and a lure that approximates the size of its normal insect diet is certainly more effective in clear water than a large hunk of shiny metal.

The size of the lure to use depends on several factors. In big streams with deep water, where the stream has a dark cast or stain, use one-quarter-ounce lures or larger, especially in the early part of the season when the fish aren't yet feeding on insects. On the smaller streams, and in big water in late spring and summer, lures of one-eighth-ounce or smaller are good.

Again, your choice of color in a lure can be affected by the time of year. In early fishing, the more flash the better; trout are less wary then and are feeding regularly on silvery-sided minnows, which many of the wobblers suggest in form and action. Streams also are much more inclined to be colored at that time, so flash is good.

However, as the water clears and lessens in flow, trout become more choosy in feeding on insect life; the flashy lure, rather than attracting fish, more often will frighten them off. You have to make your method fit the mood of the stream, approximate its food life and look tantalizing to the fish.

Dark finishes in green, gray, even all black, are most effective for fishing clear pools – at least as effective as any spinning lure can be under these conditions. As a rule, as streams slacken and waters clear, and the spring urge for food subsides, spinning on a trout stream becomes much less effective than fly casting, so it's smart not to put all your eggs in the spinning basket for stream fishing.

Bass Spin-Fishing: In streams you won't find much difference between spinning for bass and for trout. Both fish lie in much the same spots and feed on the same food with the exception that bass are more likely to have a greater interest in minnows during the major part of the fishing

Zwirz focuses intently on the rod tip for the gentle "take" of a Bahamas bonefish. When he sees it, he'll drive the hook home into the sensitive mouth tissues of the hard-fighting, shallow-water bruiser. Get ready!

Once hooked, Zwirz passed his rod to a first-time bonefisherman to let him enjoy unparalleled action. Here, the Bahaman guide "tails" the played-out bonefish, then holds tight. Spinning outfit is fairly light, top sport!

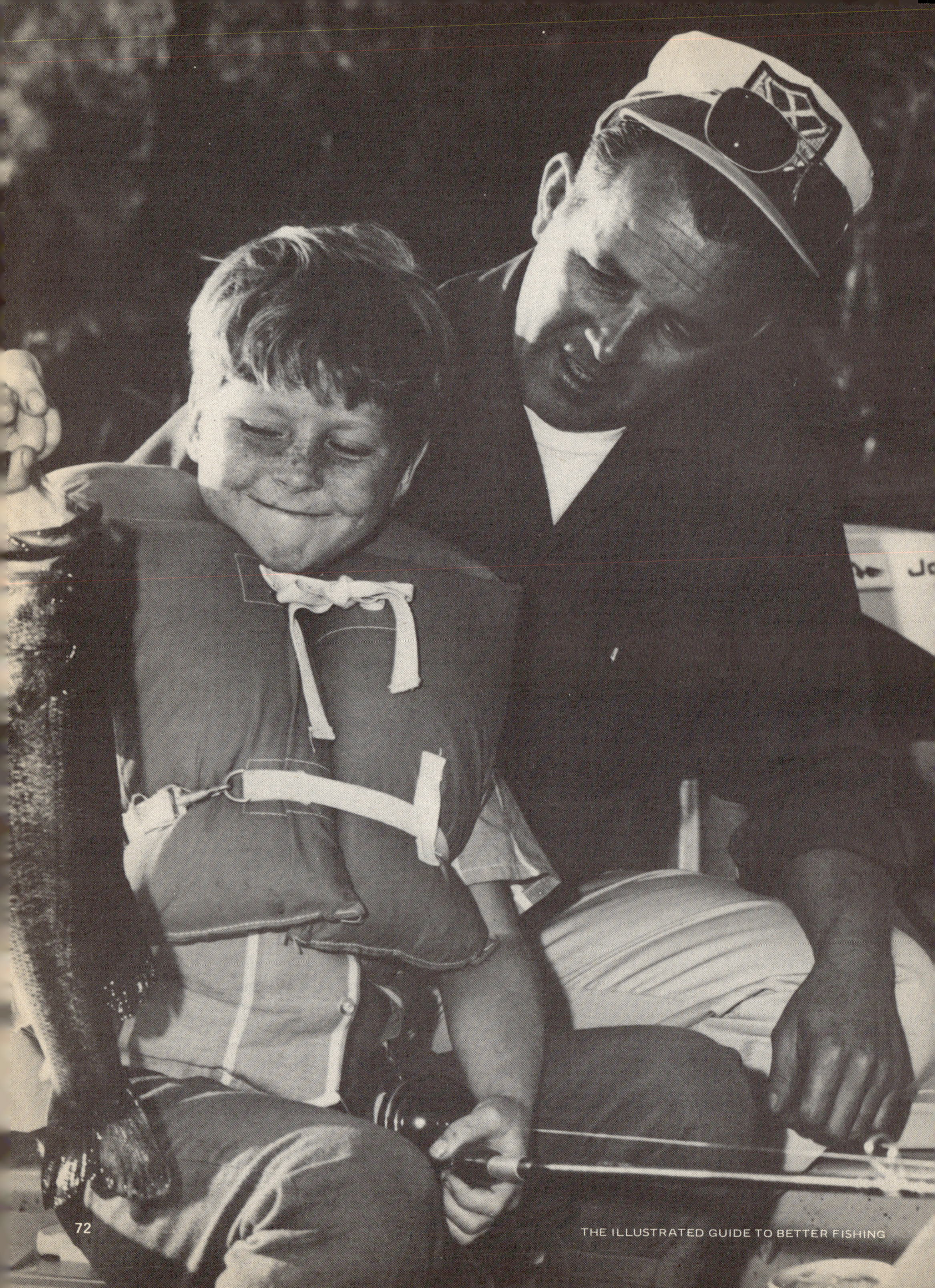

A spin-casting outfit is simplicity itself! These two New Mexico anglers find it just great for casting "hardware." The result in this case is a 3½-pound rainbow trout. Good tackle is only half the challenge, however.

season. This means fewer dead spots in the angler's year when going for bass. Bass are far more reluctant than trout to come to or near the surface in stream feeding, so keep lures deep.

Salmon And Steelhead: Spinning has done wonders for West Coast anglers after salmon and steelhead. For steelhead drifters, it's the best way of baitfishing with egg clusters and with the cherry bobber. During the upstream spawning run, steelhead work close to the bottom and that's where you have to keep the lure. The light monofilament largely overcomes the drag that prevents your doing so.

Equally important is the fact that the light line keeps the fisherman in intimate contact with the bottom and the taking fish. Though the drifter continually feels his bait or lure bumping on the rocks and gravel, the sensitivity of the line enables him to tell the difference between that bumping and the gentle tug of a fish taking the hook.

Opposite page: Few early memories surpass a youngster's first trophy fish, here a largemouth bass. Dad showed him the proper use of his closed-face spinning rig.

Heavier Tackle: Both steelhead and salmon are big, powerful fish with fixed ideas about running back to the Pacific when hooked. The West Coast fisherman likes plenty of line on his reel and a fairly long, stiff rod to put some restraint on those wildly running silversides when they decide to beat it out of the pool and away from that stinging hook. Reels of the light saltwater type, holding at least two hundred yards of ten-pound monofilament, are just about essential, and the drifting rod usually is eight feet or more in length, both to handle the fish and to work the bait effectively in the big streams.

The long rod has a sensitive tip so that the drifter can really feel what's going on as the bait rolls along near the bottom. These rods and reels also are great for fishing the big spoons and spinners used almost entirely for salmon and steelhead in Western fishing.

Salmon Spinning And Mooching: Among the saltwater fraternity you'll find increasing numbers of sportfishermen going to the spinning gear for mooching and spinning with herring and candlefish – baits dearly loved by king and silver salmon, in that order.

Both of these natural baits have been fished for years on long rods having sensitive tips, so the method lends itself wonderfully to the use of spinning tackle with its light line and fine drag adjustments. In mooching, a herring is plug-cut to give it a wobbling, weaving movement in the

Continued on page 78

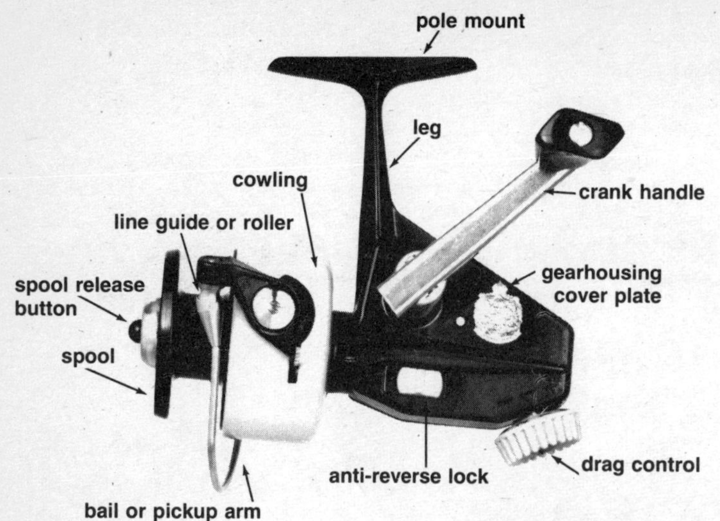

Selecting Your Equipment

Open-Face Spin-Casting

An open-face spinning reel is often best for the beginner, as it offers several advantages: It's far less likely to backlash than the revolving-spool reel, and it permits you to cast lighter lures farther and with less effort. A light-to-medium reel is suitable for the novice angler.

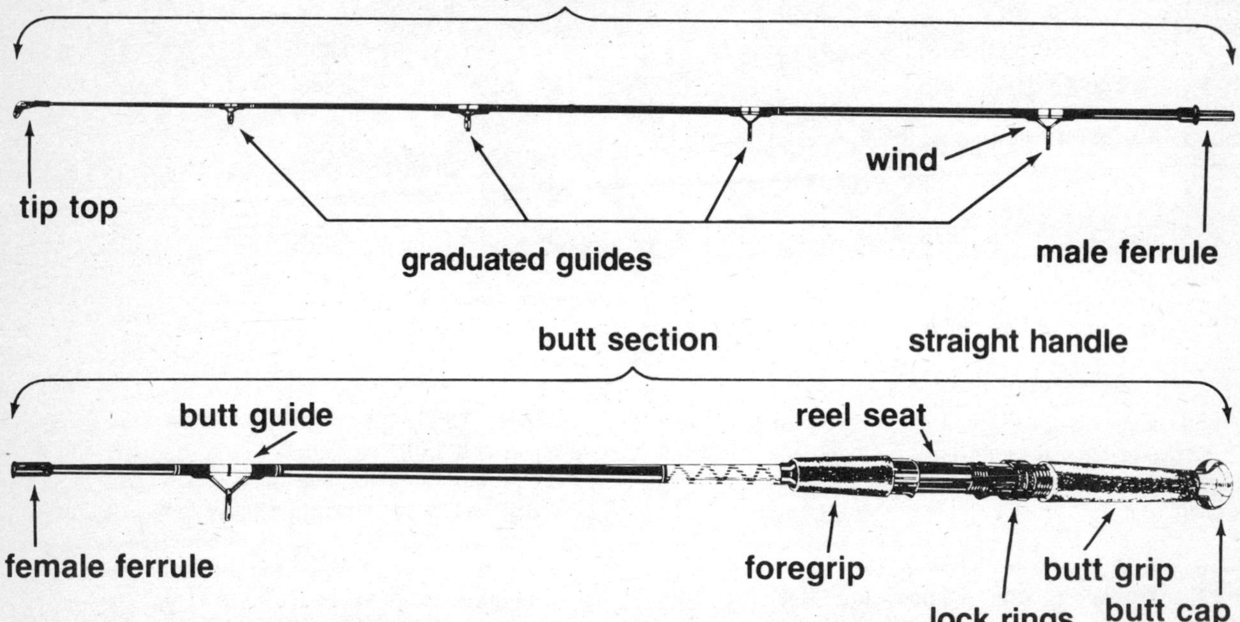

Spinning rods are characterized by straight handles and graduated ring guides, and can generally be split into five categories from ultralight to ultraheavy. Each class is determined by the optimum lure weight range of each rod. For class and general tournament purposes, use a light-action, 5½- to 6½-foot rod that is capable of casting ¼- to 3/8-ounce lures. Use the above charts to learn terminology of the rod's parts.

In choosing your line and plugs, a good general guide is to use 6- to 10-pound-test monofilament line for practice, competition and most freshwater fishing. Plugs weighing ¼ to 3/8-ounce are ideal for outdoor practice, but rubber plugs should be used indoors.

Line diameter (inches)	Approximate test (pounds)	Lure weight (ounces)	Rod class
.005-.006	1.75	1/32-3/16	Ultralight
.006-.007	2.25	1/16-1/8	Ultralight
.007-.008	3.00	1/16-1/8	Ultralight
.008-.009	4.00	1/8-1/4	Ultralight
.009-.010	5.00	1/4-3/8	Light
.010-.011	6.00	1/4-3/8	Light
.011-.012	7.00	1/4-3/8	Medium-Light
.012-.013	8.00	3/8-1/2	Medium
.013-.014	9.50	3/8-1/2	Medium
.015-.018	14.00	3/8-5/8	Heavy
.018-.020	17.00	5/8-103	Extra-heavy
.021-.024	22.00	5/8-103	Extra-heavy

The accompanying chart permits you to match or balance your line, lure and rod. This is a requirement for outstanding performance out on the water.

Making Your Play

The Overhead Cast

Grip the rod with the reel leg between your second and third fingers. Your thumb should be on top and your index finger extended. With your free hand, rotate the reel's cowling until the line roller is directly beneath your extended index finger. Pick up the line with the first joint of your index finger. Now cock the bail by flopping it open and you're ready to begin your cast. Follow the guide.

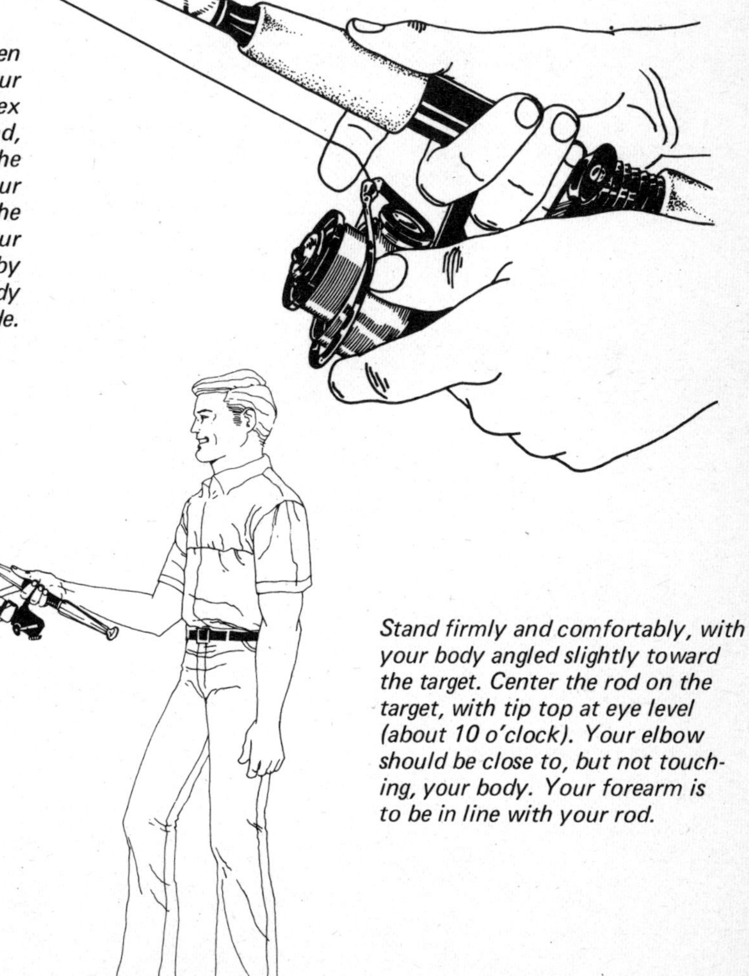

Stand firmly and comfortably, with your body angled slightly toward the target. Center the rod on the target, with tip top at eye level (about 10 o'clock). Your elbow should be close to, but not touching, your body. Your forearm is to be in line with your rod.

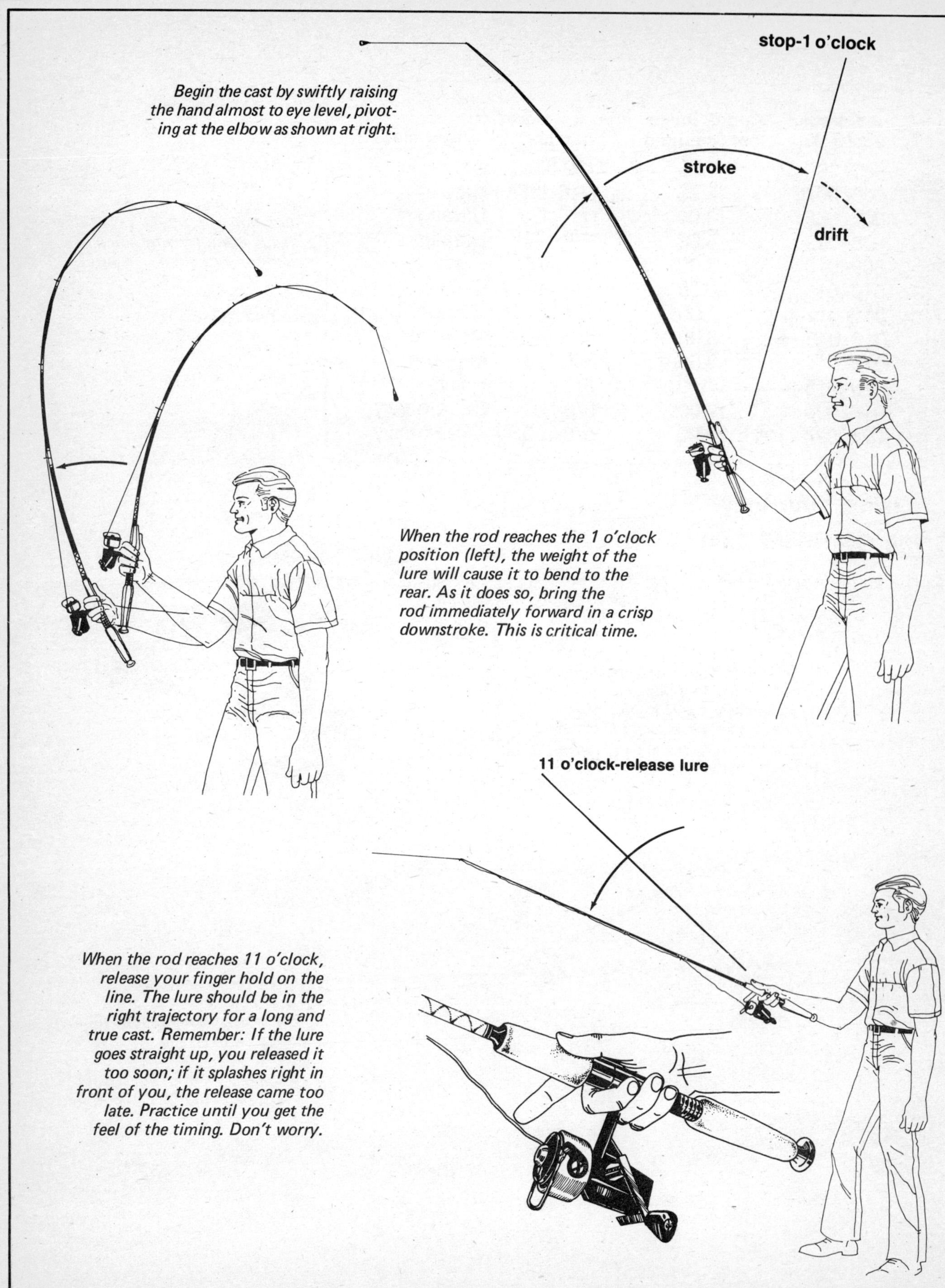

Begin the cast by swiftly raising the hand almost to eye level, pivoting at the elbow as shown at right.

When the rod reaches the 1 o'clock position (left), the weight of the lure will cause it to bend to the rear. As it does so, bring the rod immediately forward in a crisp downstroke. This is critical time.

When the rod reaches 11 o'clock, release your finger hold on the line. The lure should be in the right trajectory for a long and true cast. Remember: If the lure goes straight up, you released it too soon; if it splashes right in front of you, the release came too late. Practice until you get the feel of the timing. Don't worry.

As the lure nears the target, gently brake or "feather" the line with your index finger. The moment contact is made, simply place your finger on the edge of the spool, which creates a block that will not only stay the flight of the lure, but also help to prevent slack buildup on the spool.

As you begin the retrieve, the line guide pickup will automatically flop over to engage the line. Unlike a bait-casting outfit, you don't change hands to begin the retrieve. You use the hand that's already free for this. Former bait-casters will need to make style adjustments.

The Side Cast

The same fundamentals of timing and motion apply here as to the overhead cast, and this method is used, for example, when overhanging brush or timber obstructs an overhead type of presentation. All that you're doing is keeping your casting arc parallel to the ground. Since the arc may also be smaller, you must put extra emphasis on wrist action.

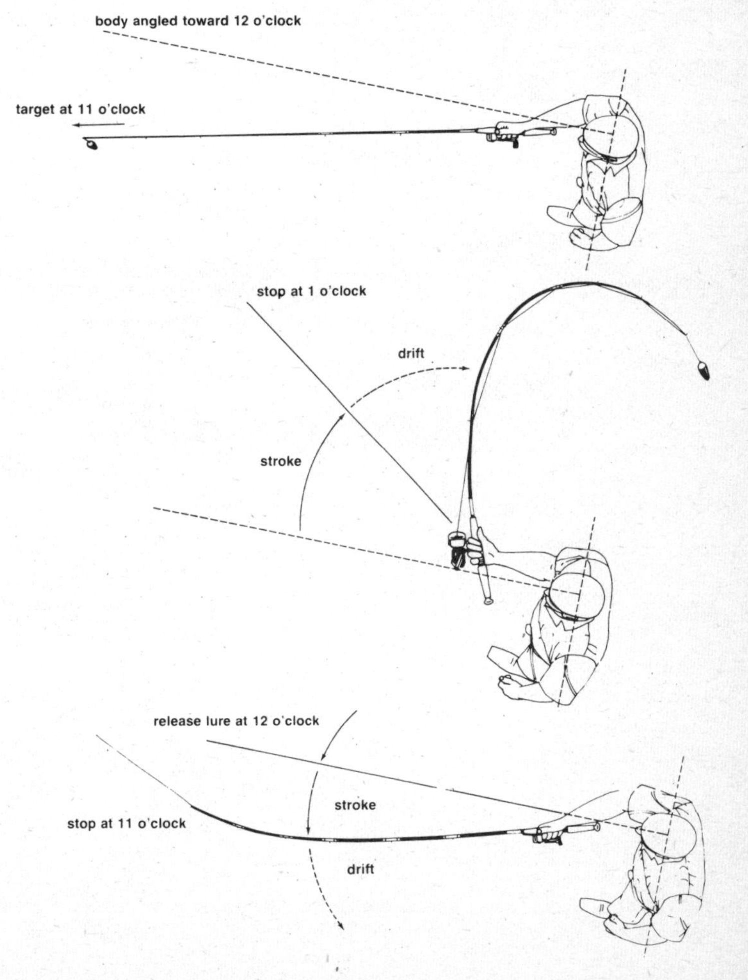

water. This is then rigged to a pair of short-shanked hooks in tandem, which are tied into a seven or eight-foot length of monofilament. A keel sinker of two or three ounces rides between line and leader, and the bait is lowered in the fast-moving tide that sends it swimming and wobbling on its way. When the tide runs well, the angler fishes from an anchored boat. When it slacks off, he mooches with his outboard, moving just fast enough to keep the bait moving.

As the term is used on the West Coast, spinning has nothing to do with the tackle used. There, the bait is a strip

Spinning has its place, but unless these casters are using weedless surface lures, the lily pads could be a huge headache. Zwirz would use a bait-casting outfit and stout monofilament to free lure if it snags, and horse big bass.

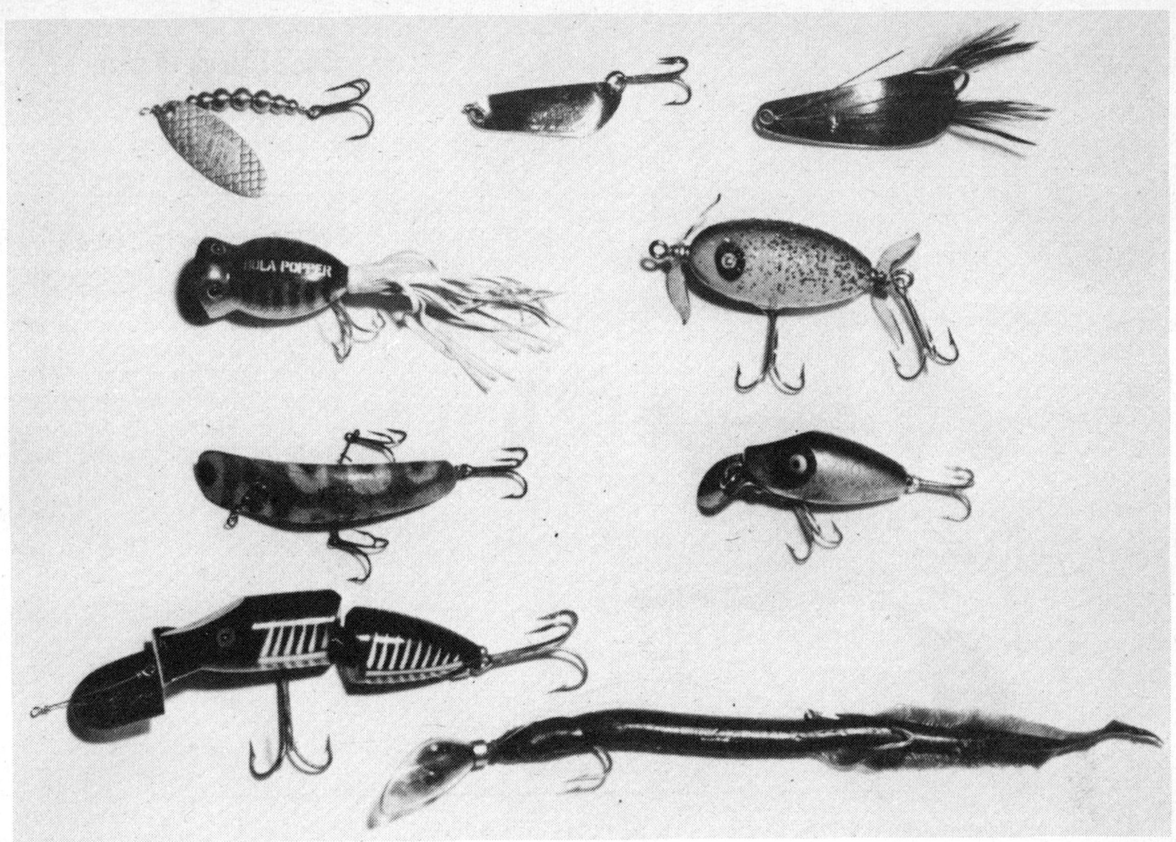

From small to medium-size and light to heavy, the right spinning rig and correct pound-test monofilament can make your terminal offering work like magic. Here are a few old favorites (above) not likely to ever lose favor with anglers.

A medium or heavy-duty spinning outfit, using heavier pound-test mono, can be used to handle the large plugs that attract big bass, northern pike and muskie. In the group at left are jointed and single-piece L&S MirrO-Lures, a couple of Heddon River Runts, plus a nameless small-fry bait imitation that just might work.

cut from the fillet of a herring or a whole candlefish is used. Bait is rigged the same as for mooching, but it is cast from an anchored boat and stripped up from the bottom with a pumping motion that causes the strip to spin.

All-around effectiveness of spinning as an angling method is demonstrated by its almost universal use in every type of fresh water and in many saltwater areas. There's no question about its deadliness in stream fishing – one reason you hear so many complaints about it from fly fishermen. On lakes and ponds, it is replacing the casting rod to a degree in those heavily fished sections where the going is tough and game fish are increasingly becoming lure shy and ultra-sophisticated.

The little plug lures, weighing from one-quarter to three-eighths-ounce, are certainly more like natural food for bass than the huge, gaudy creations the plug-caster normally needs, or at least uses, with his multiplying reel. In luring wary fish, the small lure has a sneaky way of insinuating itself into the hiding places of game fish without

Continued on page 85

Selecting Your Equipment

Closed-Face Spin-Casting

America's favorite "fishing machine" is the closed-face spin-casting reel. Its advantages include a combination fixed-spool/closed-cover design, which practically eliminates backlash, plus a thumb stop that makes line control easier. For most fishing applications, a light-to-medium freshwater rig is sufficient. Can you name the parts?

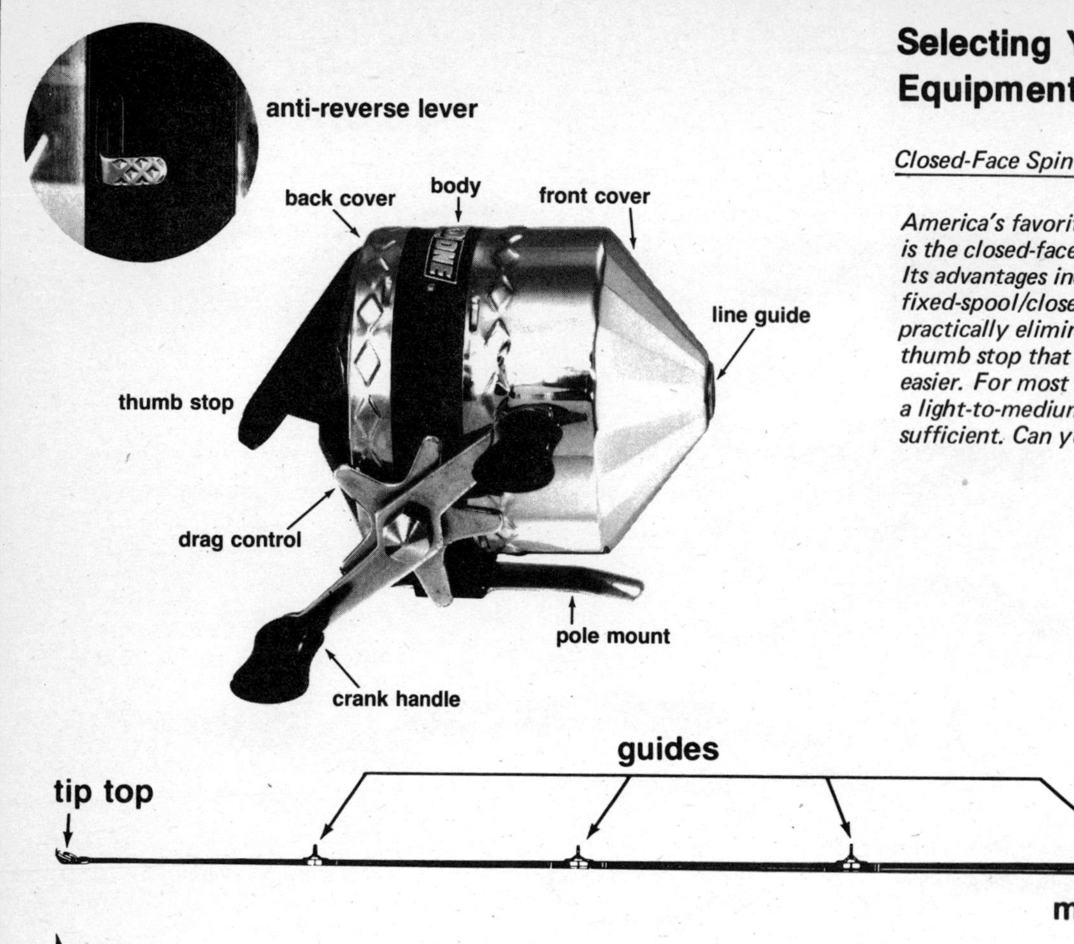

The weight of the lure to be cast, not the size of the anticipated catch, generally determines the rod to be selected. Beginners will find they learn fastest on light-action model in 5½ to 6½-foot size.

Selecting lines and plugs is important to your overall fishing success, too. Light-to-medium lines and plugs are definitely recommended. Optimum is a combination of 6- to 10-pound-test line with ¼ to 3/8-ounce lure. You should stick with monofilament line exclusively – braided lines tend to pile up inside the reel housing. Yuk!

Making Your Play—The Overhead Cast

Step one: The two-handed cast results in greater accuracy, even for experienced spin-fishermen. Using the "rod hand," hold your rod with its reel handles (left) pointing up, your thumb depressing the thumb stop. Now place your "line hand" just ahead of the reel as shown and take the line lightly between your thumb and index finger. Got it? Try this: Depress the thumb stop and let the weight of your plug take the line out. Feel it slip through your thumb and finger? Do it again, and this time use that same thumb and finger to slow the line down a bit. Now one more time, only this time stop the line dead still at 12 inches, then halfway to the floor, then just as it touches the floor. The rest is easy, and you've only just begun! Let's get on with it!

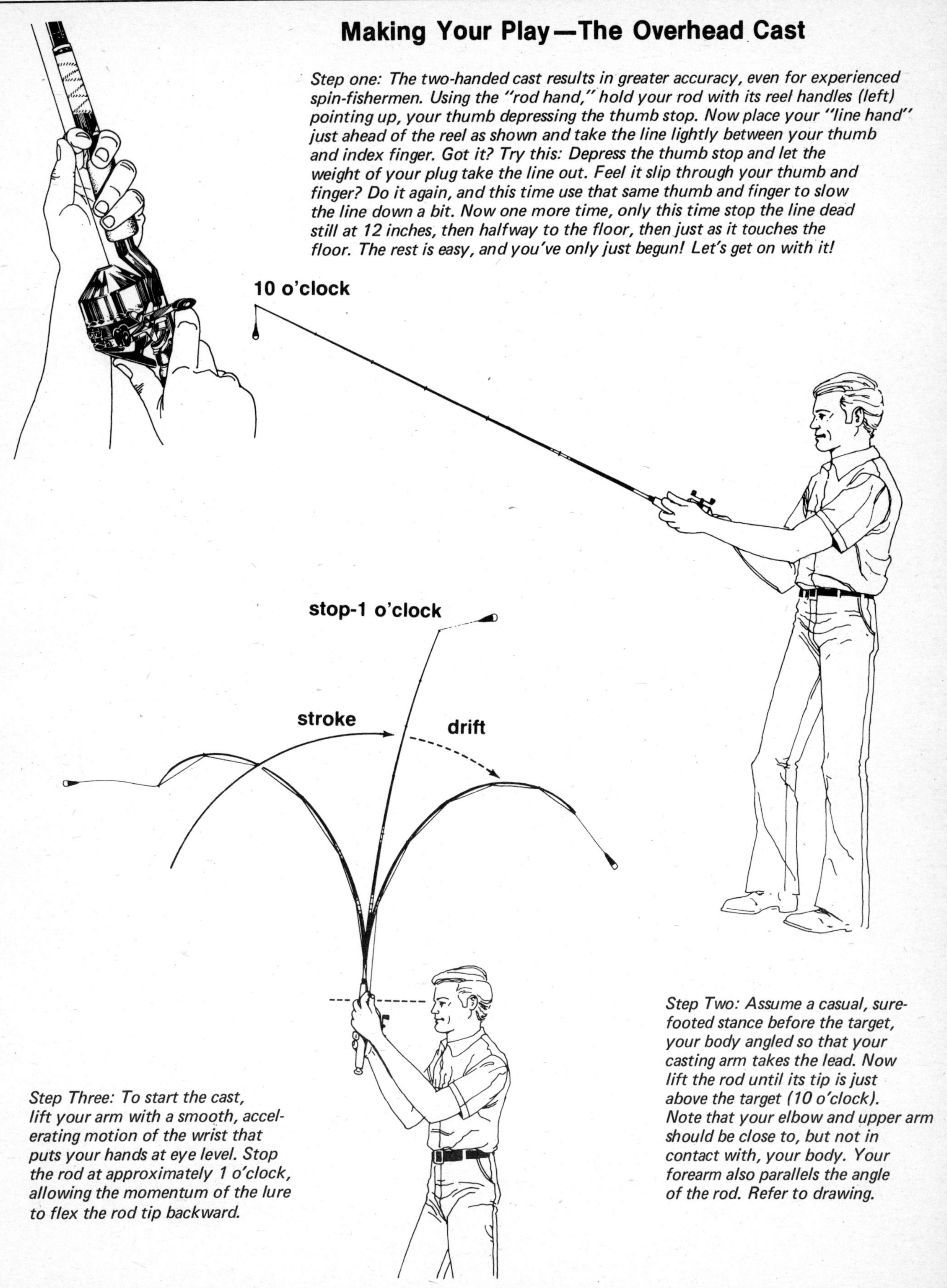

Step Two: Assume a casual, sure-footed stance before the target, your body angled so that your casting arm takes the lead. Now lift the rod until its tip is just above the target (10 o'clock). Note that your elbow and upper arm should be close to, but not in contact with, your body. Your forearm also parallels the angle of the rod. Refer to drawing.

Step Three: To start the cast, lift your arm with a smooth, accelerating motion of the wrist that puts your hands at eye level. Stop the rod at approximately 1 o'clock, allowing the momentum of the lure to flex the rod tip backward.

Step four: Without hesitation, commence the forward stroke with a quickly accelerated motion of the wrist and forearm (right). Follow exactly the same path as you took on the upstroke. At about 11 o'clock, release the thumb stop to set the lure in its flight to the intended target. Don't quit now, there's still more.

Step five: Follow through by lowering the tip of the rod to follow the flight of the lure (below). If the lure goes straight up in the air, you released the line too soon; if it chunks into the water right in front of you with a giant splash, you let go too late. Don't feel bad — even the pros do it occasionally.

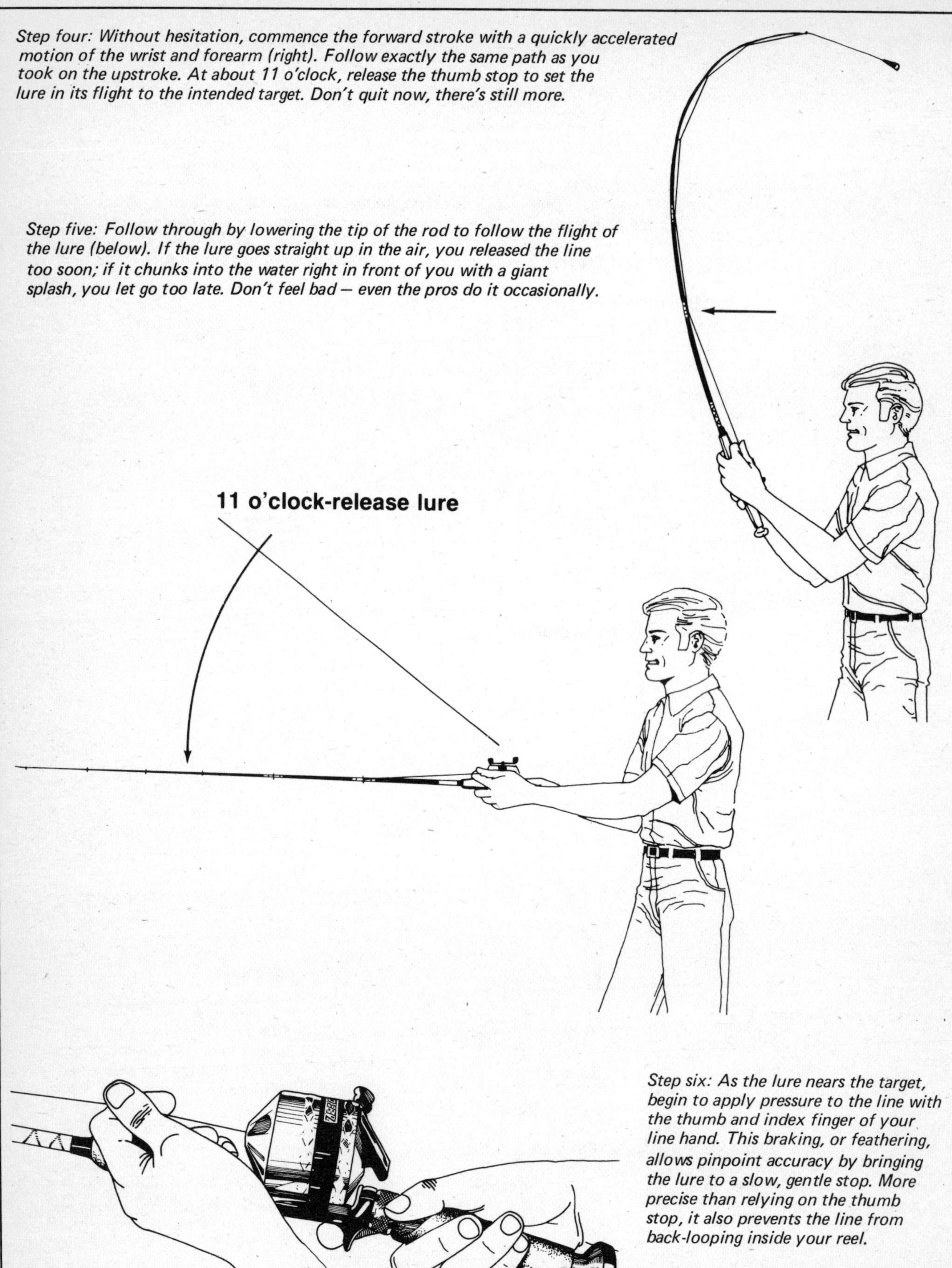

Step six: As the lure nears the target, begin to apply pressure to the line with the thumb and index finger of your line hand. This braking, or feathering, allows pinpoint accuracy by bringing the lure to a slow, gentle stop. More precise than relying on the thumb stop, it also prevents the line from back-looping inside your reel.

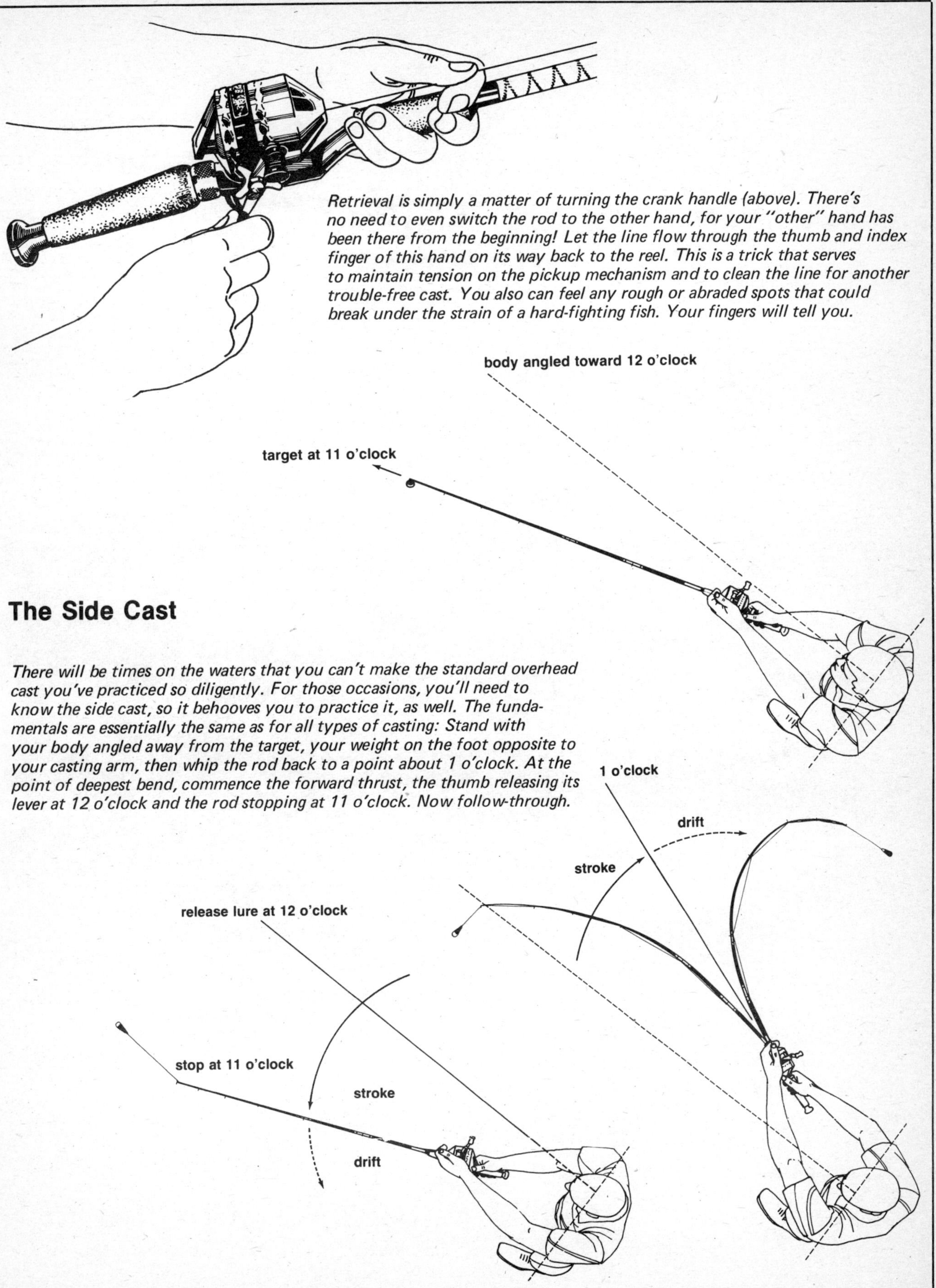

Retrieval is simply a matter of turning the crank handle (above). There's no need to even switch the rod to the other hand, for your "other" hand has been there from the beginning! Let the line flow through the thumb and index finger of this hand on its way back to the reel. This is a trick that serves to maintain tension on the pickup mechanism and to clean the line for another trouble-free cast. You also can feel any rough or abraded spots that could break under the strain of a hard-fighting fish. Your fingers will tell you.

The Side Cast

There will be times on the waters that you can't make the standard overhead cast you've practiced so diligently. For those occasions, you'll need to know the side cast, so it behooves you to practice it, as well. The fundamentals are essentially the same as for all types of casting: Stand with your body angled away from the target, your weight on the foot opposite to your casting arm, then whip the rod back to a point about 1 o'clock. At the point of deepest bend, commence the forward thrust, the thumb releasing its lever at 12 o'clock and the rod stopping at 11 o'clock. Now follow-through.

fuss or fanfare. This subtle approach is certainly a must today in thousands of lakes and ponds that take a pounding.

Fishing grows more difficult each year. While the number of fishermen steadily increases, the amount of water available for public fishing stays the same. So, as the competition gets tougher each year, the angler with the smaller lures – and the know-how to use them – has just that much better chance.

Plugs On The Spinning Rod: Spinning gear gets rid of that age-old curse of plug-casting – the inevitable backlash. Although makers of many casting reels claim their reels are free of this nuisance, few actually are. It takes a certain amount of skill to operate even the nonbacklash reels and, of course, these reels function properly only with lures having a fairly heavyweight one-half-ounce or more, which rules them out of the light-lure class. But on any sort of freshwater spinning tackle, no matter how light the plug, you can get good fishing distances without backlash.

For bass, you'll find it difficult to beat the small surface-popping plugs. As with all surface lures in bass fishing, the slow, erratic retrieve works the best. Fish bass near pads, weed beds, stumps, along brushy shorelines and under overhanging tree branches when they are most likely to be surface feeding in early morning and late afternoon and evening. With this type of lure your retrieve necessarily will be uneven; you'll be pumping the rod tip to pop the bait, taking a turn or two of the reel handle, then pumping the rod tip again.

This kind of bait-popping can, however, make a real mess of the line on your reel spool if you're using the normally springy monofilament – especially if it isn't laid evenly on the spool. It's better to use a braided nylon or dacron, or even a braided monofilament. These will lie smoothly on the reel with any kind of retrieve. If you do use the braided line, attach six feet or more of monofilament to the end of the line with a barrel knot. This will give you the less-visible connection you want and will keep the rod tip from fraying the line.

A weighted spoon cast to a passing school of 18- to 20-pound bluefish brought this action to fisherman using an open-face spinning rig. Casting from a boat is a breeze, too!

Keep Hooks Sharp: One of the disadvantages of spinning tackle is that it doesn't have guts enough to set a big hook in a hard-mouthed fish, unless the hook is needle sharp. If you're using line of six-pound test or less, your drag will be set at something less than this – perhaps three or four-pound tension. When the fish takes, your quick strike always will strip line from the spool as the hook takes hold. A dull hook with a wide barb won't set in a bass' jaw unless it's very sharp – or unless you're born lucky.

Check your bass lures for types of hooks, as well as for sharpness. If the hooks are spear-point – and these are common on lures – change over to imported trebles or doubles and keep these sharp with a hook stone. Any hook with a wide barb should have the barb stoned down or squeeze it down with a pair of pliers.

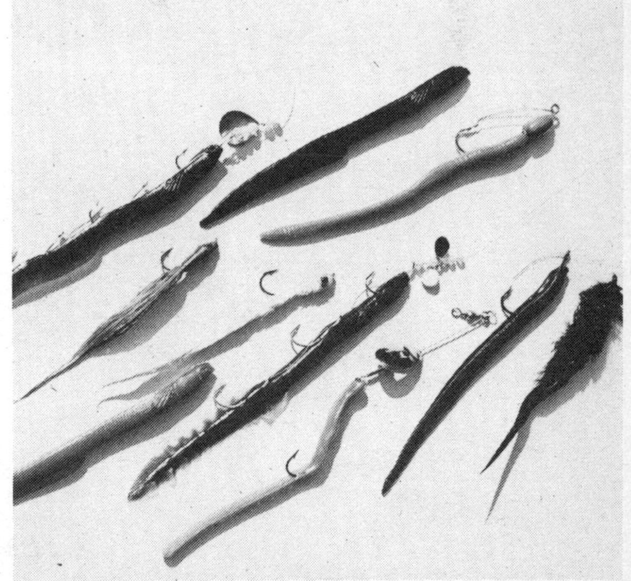

The eel-type lures, plus the newer plastic worms, will always take a share of fish, particularly largemouth bass.

Opposite page: Snook is one of the greatest game fish found anywhere in the world, and he's a natural for cast plugs or spoons. Spinning is a natural way to present them to him!

THE TRAIL TO SUPER ACTION

Chumming Is A Dirty Business, But It Can Bring Unlikely Game Fish To Your Hook!

THERE IS a seemingly elite group of fishermen that tend to look down their noses at those who would stoop to the practice of chumming. They often remain fishless while those who cast ground-up bait fish to the waters usually come in with loaded fish boxes!

However, there is far more to successful chumming than tossing ladles full of ground bait over the side. In fact, it's sort of an art closely akin to wrestling 'gators or milking cobras! It is an art form that makes more landlubbers seasick than all the rough seas since the invention of the boat. It is a messy job for the man with the chumming assignment. One guest on my saltwater sportfisherman, the *Gallant-Charger*, lasted exactly sixty-eight seconds before draping himself over the rail as though struck down by an invisible sledge.

Still, when all of the nicer strategies have failed,

Opposite page: While author and his wife fished a second boat along southern shores of Cat Island, the Bahamas, Captain Jerry Lewless and Oakley Bidwell bring in Allison tuna. Like blues and other game fish, tuna can be brought close by chumming or can be trolled. Left: 'Way up north in Nova Scotia, angler works a giant tuna that was enticed by chum line.

You should never attempt to boat a giant tuna with just your wife aboard, or alone. It's a job requiring lots of manpower to horse up to a half-ton over the side. Even with gin pole block and tackle setup, this is a backbreaker!

chumming can do minor miracles for anglers fishing not only saltwater species, but freshwater as well. This method tends to attract fish within range of the baits or lures of fishermen and has far more applications than many might suspect.

An exhausted Zwirz watches as four trophy sharks are taken off small runabout he used. Shark at left presented quite a problem, as did the mako on foredeck — not easy to get aboard the small boat. They were chummed close to big baits.

Basically a technique utilized by the still-fisherman, chumming lends itself to live-line or float-fishing techniques. Anyone who believes chumming is little else than a haphazard method of throwing over ground bait to attract a few fish is more wrong than right. Surprisingly few fishermen have learned much about its amazing productivity, unless they have gained experience by actually putting the method to use under varying circumstances and for a variety of game fish.

This method will attract most any fish you care to name; especially saltwater species. Stripers, bluefish, pollock, yellowfin tuna, cod, blackfin, amberjack, bonito, barracuda, king mackerel, jack crevalle, sea trout and even the wily snook seldom pass up the opportunity to come into a chum line and feed on the apparently free goodies. Sharks also tend to move into the scene from time to time, as will an occasional marlin, sailfish or swordfish.

Creation of chum calls for some type of bait fish to be passed through a meat grinder. This chum then is ladled overboard at spaced intervals in small amounts, based upon the speed at which the tide or current is moving. To stretch the chum, some anglers mix in seawater so the chum takes on the appearance of loose hash.

A great many types of bait are utilized in producing chum; to some degree, this depends upon the geographical region and the availability of certain baits at a given time. Such species as mossbunker, herring, anchovy, clam, shrimp, sardine, smelt and menhaden may be ladled into the sea, although the choice of chum makings may depend upon the specific species of game fish sought.

Once continuity of the chum line is established, one must take care that it does not develop a break or open area. Fish will move up an unbroken line of chum practically to the boat's hull, but should it become broken, it becomes necessary for the entire process to be repeated

A typical chumming setup on a party boat: machine grinder (lower right), and tubs of mossbunker or similar oily bait fish. The mate here unhooks a small bluefish just caught using this most successful fishing method.

until the unbroken chain of food draws fish into range of baited hook or lure.

With chumming in an unbroken line so all-important, you often hear much hollering and complaining if and when another boat crosses or anchors down-current from the boat that has already established its chum line. The simple movement of water created by a boat crossing a chum line can cause a washout of the trail of ground fish-feed. This takes all the magic out of the work under way.

It is possible to do your chumming off the boat's stern, however, it usually can be done more efficiently from a position along the side and in the forward section,

Left: Mate grabs the leader and prepares to hoist aboard another bluefish that was attracted by the chum line. Below: "This is a very busy mate on a party boat," Zwirz comments. "One minute he mans the chum ladle, and the next he hooks a scrappy bluefish for a little personal fun."

In Florida's Ten Thousand Islands, Zwirz was seeding tarpon holes with cut bait when shark grabbed his baited hook. Landing him was rough job on open-face spinning gear!

especially if the current or tide is running strong. Calm days are perfect for working the chum line. Once anchored, the boat rarely weathervanes in any direction but that dictated by tide. On the other hand, one is hard pressed to keep an acceptable chum line going if the wind is blowing in a different direction; this will cause most any boat to yaw, first one way, then another.

For this reason, knowledgeable fishermen bring along two anchors. The first is lowered to the bottom in the usual manner so that it holds firmly. The boat is then run ahead and off to the side of the spot where the first anchor is positioned. The second anchor is put over the side and the boat allowed to drift back slightly before this line then is made fast.

The boat positioned in the apex of a secure triangle, the anchors will hold the craft steady, bow facing into the tide or current. Positioned with no problem of yawing, the chum can be ladled over the stern with no fear of breaking the feed line.

The chum line established, the anglers get their baited hooks out into the area. In this situation, utilize the live-lining method of presentation in which your baited hook is allowed to drift back with the current. Normally no sinker or added weight is used, though the bait can be held at a specific level by means of a float for some species.

Possibly no other fish receives more coaxing with chum than does the ever-popular bluefish. Up and down the coasts, working fishermen feed the menhaden into the grinder where it is churned to a pulpy consistency, then mixed with just the right amount of sea water.

Then starts the ritual. Once the school of blues moves in along the trail of bait, fishermen usually have a fairly long, rewarding session with these hard-fighting bait choppers.

The wise old heads generally have rigged their tackle in about the same manner; one is likely to see Eagle Claw or Mustad Beak hooks ranging in size from 3/0 all the way to 8/0. Hook sizes depend on the size of the blues expected at a specific season in a given area. If the fish are running in the two or three-pound class, a 3/0 hook will handle them nicely.

For blues running five to seven pounds or larger, a wise decision for the angler is to move up in hook size to the 8/0 for the mean ol' tide runners. If the blues are not yet skittish about terminal tackle, use a short section of wire between your line and the hook. A heavy bluefish can chop through an angler's line.

An odiferous mixture of catfood and ground trash fish was satisfactorily employed to seed Kentucky Lake for crappie.

The Caribbean gives up one of several grouper, wahoo and barracuda chummed along a coral area in deep water.

Once the blues realize that there are baited, wired hooks anywhere they look, they begin getting line-shy. It is not rare to find the school passing up cut baits presented with the added wire. Often one fisherman hooks into one fish after another, while the fellow standing at his elbow enjoys only an occasional wary strike. It is the angler sans wire who was having all the action. When the action is heavy and big fish are everywhere in the chum, all you need worry about is keeping your own hooked blues clear of other angler's lines.

Still after tarpon, author instead puts a small snook in the net. Glad Zwirz enjoys his tarpon-fishing frustration.

Most individuals fishing blues in a chum line, either from a party boat or private craft, tend to steer clear of light tackle. They owe this courtesy to their companions. There just isn't any way to handle a big blue with overly light tackle when fishing shoulder to shoulder. Most outfits include rods that measure six feet in length, not over seven.

There is a wide selection of reels and any of them of conventional medium-size would be satisfactory. It should boast a reliable drag control and be capable of spooling from 150 to 250 yards of 40-pound monofilament. This same basic outfit will serve nicely whenever you troll for blues or for such species as albacore, bonito and in most striper-trolling situations.

Whenever I fish alone or with no more than two other fishermen, I bring along lighter tackle. It allows more sport. For still-fishing or trolling, such a rod has a four-ounce tip section nicely balanced with Penn 2/0 Senators. Each of

After hauling aboard and releasing forty blues of this size, author grimaces while holding one aloft. Chum line was the potent medicine on Long Island Sound, Connecticut (above).

Zwirz did the chumming off New Jersey while companion tried his luck with the fly rod. Instead of a school of bluefish, he hooked hard-fighting bonita that stripped 300 feet of backing before angler could cool him down!

In a rare photo, this single, unwary bonefish gobbles torn-apart shrimp that guide spread around bottom near boat. He eventually grabbled the whole shrimp angler offered. Most bonefish would have spooked at the photographer.

these can be spooled with monofilament or with up to two hundred yards of 30-pound Dacron or braided nylon. Fishing solo, I'll use either a Fenwick or Heddon popping rod coupled to the Ambassadeur 6000 reel.

Mackerel are not at all shy about showing next to the boat when tiny scraps of herring, mullet, menhaden or squid are ladled into the sea. A mess of pilchards or anchovies do well for West Coast anglers looking for fast action on yellowtail or white sea bass. Nor should one underestimate the drawing power of such tidbits as live grass shrimp. They will draw sea trout from acres away and hold them close while you fish them with bait or cast to them with a small pearl metal squid tipped with a piece of shrimp.

Fishing such spots as the coastal Carolinas, Florida, Mexico and the Bahamas, I've experimented with various chum baits. Some I've used in the traditional chum line, while others have been put to use in either a chum pot or chum bag. The latter two coax the lineup of bottom feeders/reef fish into range of my baited hooks. I've hooked into giant groupers, jewfish, barracuda, tarpon; even the mayhem offered by an outraged giant ray.

Crushed mussels lure a fair share of California corbina and flounder. Fluke, on the other hand, seem to go more for ground mossbunker, while ground clams in your chum pot can be pure magic when it comes to tautog and sheepshead. Most species relish a particular bait more than others, but there are times when a given ground bait will coax in the darndest lineup of fish you'd care to imagine.

There was the time I was trying to entice cruising tarpon within reach of my fly rod. It was off the port of Caracas that my guide and I began breaking up blue crabs and tossing them all around the boat until a great shadow zoomed under the boat. It was a sleek, white marlin cruising looking, I think, for the smaller fish that were coming in to feed on the crabs.

After ten minutes of casting a five-inch streamer ahead of his path, he struck at it savagely. And I struck back so hard that my rod snapped off right at the butt. Never will I forget that first contact with a marlin on the fly rod, brief though it was.

Another time, I seeded an area on an Eastern impoundment and began fishing for white perch. Instead, I found myself rushing home to show off a twenty-seven-inch brown trout that found my mixture of ground worms, oatmeal and sand.

CHAPTER 7

READING THE WATERS

The Fish Are There, And Proper Knowledge Can Help Sort Them Out

Opposite page: Fish occupy only ten percent of the total available water acreage, and trophies like this one fewer still! Salmon and trout in Canada's Miramichi take different positions in the stream (above), and anglers who know the difference will have best luck. Study bottom cover, too.

PROPER READING of fishing waters remains one of the more essential talents relating to consistent angling success. The fisherman capable of determining what's going on *beneath* the water's surface has won a major part of the game.

Most all sportsmen who have given serious thought to this basic subject realize there is a marked difference between just casting and productive fishing. Successful anglers accept this fact and learn their art carefully. A fair part of this difference lies in the angler's ability to determine, by looking carefully at a lake or a stream, just what is happening under the surface and how it will help or hinder his fishing.

Streams, other than tiny brooks, are extremely complex in the depth and flow of their currents. Each variation in stream movement has some definite meaning that almost precisely fixes the way you'll fish, the size of the lure and, in some cases, even the fly pattern you'll select. And every species of fish has a special liking for a certain type of lake or pond or a particular basic situation in a stream. One can learn about these likes and dislikes only by careful observation while fishing. Take time out from casting to see exactly what's going on. It all follows a fairly logical pattern, if you know what it is you are seeking.

Assuming you're on a stream known to have more than one species of trout, it becomes possible to pick out the location where you are most likely to find one species more than others. Many streams hold three kinds of trout, many more at least two kinds, particularly in Eastern waters. Quite often, one fishes differently for the varying species of trout right in the same areas of the stream on the same day.

About ten years ago Glad, my wife, and I were working wet flies on a well known Eastern stream that has both

Zwirz, fishing West Virginia in late summer, searches out cold spring holes to find smart smallmouth bass and trout in normally warm waters. He knows big fish seek out colder waters and will check topographical maps for them.

brown and brook trout in about equal proportion. The average size of the browns here is larger. This stream holds an occasional rainbow, as well, but they are encountered so infrequently that they come as a special surprise.

On this particular day, the brown trout weren't stirring. Insect life on the stream was sparse, the only flies evident being small dark caddis winging their way endlessly upstream in little groups of two or three; nothing spectacular at all. The larger browns just weren't going to be interested until late afternoon or evening brought new mayfly or stone fly action.

However, we had started at sunup and already had decided on a full day's angling. It was early June. The stream level was normal, the water clear and the sun bright, with a cool breeze from the West stirring the leaves on the hardwoods throughout the river valley. In short, it was an excellent fishing day.

As anglers who knew the stream well, we headed first for the section well upriver where we knew the brown trout lived. However, we worked the water hard, fishing the deep runs and the heads of pools with most of our favorite flies for several hours, without stirring the yellow sides of a single brown trout. But we did take several pink-flanked brook trout. None of these were over ten inches, unworthy of keeping.

Left: Realizing a trout was lying in depression behind rock to escape primary flow of river, this fly fisherman drifted a nymph pattern to trout's feeding position — with success! Right: Nice-sized bluefish was taken after angler learned this spot was in a channel leading to nearby river filled with bait fish. Big blues used this route.

Nova Scotia jetty fishermen know well that rocks hold crabs and other bait fish that attract stripers, blues, blackfish. Surf keeps bait loose and moving — great spot for action!

As the morning passed, we faced the fact that it had to be brook trout or nothing, so we changed tactics, switched to smaller flies of a different pattern and began to work the pocket holes behind the big boulders by sinking the fly deep, then switching it to the surface of the water.

Soon I had a pair of nice native trout better than a foot long, so I decided to open them up for a look at their day's diet. To my surprise, I found these fish well padded-out with large black, winged wood ants. Apparently, this was the ant's mating time and, in moving along the banks, many were falling into the stream. Brook trout seem to like ants better than any other species of trout, though why any trout likes them is difficult to understand; they're filled with bitter formic acid.

However, it seemed to make sense to imitate the color, size and form of these ants, so I trimmed-up a No. 8 Leadwing Coachman and Black Gnat and fished these deep. I was still stubborn enough to feel the brown trout were feeding on these, also, but as it turned out that just wasn't the case. For another hour or so both of us worked our pet brown trout lies without a touch!

Finally, we gave up on the browns and moved downstream to a spot where a large cold-spring brook poured into the river. Downstream from this mouth, the river holds a long stretch of big-boulder pocket water, ideal for brook trout. From this stretch we brought our total catch of brookies to sixteen, the largest two a bit over

Opposite page: One fine trout from a Maine river! Hot weather, a deep pool and heavy oxygen brought this lunker to the location, where a skillfully offered fly got him.

Shadows, rock bottom and boulders spelled smallmouth bass during late afternoon's outing. Such knowledge paid off in finding the fish, where many anglers come up empty.

An undercut bank in the shade that's free from most predators and high in oxygen (from the white water) is a prime hiding and holding area for good-sized rainbow trout. Besides a big fish, smaller ones are close by.

seventeen inches long. I hooked only one brown trout during the entire day and certainly would have had poor sport had we not concentrated finally on the brook trout.

In any stream where you'll find brookies and browns and/or rainbows, the brookies play second fiddle. The bigger browns and rainbows will bull them out of the best locations, the browns usually taking over the best spots and the rainbow, if any, taking seconds. So, look for browns in the deepest runs, at the tail of the riffle coming into a pool or wherever the combination of good cover and constant food supply is obviously the best. Deep water furnishes the cover, current flow furnishes food.

Brook trout usually are shoved out of these choice spots to the areas below the middle of the pools or runs, off to the side of the heavy pool riffles and in the little back eddies behind the big, projecting boulders. The rainbows take over the fastest riffles, usually finding a depression in the bottom where they can lie out of the primary current, which moves over them carrying the food supply.

Obviously, there is no hard and fast rule about exactly where you'll find each type of trout. Any trout picks his feeding spot with a view to protective cover – deep water, overhanging banks, logs, stumps, ledges or boulders – where he can hide, yet obtain food coming within reach with minimum effort. In a one-hundred-yard stretch of almost any stream, you'll probably find every species of trout that uses the stream at all. It just helps greatly to be able to know where they lie, for much water in every stream is barren of the sizeable game-fish you wish to catch.

Wide, shallow riffles or slow, shallow to medium-depth pools hold few trout except the smaller ones, especially during warmer weather. Flat, open pools, with sand or small gravel bottoms lacking fairly large rocks, also are poor locations to look for trout. These fish are naturally more timid than other species, continually seeking protection from ospreys, eagles, herons, mink, otter and raccoon, as well as human fishermen. And, since they depend on the flow of water to bring food, you'll need to look for them with this in mind.

Certain types of streams are more favorable for one species than others. In a slow-moving meadow stream, which tends to warm up considerably during the summer months, you'll find browns and browns only. If you want to catch rainbows, seek the fastest streams where the clear water is moving continually from one series of rapids to another. Since rainbows need plenty of oxygen, you'll find them in turbulent flows which maintain a cool temperature during the hot months. The presence of turbulence keeps the oxygen content high.

Chain pickerel in East Lake, near Manns Harbor, North Carolina, look for their idea of ideal cover, in this case a stickup protruding from a weedy bottom section.

Brook trout, oddly enough, seem to have more cosmopolitan tastes than other species. Just so long as the water stays cold – 70 degrees Fahrenheit, or less – you'll find brook trout in the slowest of wilderness brown-water streams as well as the fastest cascades of mountain brooks.

Fishermen who prefer lake fishing have more trouble locating fish, since different species live at different levels, depending on the water temperature. The reason for this is the oxygen is the most important thing in life to a fish, next to food, and water's oxygen content is determined chiefly by its temperature.

It's generally known that smallmouth bass, walleyes, northern pike and muskie don't do well in warm-water lakes. But largemouth bass and almost all species of panfish can tolerate the heat of Southern climates, thriving in lukewarm water. Obviously, you won't fish in shallow, warm-water lakes and ponds for smallmouth bass or walleyes, landlocked salmon or any of the trout species. But it helps to know where to find the fish you're after in lakes where they are known to be.

For example, you'll be wasting your time in fishing the shallow weed beds and lily pads for smallmouth bass in hot weather; they're certain to be in deeper water. But these are the spots for taking largemouth bass, pickerel, pike and also panfish. So the depth at which you do your fishing will have a great deal to do with the type of lure or method you use.

In addition to depth and to changing temperatures as the fishing season progresses, the relative clarity of the water itself has much to do with your choice of lure and method. This is because the depth at which a fish can readily see your lure is largely determined by the clarity, though there are other factors; such as cloudy weather, heavy riffles and the sharpness of a particular fish's vision.

In bright sunlight in a clear-water lake, a white plug can be seen readily at a depth of twenty-five feet. The same plug in dark brown water can't be seen much more than a yard away. If and when a lake is working, this visibility is, again, cut down by half, so your lure would need to pass within a couple of feet of your fish for him to see it at all. Under these adverse conditions you'll need to space your casts closely together as you work any given part of the lake, in order to be certain that your fish could see it.

Even farm ponds offer variations like greater depth areas, springs, and vegetation or cover. Knowing the bottom cover adds up to stringers such as this taken by Oklahoma angler.

Naturally, these variable conditions in lake waters have a great deal to do with the way you will cover them and what size and color lure you will use. Waters of many degrees of brown are found in great fishing country. Along with cover, food and oxygen supply, this must be considered carefully when reading your water. Consistent success depends upon it!

CHAPTER 8

The author poses with four trophy lakers dredged up from deep-water channels of a Northwest Territories' lake in Canada. Even fly rod can be rigged with breakaway sinker allowing deep presentation of bait-fish imitation fly.

OVER THE past ten years or more, numerous articles have been written about structure fishing, plus the importance of both water temperature and oxygen in the life cycle of popular fresh and salt water game fish.

Though world-wide research has been taking place in both fresh and salt water, possibly no facet has been more widely studied than that of the ever-expanding salmon fishery of the Great Lakes. These trophy-size salmon have been caught in water as deep as a hundred feet. Best success seems to require a slow troll at this strata and there are seasons when both chinook and coho inhabit these same depths. During the spring, these same fish are taken consistently well within thirty feet of the surface. Great from sporting aspects, this doesn't solve certain unique problems that exist when depths from forty to a hundred feet must be explored with artificial lures or natural baits.

Lake trout and even largemouth bass undergo periods when only a deep presentation will produce results. The laker is notorious for this during the warmer months, lurking far deeper than many fishermen can believe. Just as unbelievable to some in search of a Toledo Bend Reservoir hawg bass, is the fact that steamy weather will drive the bass to depths as unusual as fifty feet. Miss their strata of

THE DEEP & THE DEADLY

Think Fathoms, Not Feet, When After Big Fish. Here Are Some Tips On Reaching Bottom!

Trolling from three to 80 feet deep, the Doelcher Fish-Seeker permits presetting for desired depth. They are inexpensive and durable, for long periods of service.

Luhr Jensen downriggers installed on Zwirz' Gallant-Charger. They have greatly improved catches, particularly during hot weather periods in both fresh and salt water fishing sites.

that day by only eight or ten feet and you go home fishless.

Northern pike and muskie are two more species that may lie suspended in twenty or more feet of water, often on shelves off points, or close-in to protective cover in channels and river beds. This is often the case with the heavyweights throughout hot summer periods, while a cold winter makes this depth more tenable than water nearer the surface.

The need for proper presentation of baits and lures for a number of saltwater species has brought many a fisherman to realize that rigs trolled for grouper, deep-roving tarpon and many more of the true big game species often will produce at greater depths than once supposed.

If you are able to settle for a simple, weighted sinker, and are to still-fish, all the better. However, if you must troll extensively, cast and retrieve over and through bottom cover, the ritual of presenting baits and lures becomes a technique that must have its own built-in sophistication and finesse along with an imaginative assist.

Much of what has taken place in the field of bait/lure presentation research has been due to the increasing use of downriggers for fishing boats working the Great Lakes bonanza. The use of two or more downriggers on today's fishing machines has been spreading from the salmon grounds to this continent's lake trout waters, as well as on northern pike and muskie fishermen's boats. Saltwater anglers are using them when trolling deep for stripers and blues and other gamefish that feed in fast tidal rips and channels – normally tough spots when it comes to keeping a rig working deep and true.

For trolling at any depth from three to eighty feet, the Doelcher *Fish-Seeker* depth controller is an inexpensive, lightweight device that permits fishermen to control lure depths without sinkers. Of tough polypropylene, it is virtually indestructible.

When a fish strikes, the Fish Seeker automatically flips over and surfaces. There is no need to reel it in if it hits a snag; just give the line some slack and it will dive to the pre-set level. Trolling depth is controlled by attaching your rod line and leader to different holes in the Fish Seeker's fins. These holes are static-tested to eighty-five pounds for durability; an instruction sheet tells how to adjust your lines for any desired depth. The Fish Seeker can be used for bass fishing, too.

Available in two sizes – one-half-ounce for small-or-medium-size lures or baits, and one ounce for large lures/baits – this handy device comes in colors of blue, red or yellow from Doelcher out of Mission Hills, California 91345.

The downriggers on my two boats are from Luhr Jensen; a long arm configuration seems to work best on larger, big water boats, the shorter arm models with bass boats. These accessories have improved my scores when temperature necessitates deep water tactics. Not only do these units work without any foulups, but by way of their individual

Distaff half of Zwirz angling team coordinates Lowrance Depth/Fish Finder unit on top left of console with short arm downriggers on their super bass boat, dubbed Mindy.

line meters, show exactly at what depth my heavy drails are in action.

Having been a guest on Johnson Motors fantastically equipped super-fishing machine, I've seen their four Lowrance units in action. Not only do they work like charms for controlling depth, but give accurate water temperature readings at whatever depth they are running the lures for trophy-size Great Lakes salmon. For the record, where once there were few companies in the downrigger business, today there are now a number from which to choose.

For lesser depths, some anglers are using all manner of well designed torpedo shape or bell-shaped sinkers to present live or natural baits where the big ones lie in wait. I have found Water Gremlins' *Snap-Loc* sinkers an instant assist for going deeper without fuss. When presenting lure, fly or bait at deeper-than-usual depth, a three-way swivel or a sinker release setup is easy to rig, allowing varying leader lengths to suit the action of the bait.

For big-water salmon, anglers often use one of three simple rigs: the sinker release method; a dodger/spinner technique, or the old standard whereby a weight hangs from the three-way and lure and leader are attached to the appropriate swivel eye. For terminal gear in sport salmon angling, rigs are numerous, and with the differing arrangements, one can go from a few feet sub-surface to presentation at the maximum required depths.

Dan Gapen, owner of Gapen's World of Fishing in Big Lake, Minnesota, came up with an idea called a Bait-Walker.

Getting deep with standard fishing tackle was Gapen's goal, without downriggers or the associated cost! You can't cast with a downrigger and Dan Gapen wanted to cast if he wished, troll if that was the best method for the species, natural habitat and general conditions.

Floating plugs, deadly as they are these days, are winners. They win heavier purses when you can run a wobbling plug below ten feet; an often neglected requirement for trophy fish. A 1½-ounce Bait-Walker with a 3½-inch Rapala or Rebel lure, or one of the Bagley baits allows the angler to feel the action of the plug in the upper Bait-Walker wire at depths to seventy feet!

Beneath Great Lakes waters swim huge populations of walleye, smallmouth bass, northern pike and crappie, a bountiful crop awaiting harvest. But the old saying that "ten percent of the fishermen take ninety percent of the fish while ninety percent of the anglers take but ten percent" has a sound foundation.

One problem facing the angler today is getting down to the fish. Many rigs have been made over the years to get down deep, but have presented the angler with another problem: snagging. If a sinker got you down on bottom, it also got you fouled in the rocks, brush or logs. This discouraging factor forced most to return to the storybook style of angling.

The first objective for Gapen's Bait-Walker idea was to produce a sinker weight form that would walk over rocks without snagging. The next was to rig some type of wire-form above the lead which would elevate the line off the bottom, preventing snarling and catching and allowing free line movement. Lifting the line off the bottom also would project the bait or lure automatically to a position more desirable from a fish's point of view than a bait working on the bottom.

Wire from a spinner bait rig was reworked to give life and proper curve. This would accomplish the desired elevation off the bottom if a proper lead form could be designed. To the upper end of the form a crane swivel was added. To the bottom, a bell style sinker was moulded. Thus, the first working model was formed. Next, the

Fishing companion prepares a Riviera downrigger for use in salt water after striped bass. Forty to fifty yards of line were let out before connecting line to outrigger release. This is a necessity, since stripers are wary and wise.

A closer look at the Lowrance graph-type depth/fish finder and downriggers that give temperature at depth fished, plus amount of line released. This accuracy is often essential.

rockiest place in Minnesota – below the dams on the Mississippi – was chosen for testing.

During the first tests the discovery was made that the rig held line off the bottom, but it rode heavy and hung up. By backing up, the angler almost always could get the rig to pull loose. With several more weeks research, all but the flat back of the now-marketed Bait-Walker had been designed. Rock snags were no longer a problem; the new rig bounced happily over ninety-seven percent of the meanest rock reefs and river structures that lakes of the upper Midwest had to offer. However, the new rig seemed to drag heavy; the two-ounce size felt like two ounces.

Correcting the drag problem was accomplished one day when Gapen accidentally cut the back off a rig being tested. Reduction of weight was accomplished, but the big plus was that the Bait-Walker no longer dragged. What had once been a two-ounce sinker now had the feel of a three-quarter-ounce weight. The lucky discovery created the exact design he had sought. Cutting off the rig's back provided a method by which water pressure from behind helped propel the rig forward, while this flat back made the rig ride upward with the upper arm riding horizontal to the bottom. Only the tip of the lead sinker touched bottom, reducing bottom friction considerably.

Originally, the Bait-Walker was designed with live-bait fishing in mind, but several discoveries have been made since the birth of this new rig. With the Bait-Walker, floating plugs such as Rapalas, Rebels, Norman Minnows or Redfins can be worked over rocky lake bottoms in depths up to fifty feet. These floating plugs always had been a problem to the angler attempting to submerge them to any depth. Three-way sinker devices, split shot and lead weights in many configurations have been tried with little success. Shot often got floaters down, but became snagged in obstructions and didn't run the lure in a true form. Sinkers killed the plug's action and became snagged at the slightest contact with obstructions.

During July 1978, a pair of walleye anglers on Mille Lacs Lake in central Minnesota tried a small Rapala, then a small Rebel behind a Bait-Walker. Theory was, if this rig was snagless, it wouldn't get hung up. It ran like a keel sinker, so it should hold the floating plug in a straight line. Even if the plug wanted to run to one side, the rig would hold it straight. The new concept worked. Not only did the Bait-Walker hold floating plugs at depths of twenty feet or more, but allowed the angler to feel these little baits vibrating no matter what the depth.

Drop-back line length has been a bit of a problem, but thirty-six inches was soon settled on. Besides working this style lure just off the bottom, the new rig produced its first limit stringers of walleye while deep trolling. Since those first tries with floating plugs, word began to spread and a pattern has developed: each size plug works best with a given drop-back line.

If you intend to use a floater with a length shorter than three inches, drop-back line need be no longer than thirty-six inches; thirty-two inches is ideal for maximum performance. A three to 4½-inch floater requires drop-backs to forty inches. Longer or shorter drop backs could be used by six inches either way, but forty inches seems to do the best job under most conditions.

A plug longer than 4½ inches should be tied to a drop-back no shorter than forty-six inches. This length allows large lures a chance to work as the manufacturer designed them. Big-lipped muskie plugs such as Bagley's B series might be given even greater drop-back line length.

The deeper the floating plugs are driven, the more buoyant they become, a factor which eliminates any chance of the plug's digging into snags. This fact was established last summer while trolling for lake trout on Big Trout Lake in northern Ontario. Our party was using a six-ounce Bait-Walker with nine-inch Bagley Bs with the huge lips. With a four-mile-per-hour troll in progress, the rig ran at fifty-seven feet; fifty inches of drop-back was used. We knew just where our rig was running by watching our locators. When crossing a fifty-five-foot rock hump, our rig would touch bottom. The Bait-Walker always bounced across the hump's surface; not once did we feel the B touch.

To prove the water pressure effect on floaters in Big Lake near Gapen's home, underwater diving gear was used

Within sight of Johnson Motors' plant, their research/ super fishing boat is readied for Great Lakes sortie. Most anglers aren't fortunate enough to have this gear.

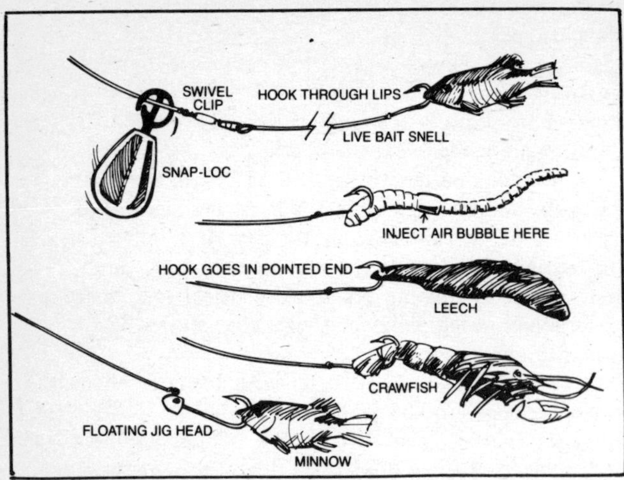

Water Gremlin's Snap-Loc sinker is yet another inexpensive setup for presenting lures/baits when depth isn't excessive.

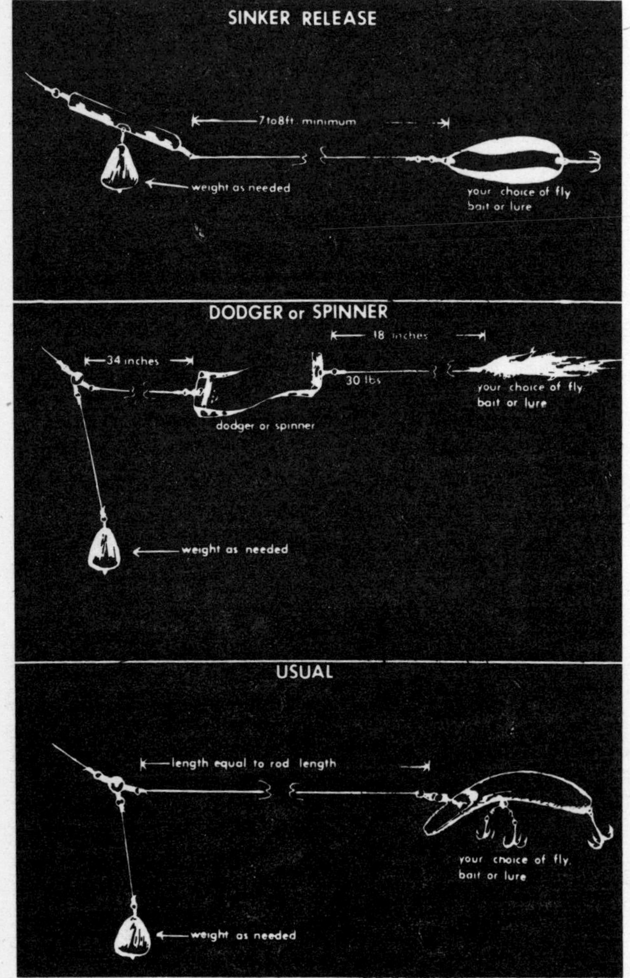

Three types of fishing hookups with specially rigged weights and sinkers that are used for salmon or lake trout. You're free to choose lures, flies, or use bait.

Zwirz hefts aloft 24-pound lake trout he coaxed from deep, clear waters of Canadian lake. A shallow presentation of lure or fly would not have brought the strike — or action! Keeping clear of weeds is feature of Bait Walker (below).

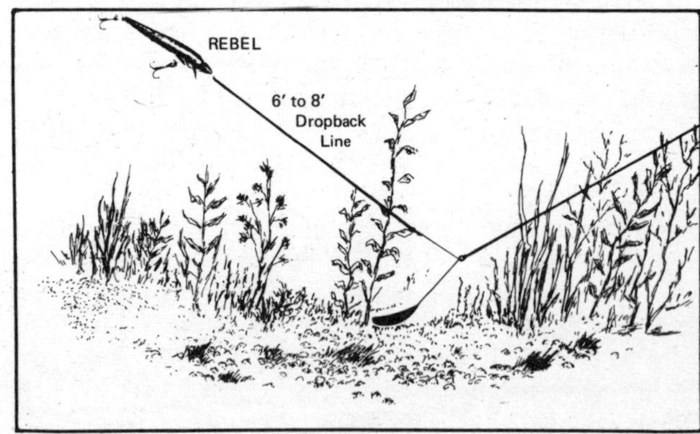

to confirm that, once a floating plug goes below twenty or twenty-five feet, lip size has little bearing on how much deeper the plug can be driven. Water pressure is the controlling factor. Only plug size could vary the plug's depth control.

When working plugs such as Rapalas and Rebels, rig weight determines how deep one can work successfully. Floating plugs work best with a specific size between certain depths. The angler can use a heavier weight in shallower water if he desires. Often the technique is beneficial in working structure which varies greatly in depth. If you run from six feet to twenty-four feet within a few yards, the angler might want to run a 1½-ounce Bait-Walker rather than a three-eighths-ounce, which would work best in six feet. By using the heavier weight, he is able

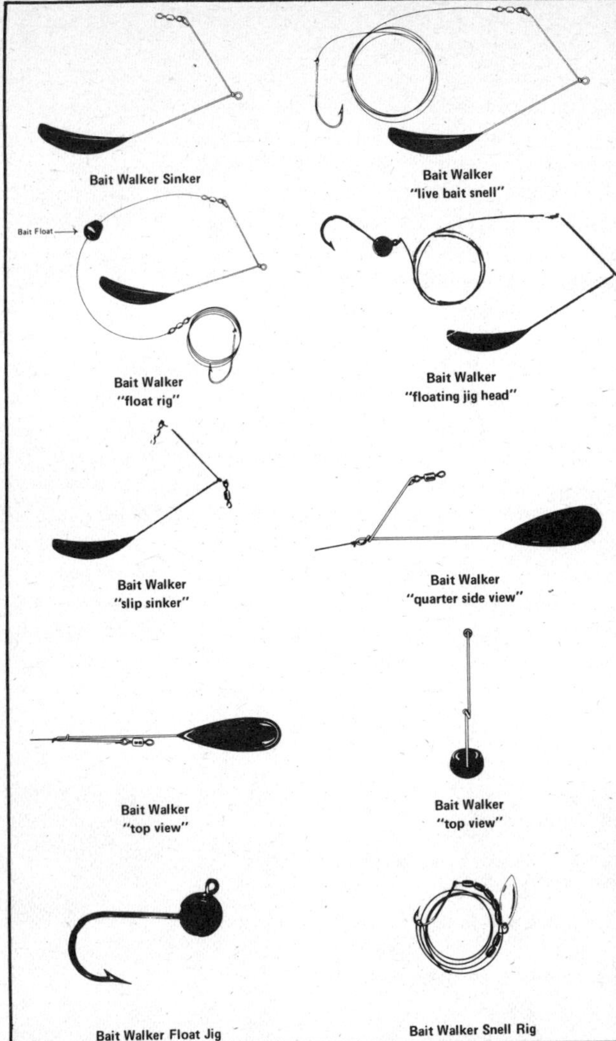

The Bait Walkers are available in many configurations for just about any fishing situation. They take fish!

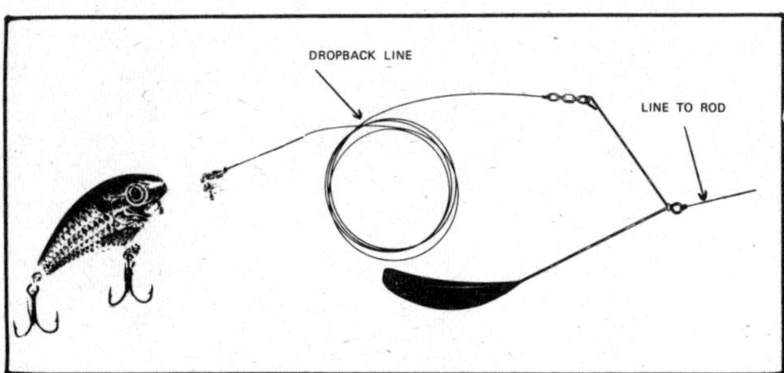

Bait Walker, long-lipped plug and drop-back line make it possible to attain depths like never before – snaglessly!

to travel the downhill slope and control his plug on the bottom at all times.

Sinker float occurs when a rig comes from shallow to deep and is unable to follow contour due to lightness. It will literally float through the water a number of yards before reaching bottom once again. If fish lay at the bottom of the structure being worked, your lure passes too far above them to be effective. The heavier rig eliminates this problem.

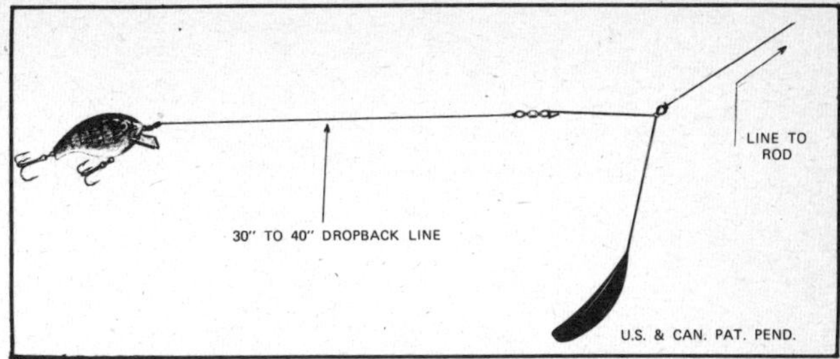

Snag-free Bait Walker works deep lakes and river bottoms with shallow-running plugs, crank baits or natural baits.

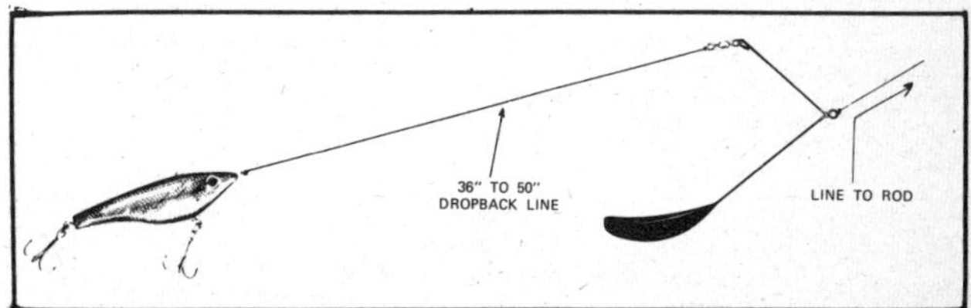

Trolling shad-type lures for suspended fish can obtain great results. You reach fish that previously you'd have missed.

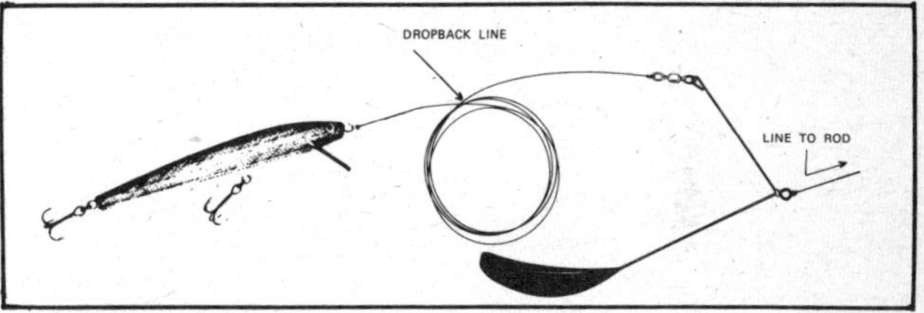

Flotation plugs so deadly on muskie and northern pike can "get down amongst 'em" with Bait-Walker and drop-back line.

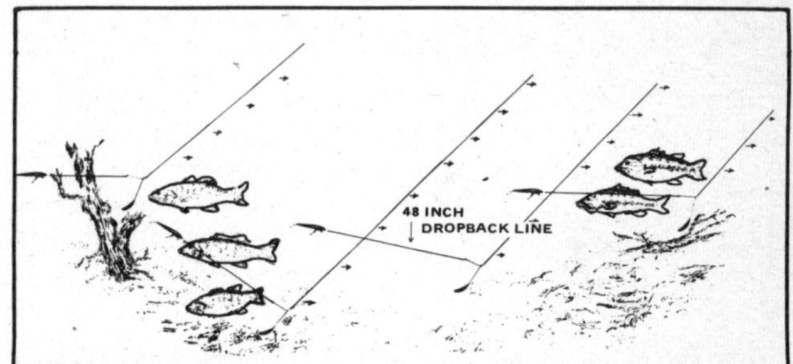

Mental adjustments are needed with this rig, but author says you develop "sixth sense" for it. Try 48-inch drop-back line when seeking bottom-hugging trophy black bass.

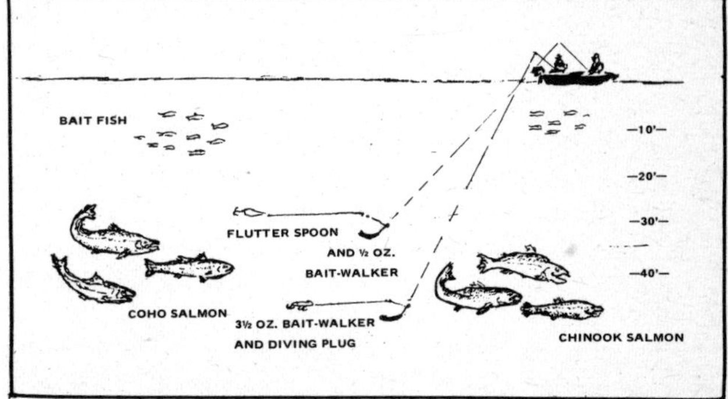

In spring when coho/chinook salmon are within 30 feet of surface, Bait Walker, 14-foot boat and 6 to 18hp motor makes this setup "poor man's downrigger." Use 5- to 7-foot drop-back line and salmon fly, spoon or floating plug.

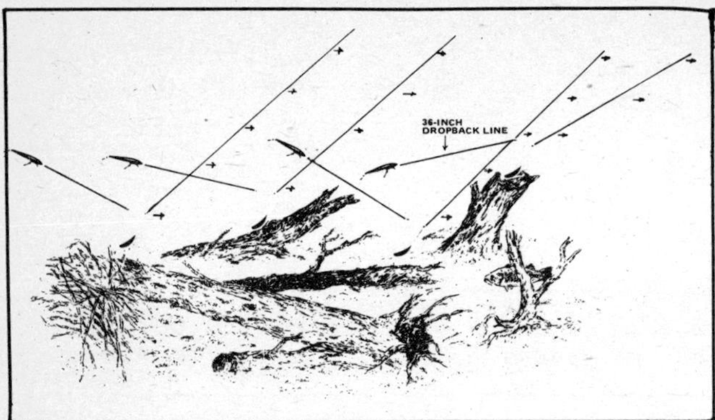

Water pressure and lure design, coupled with appropriate drop-back length, keep lure clear of snags like brush, logs.

Depth Chart

Size (ounces)	Water Depth (feet)
1/4	3 to 8
3/8	5 to 10
5/8	8 to 16
1	10 to 20
1½	16 to 28
2	20 to 34
3½	30 to 50
6	40 to 70
10	70 to 90

There are other factors such as speed and line weight to consider when working floating plugs behind Bait-Walkers. The faster you troll or retrieve, the shallower your rig will run; the slower you go, the deeper. If using six-pound line one time, then twenty-pound the next trip out, depth will vary. But Gapen has devised a rule of thumb which seems to work. Once you establish a pattern with speed and line weight for a starting point, you add or subtract a foot from running depth for each four pounds of line increased or added on each mile an hour of speed added or decreased. You soon find that you acquire a sixth sense in determining what size Bait-Walker should be used with line, speed and lure.

Example: Traveling at four miles an hour with a 3½-ounce Bait-Walker, twenty-four-pound line is being used with a seven-inch normal-lipped Rapala, Rebel or Bagley. You are trolling 120 feet of line behind the boat and you have a forty-eight-inch drop-back line of eighteen pounds between rig and plug. According to our tests, your setup should be traveling forty-two feet below the surface. If you are watching fish on a locator in that forty-foot level, they should be yours.

This factor caused Lake Michigan anglers to latch on to this new rig for salmon, lake trout, steelhead and brown trout. Those unable to afford expensive downrigger equipment soon began to use the new device, flies, spoons, plugs and jigs rigged behind it. Soon the bright orange devices were nicknamed the "poor man's downrigger." It was during this innovation that the 3½ and six-ounce sizes were developed. Presently, a ten-ounce is being tested for line drag and rod pull.

Ten ounces, or even six, may seem like a lot of weight to load on a rod. But the key to the success of Bait-Walkers is the fact that they work for you by forcing themselves forward via water pressure from behind; that old airplane wing theory. So far, prototypes of ten ounces have scored a complete success. Fishermen will be able to work water depths in the one-hundred-foot bracket with stiff bass or muskie rods loaded with twenty to twenty-five-pound line. Drag weight on this heavier model proves out at about 3½ ounces.

For the cat fisherman, the new Bait-Walker rig has become a boon. Rocky rivers where channel cats lay are easily worked sans snagging. Those who straight-line cats directly behind a boat or downstream with the current find that a Bait-Walker loaded with a chicken blood bait in chicken liver on a thirty-inch drop-back will tilt up just as if being trolled. Catfish tend to come in from downstream, mouth their bait, move forward three to five inches, rest and mouth the bait, then begin to back off downstream. When the cat walks forward, the Bait-Walker will tilt forward to signal the angler that the fish has bait-in-mouth. Tension on the rod tip will lessen, slack line signaling that it is time to set the hook.

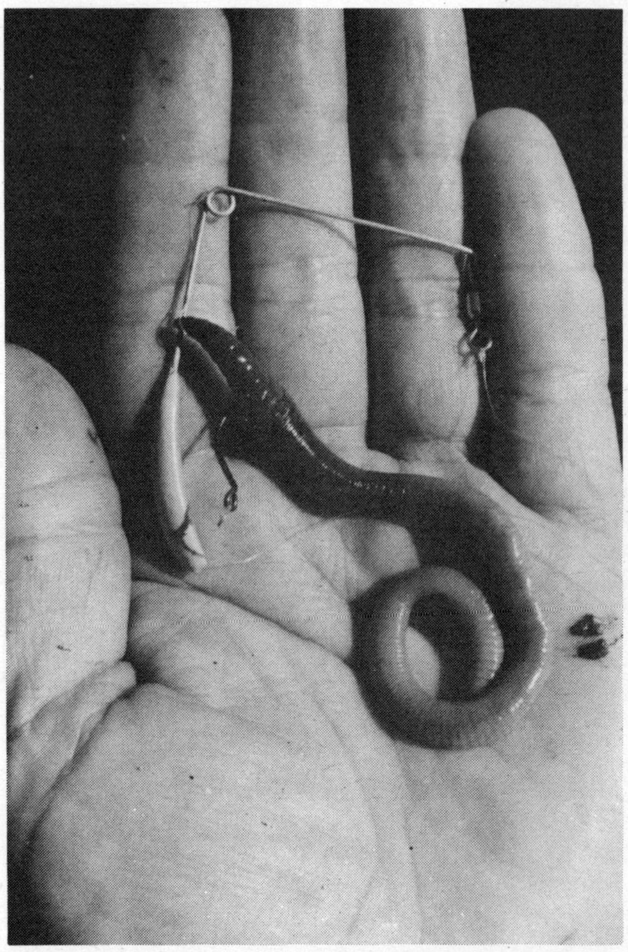

Correct way of rigging Bait Walker with live nightcrawler is shown above. With no friction, fish mouth bait longer.

As to why the Bait-Walker is so snagless, it's best explained this way: Nearly all other bottom walking sinker devices have their point of pull either through or on the upper edge of their construction. This causes them to pull into a crevice or obstruction. The Bait-Walker's design is so that the point of pull is elevated high above the main body construction; when hitting an obstruction, force is exerted upward to lift the weight up and over any would-be snag.

One other determining factor contributes to this rig's snag-free posture. Bait-Walkers hit waiting obstructions with the sinker weight flat on, not in a pointed manner. The rounding of the Bait-Walker's lead body also contributes to its snagless profile. But all this would not be possible if that flat back didn't position the Gapen walking sinker properly. That flat side behind the lead weight is the key to making it work.

Bassmen working Dale Hollow Reservoir found that, by positioning their boat atop the shale and rock structures, then casting into deep water, the Bait-Walker offered excellent control. Boat position could be in as little water as six feet while casting target depth at times reached sixty-five feet. Rig size varied from 1½ to two ounces while drop-back became less than twenty-four inches. This short drop-back line afforded the fisherman freedom from tangling while casting the somewhat cumbersome arrangement. Sidearm delivery seemed best, similar to casting live bait.

Hitting water, the rig soon would drag the resisting crank-bait down to the bottom. Water pressure on the floating crank held it high, while the Walker worked its way upward along the rocky shale structure. By retrieving in short spurts, anglers were able to give the crank-baits an erratic up and down zig-zag action. While being reeled, the plug would dart toward bottom. Once the pause came in retrieve, the crank-bait would be forced rapidly upward by water pressure. This tantalizing action bass found hard to resist.

The snagless rig allowed the angler to get down along the structure where suspended fish lay. Crank-baits work well on bass, but will not travel deeper than fifteen feet or so. The winter fish in Dale Hollow were down between twenty-five and forty-five feet.

A special retrieve technique resembled migrating crawfish or minnows as they might dart along the structure in an attempt to reach shallow water. Direct contact from rod to tip to the crank may have been a key factor. The angler was able to feel the slightest fish rap when one attacked his lure. This was due to construction of the new rig in which the upper wire arm is part of the line, not part of the rig. Thus the slightest vibration is signaled up the line. If a crank was on its way up during the pause and a fish struck, the angler immediately felt it.

During the following spring, more bass fishermen began to use the new rig. It was soon discovered that if a drop-back line in excess of five feet was used on floating cranks and plugs, Bait-Walkers provided a means by which the bassmen were able to work these lures above stumps and brush. Here the lure would have to be left to float free, while the rig was worked slowly up and over the wood construction. Water pressure on the slow-moving lure kept it free and clear.

Kentucky Lake in western Kentucky was the proving grounds for this particular method. In the middle of the big reservoir lies a stump-infested mound of ground which has eaten tons of jigs over the years. A.A. Toney, a noted bass angler from the Kentucky-Tennessee area, was the first to utilize Bait-Walkers for brush and stump floating. During April and May, Toney produced several stringers of bass that exceeded the fifty-pound mark, using one-ounce Walkers and floating Rebels.

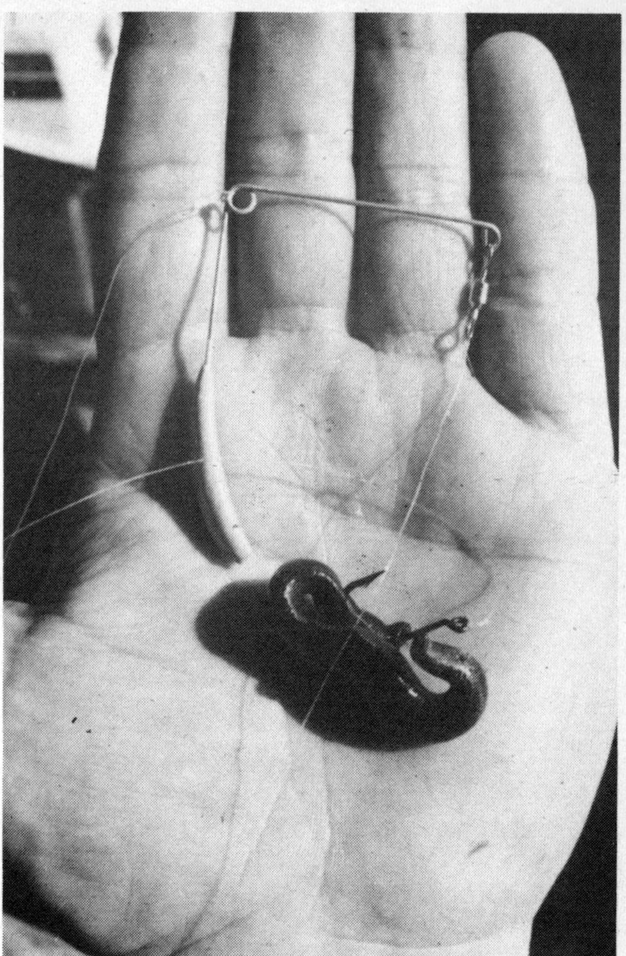

Alternate way of rigging nightcrawler that produces good results. Anglers can always feel bait with this rigging.

Toney harvested huge stringers of crappie from these central lakes using a similar method. Instead of a long drop-back, Toney used one about forty inches and reduced plug size to the smallest he could find. Casting into the stumpy area, the retrieve would be ever so slow till reaching the outer edge of the stump field. Once there, the rig was allowed to drop down along structure where crappie were encountered or Toney knew they'd been passed by. Again, direct line contact from rod tip to lure was of utmost importance.

Floating plugs become more buoyant the deeper they are worked. Thus, those who worry about a deep-lipped or a shallow-lipped plug hanging up behind the new rig can forget it. In most cases, even if the plug reaches bottom, its lip will hit first, causing the lure to veer off and upward to wiggle on its way. This occurs mainly in shallower water. Gapen doesn't make the claim that you can't hang up an

Don Gapen, inventor of the Bait Walker, shows what his invention can do on big bass. A poor man's downrigger!

artificial while using his rig, but changes of doing so are reduced.

Working floating lures over weeds can be accomplished via the Bait-Walker/floating plug combo. By using long drop-back lines – 4½ to 7½ feet – working slowly over weed structure, the angler is able to float his plug above the weed tops. Because of direct contact between rod tip and bait, the striking fish are felt easily. This method is not recommended where weeds touch surface, but rather where short eel-type or sparsely growing pickerel weeds reach heights of two feet or less.

Striped bass, acclaimed by many to be the hottest new fish to hit our market, is fished best by trolling. Though many fish are taken by jigging or when stripers appear on the jump in lakes such as Beaver in Arkansas, or Lake Mead on the Arizona-Nevada border, the biggest stripers are caught by trolling. Recently the Bait-Walker has begun to show up in this new market. Striped bass fishermen find this new rig works lures such as big Rebels or Bagley's big Bs down in the deep waters where the better fish lie.

As with salmon, the Walker becomes a downrigger of a sort. It holds plugs at depths otherwise unreachable with conventional methods. No line twist occurs; the rig runs flat and straight out behind a trolling skiff, and if trolling speed is constant, any given depth can be maintained providing the Walker weight is correct.

Anglers working stripers have run as many as four lines behind, a feat never before accomplished with diving plugs. Snarling and twisting always had been the problem, but with this rudder-like device the problem has been eliminated. Many fishermen after stripers have found that soft plastic-type jigs and lures with vibrating tails, such as made by Mister Twister and Bass Buster, do well for the reservoir striped bass worked deep behind a Walker.

Last summer, Bill Binkelman and Dan Gapen worked Lake Kagagami in northern Ontario. Kag is a lake where walleye run better than average, three to four pounds. Most Canadian lakes average fish nearer to a pound and a half.

Slip sinkers always have been part of the American anglers' repertoire. Walleye anglers across the northern tier have been using this device to work the slow-feeding walleye for as long as I can remember. First came the bell sinker style, then the egg sinker, finally a sophisticated flat-bottom-style rig with upturned lead eye which did a good job of feeding line to the wary walleye. Each seemed to work better than the one before. Because previous bottom-walking sinkers had holes directly through their lead construction, the problem of lead chafe or friction caused by the line running through the lead hole was a major factor to cause walleye and catfish to drop bait.

The other problem was friction caused by the lack of elevation off the bottom. All of them held line flat on the bottom, forcing this line to run over any friction-causing material which might stand in the way, as a fish began to take line. By placing either a snap swivel or adding split ring and swivel to the forward end of the Bait-Walker, where normally you'd place your line, this new rig can be made into a slip sinker. It does several things for the angler which previous bottom sinkers did not!:

Line friction is eliminated when rod line is run through the smooth nickel-plated swivel eyes. Swivels move in all directions allowing line to follow angles to which fish or water pressure might force the line to move. Line is elevated off the bottom so that no bottom contact is encountered when line pickup occurs. This is a result of line being lifted off bottom by the L-shaped wire form which protrudes above the weighted bottom on the Bait-Walker. The rig will always sit upright on the bottom with its arm pointed toward the surface.

Rigging is simple. Run the rod line through both end eyelets of the two swivels. Place a bead, shot or swivel for a stop, preventing your rig from running all the way down to the hook. Most fishermen find that thirty inches of drop-back for live bait is sufficient. For those wishing no loss of equipment when a hook snags the bottom, a swivel can be placed for a stop, then placing a lighter drop-back line behind it. Once the hook becomes embedded in a log or root, it is a simple matter of pulling; break off the hook attached to the lighter line and replace it with a new one.

Among the most significant of the new floating riggings are the floating jig heads. They come in a variety of sizes and colors and perform to get live bait up off the bottom. When selecting a floating jig head, make sure the eye points downward in an opposite direction to the barbed portion of the hook. Also make sure the biggest part of the buoyant portion of the float is on the barb side, forcing the hook point to ride upward with the barb away from the bottom, another way to prevent snagging. Fluorescent colors such as

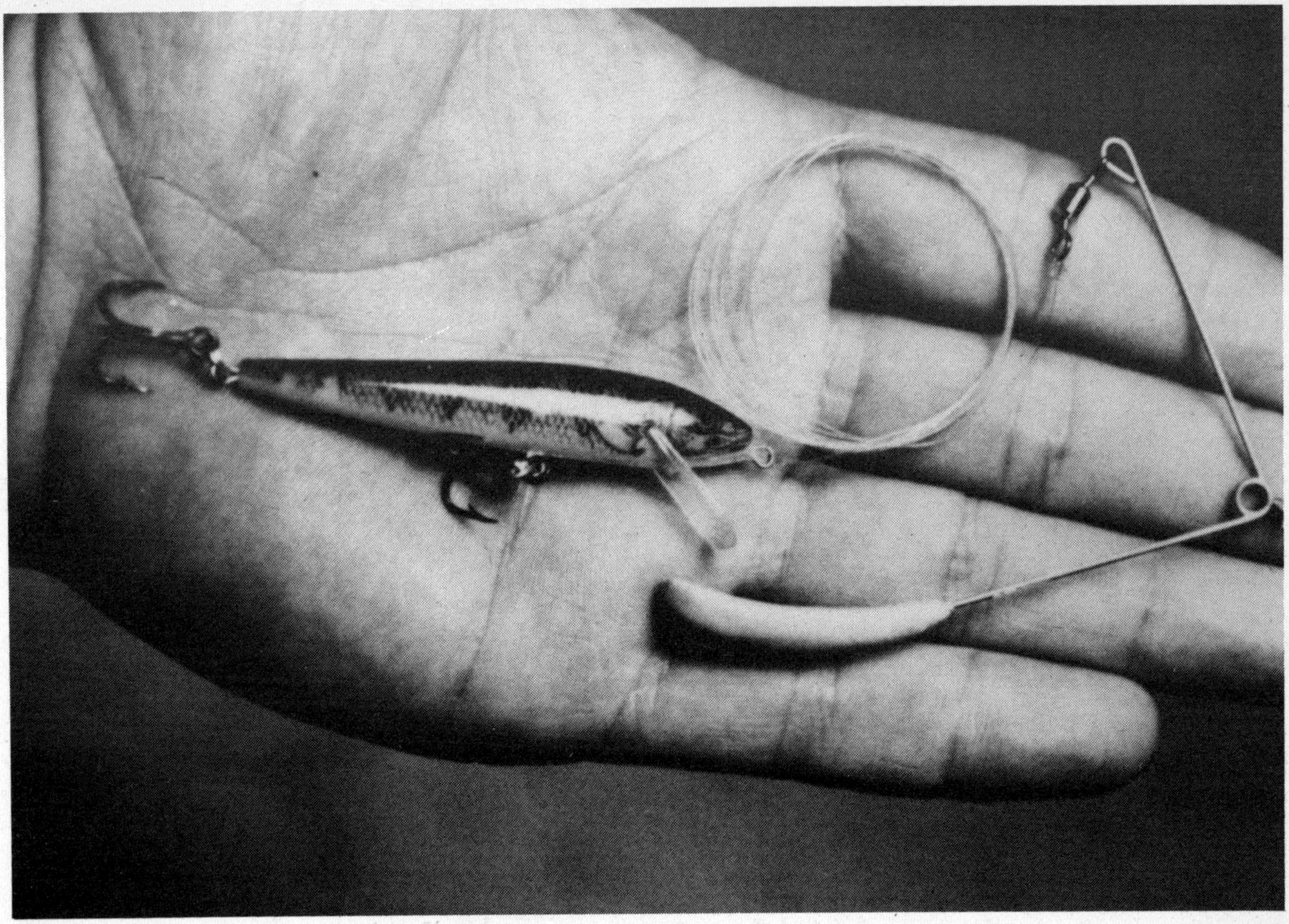

This is typical of riggings discussed in text. Shown are Bait Walker, lure and drop-back line for species sought.

orange, red and yellow-lime seem the best producers.

Commercial rigs with round or oblong foam moulded on the drop-back line work well. But if you find a need to make your own floating rig, use an old ice-fishing float. Run it halfway up the drop-back line, place a piece of toothpick or matchstick in it and you have an excellent floating rig. I've used everything from red cricket bobbers to stripped ice fishing floats. All take fish.

The Bait-Walker is not a cure-all to the complex problems that face the modern angler, but Dan Gapen has come up with a device that eliminates many problems for the angler who realizes the greater number of fish live most of the time in the deeper waters of our lakes and streams. Application of Bait-Walker techniques should prove its value during the hot summer and the cold winter, when fish hang deep. Most fishermen will find that the Bait-Walker works twelve months of the year.

Wary fish can be fooled by Bait Walker, since drop-back line line isn't near the weight. Bait floats more naturally.

When this feathered jig hits the water and angler finesses it with rod tip and retrieve action, it will come to life and resemble some living type of food on which fish like those in the foreground feed. This is Florida.

LOOK-ALIKES & NATURAL BAITS

Either System Of Fish-Taking Requires That You Be Smarter Than The Fish And Know More About Your Bait!

THOUGH MANY a lure maker might pray that it be different, natural baits take the greatest number of fish. This reference encompasses both the live variety as well as preserved baits. To a lesser degree, we can include those rubber or plastic creations that duplicate a natural bug, aquatic insect or terrestrial critter.

Today, there still are more fishermen who use only natural baits than there are fly fishermen, spin casters and plug tossers combined. The accomplished angler never limits himself to any one form of tackle or to any simple method. However, one must respect any fisherman who has become proficient with natural baits, then broadens his scope to include all the methods and tackle that make fishing the never-ending challenge and source of pleasure that it is for so many of us.

Fishing with these baits can be exceptionally productive: a good bait fisherman on a trout stream is someone to be reckoned with.

Although we will only touch on the handiest, most popular freshwater baits, the world of saltwater fishing often depends on the use of specialized natural baits to an even greater degree than required with many freshwater species.

Assuming that most anglers have gone fishing at least a few times during their younger days, it's a safe bet that at some point they dug a can of worms. I well remember that this served as my admission to the sport, until I received my first fly rod and a small selection of flies at the age of 12. A carefully fished worm still puts a share of wilderness trout in my camp fry pan.

There are two schools of thought about how to put a worm on a hook. Some fishermen prefer to impale a worm just behind the head, then over and over again at about one-inch intervals. They feel this method helps hide the hook and is more difficult for a crafty fish to steal. A second group prefers to run the hook through the head and continue pushing the hook through until both the bend and shank are covered. The remainder of the worm trails along in a natural position.

Some bass plugs are so lifelike that they seem to be real. This doesn't mean that bass won't strike at some odd-looking lures, but the strike may be just reflexive action.

The latter method, I feel, looks more natural in the water. I lose a few worms and miss some short strikes, but I also fool a few wise bruisers that might not accept a tightly massed worm. Incidentally, some anglers believe in quantity and rig two or even three worms on a single hook.

Worms are great when used with a plain hook, especially if fishing for trout. Panfish often respond to a worm cast or trolled behind a spinner.

When casting with worms, it is important to learn the gentle, pendulum cast. With this easy swing, one does not tend to snap the bait off the hook as one might with a snap cast. Worms are most productive when fished on fairly small hooks. Sizes 12, 10 or 8 are best and the type of hook

Holy Toledo, what a hawg! Once the angler learns how to manipulate an artificial lure, he can expect to fool wary old fish like this bass (above). Squirming crayfish (left) and hellgrammite in photo below have been duplicated by artificials. But until you present lure in lifelike fashion, you'll come up empty. Author defies you to tell whether nightcrawlers below right are real or imitations. If you can't tell, it's hoped that your quarry can't, either! The king-size worm remains one of world's popular baits.

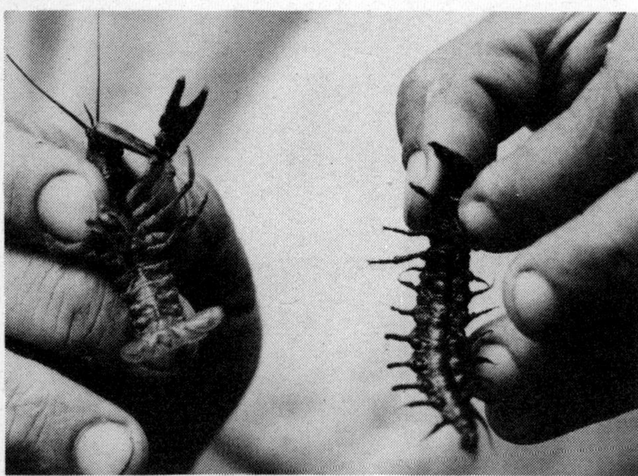

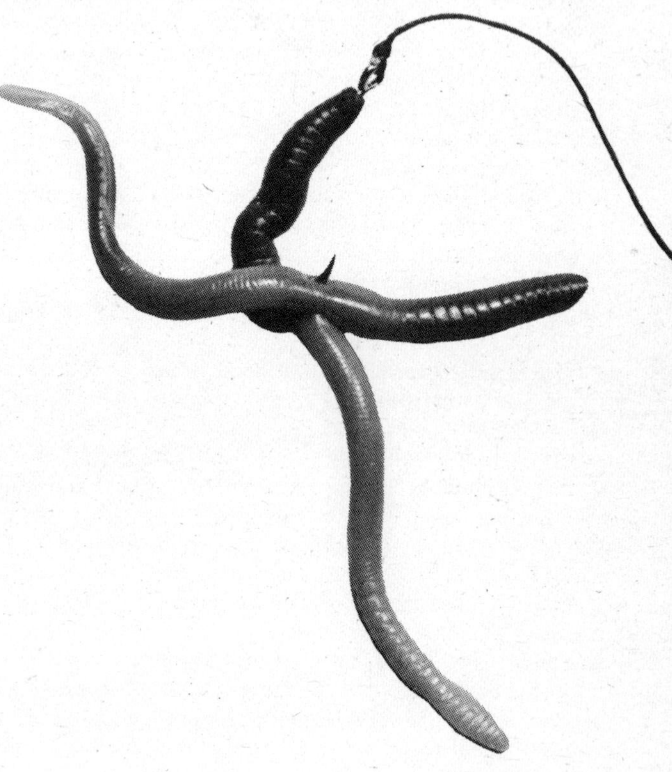

known as a bait-holder is tops. It features two little barbs on the shank that hold the worm up on the hook.

After a summer shower, big trout go crazy over five or six-inch nightcrawlers. Bass are partial to them at just about any time. Eels, bream and you-name-it will join the chow line for the big crawlers. You can hook them pretty much the same way as the worms, but I recommend fixing them behind the collar, then once more about two inches back. They're more secure that way and look more natural to a waiting fish.

Cut up, the nightcrawler is perfect bait for any of the panfish and for the typical hatchery-type trout. Many anglers use bait-holder hooks in No. 4 and No. 6 sizes for big bass, in No. 10 and No. 12 for the cut baits.

To a fisherman, minnows include almost any bait fish used to catch larger fish. Normally, however, the term refers mainly to forage fish of many species ranging from one to five inches in length. Minnows are winners for the same reason big trout eat smaller trout and bass grab other fish: cannibalism is a key to survival in the world of fish.

Freshwater shiners are a popular bait in many parts of the country. Easily caught in drop nets or in minnow traps, they're sold in many tackle shops. To keep them, one needs a minnow bucket with an aerator or, at least, the bucket and a supply of OTabs. OTabs release oxygen into the water, thus acting as an aerator. The more water, the longer

This look-alike from Action Lures is called the Breathing Crawfish and certainly resembles the genuine article on the opposite page. Note weedless hook arrangement, a necessity.

This look-alike leech, a bait made of pork rind by Uncle Josh Bait Company, even feels real and can really hammer the finicky fish that include this annelid in their diets.

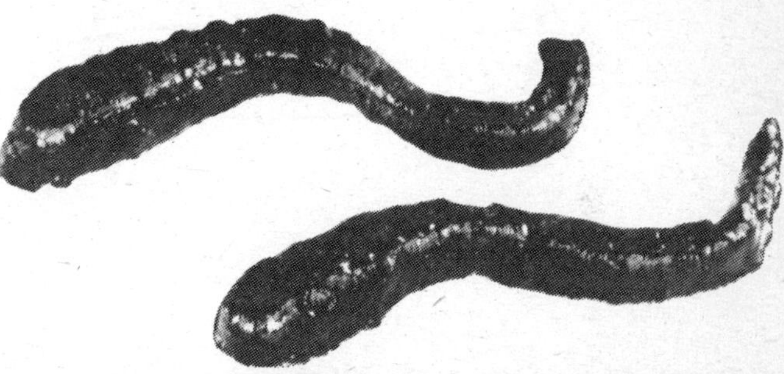

Frogs, grubs, salamanders, crickets and some terrestrial insect imitations can be deadly when properly rigged and presented (below). Read about insect behavior, appearance.

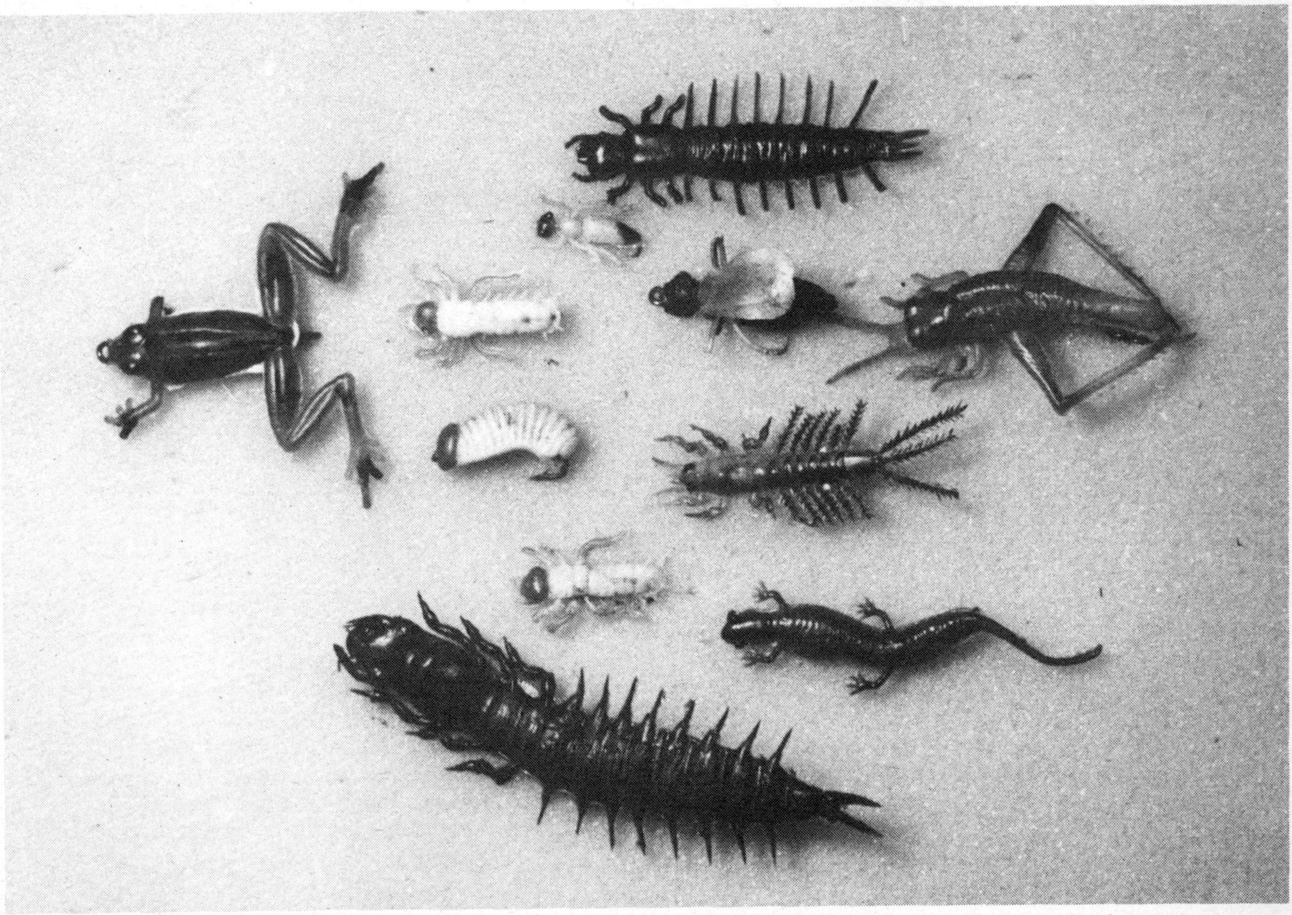

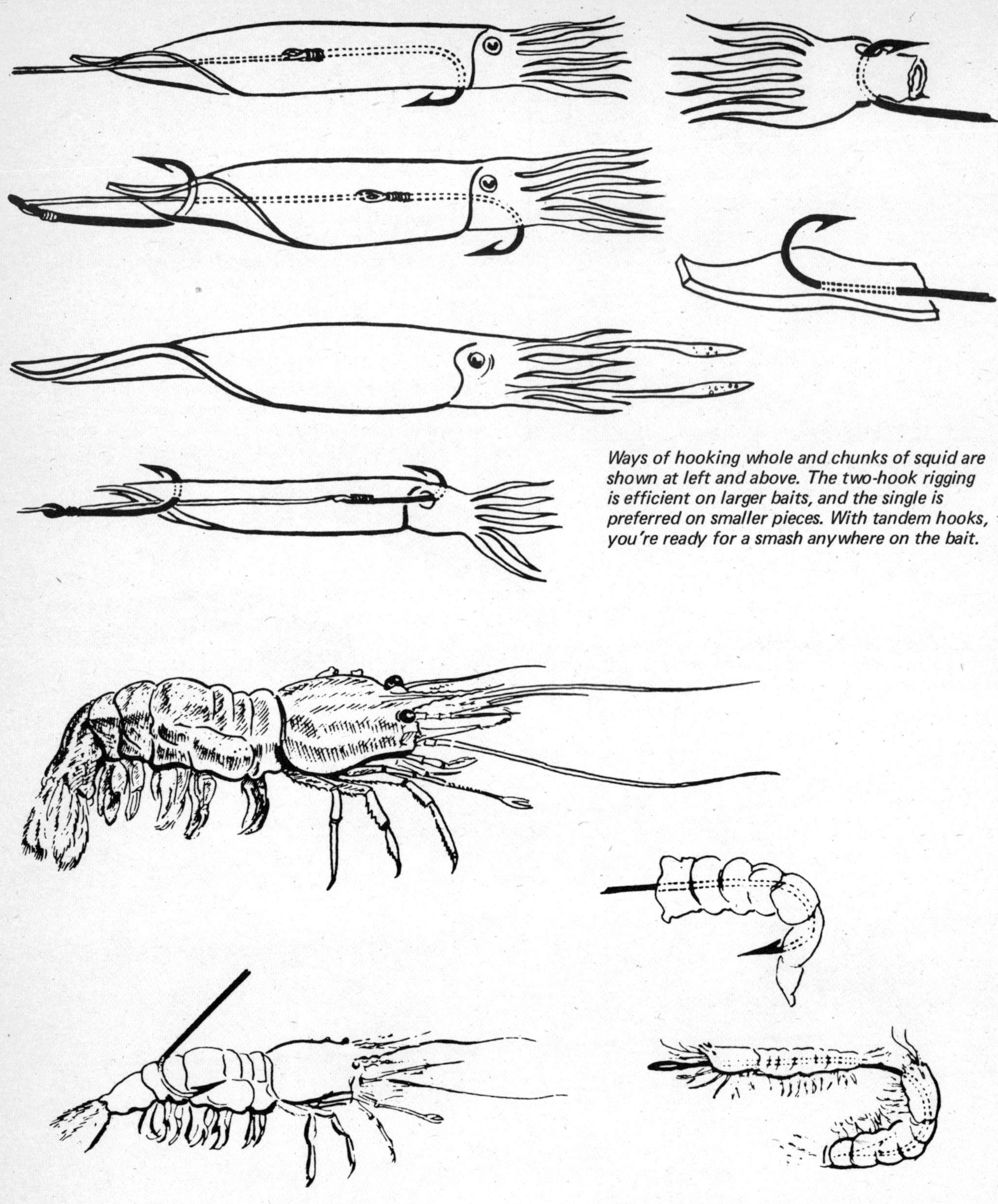

Ways of hooking whole and chunks of squid are shown at left and above. The two-hook rigging is efficient on larger baits, and the single is preferred on smaller pieces. With tandem hooks, you're ready for a smash anywhere on the bait.

The edible shrimp that you see in the fish markets makes a fine bait, and shown above are three rigging sets that depend on the size of the shrimp used. For still-fishing, hook shrimp through tail (bottom left). This enables shrimp to retain mobility. If using large shrimp for small fish, remove the tail and shell, then thread on hook (top right). When using tiny prawns, thread several on the same hook, as demonstrated at the bottom right.

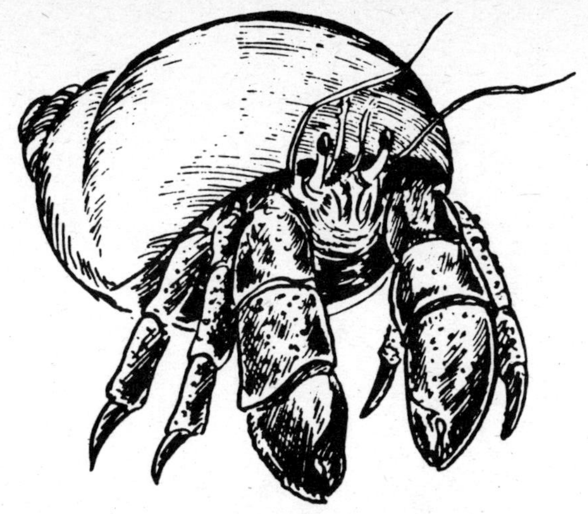

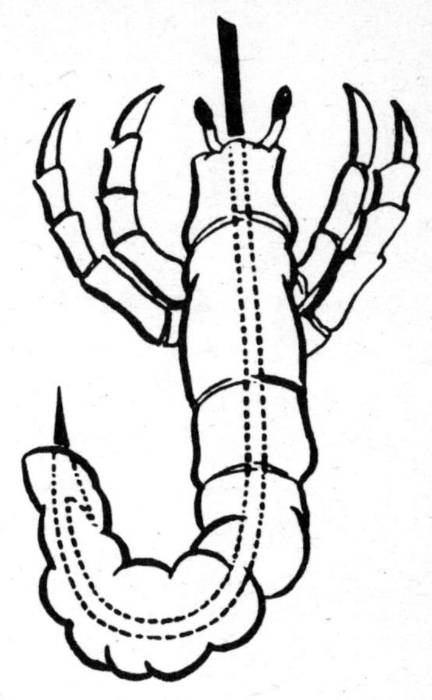

The hermit crab, an undersea squatter that lives in abandoned shells, makes a good bait when hooked in manner shown at right. You can pick them up along both coasts in shallow bays and inlets, or tidal pools.

To hook the hermit crab, you've got to get him out of the shell. This is done by cracking it or applying heat, and you'll be surprised at how tenaciously he clings to shell. Now break off the large claws and run the hook through the body as shown above. Be careful you don't hook yourself!

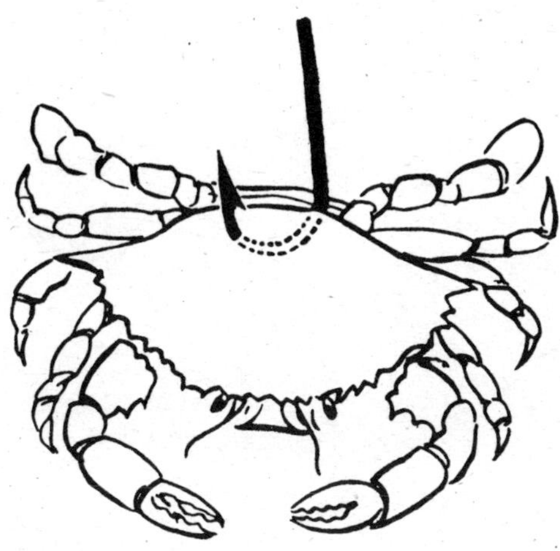

As a natural bait, it's hard to beat bottom-working crabs. Small, whole crabs are best hooked to stay alive for your bottom fishing. First break off the large claws, then run hook through the top shell from below (above drawing). An alternative is to hook through side by leg, as shown below.

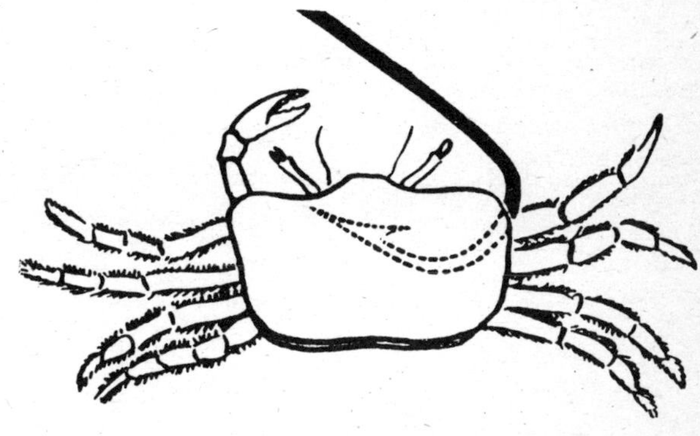

To hook the fiddler crab, first you must break off the large claw and insert the hook into the body at the break, threading it on. Another way is through shell from below, similar to illustration immediately to your left.

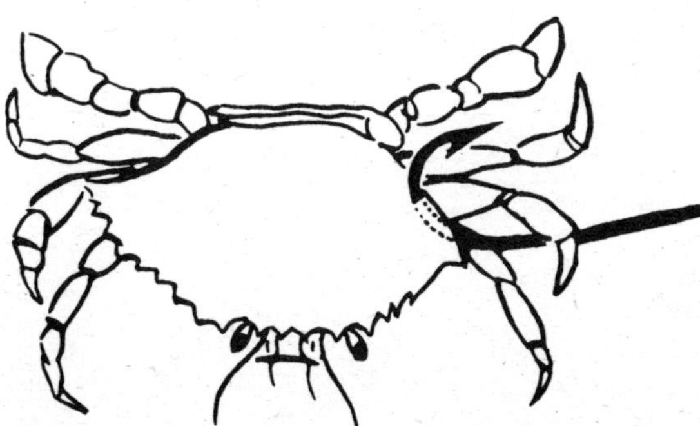

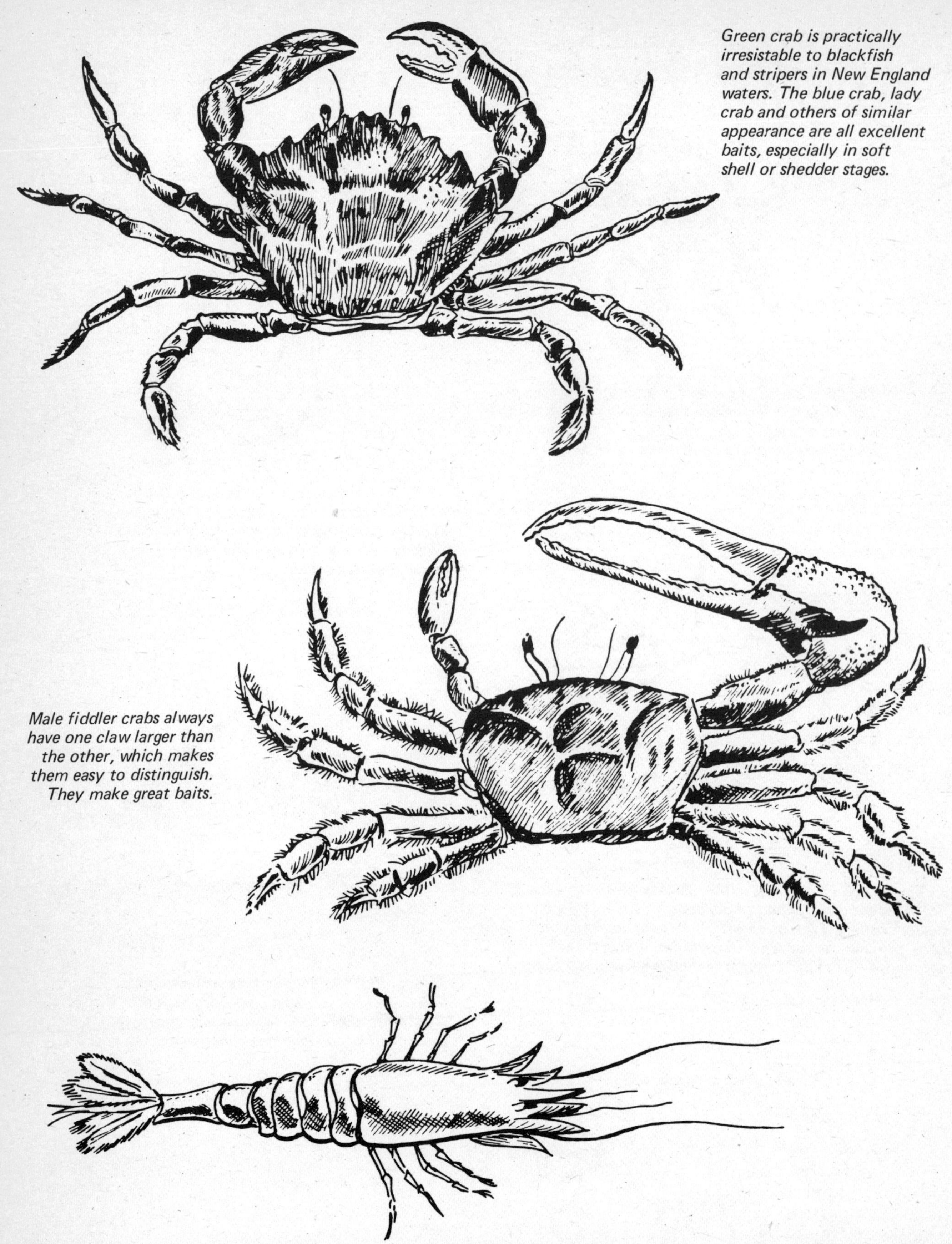

Green crab is practically irresistable to blackfish and stripers in New England waters. The blue crab, lady crab and others of similar appearance are all excellent baits, especially in soft shell or shedder stages.

Male fiddler crabs always have one claw larger than the other, which makes them easy to distinguish. They make great baits.

Tarpon, snook and bonefish will take the sand shrimp, and most bottom feeders will happily inhale them, too. They hang out near shore in seaweed, grass, or among rocks, and can be caught in dip nets or seines.

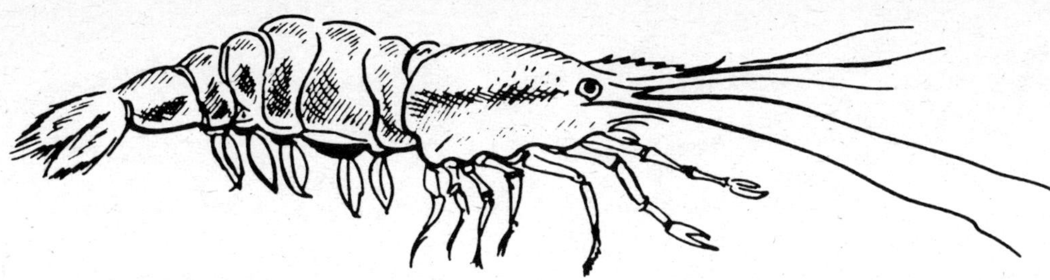

You can distinguish the prawn from the sand shrimp by size, the prawn being about 1½ inches long on average. Often called grass shrimp, it's a deadly bait for chumming for weakfish. Drop one or two into flow of tide occasionally.

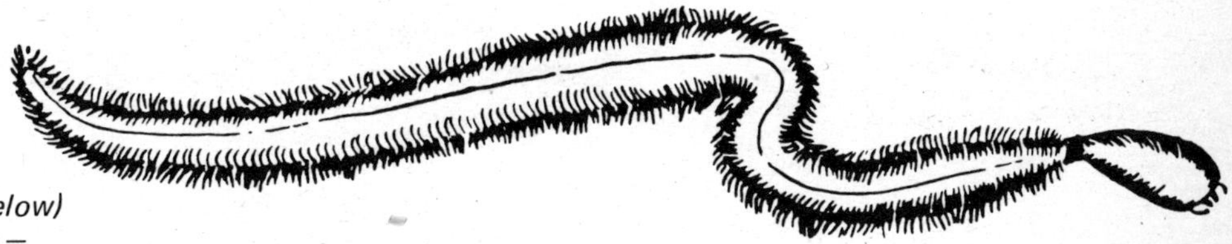

If you can get sand worms (below) or blood worms (right), do so — fish go absolutely crazy for them.

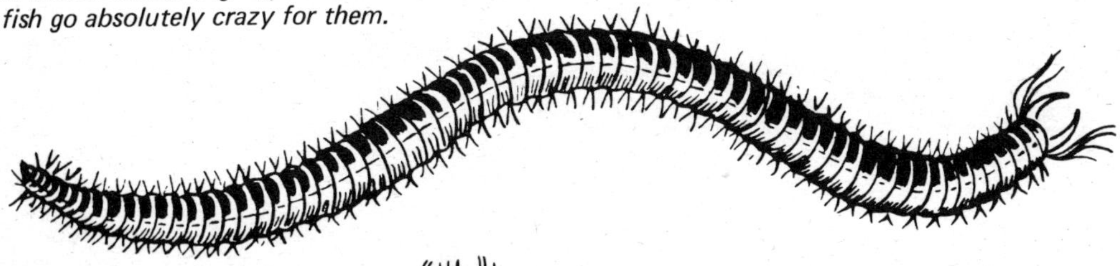

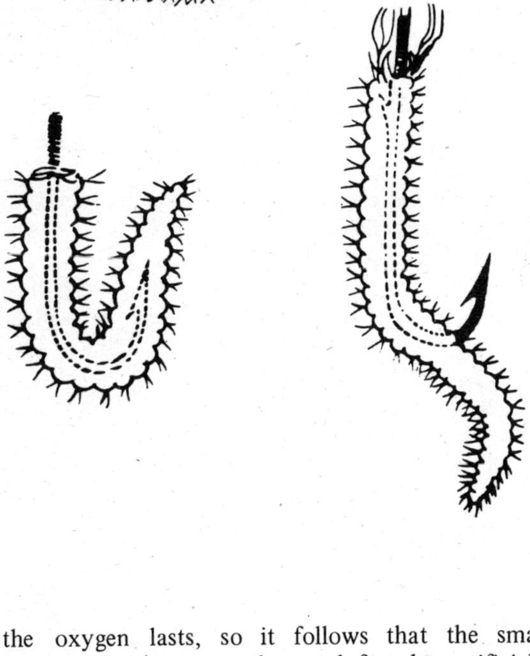

Two ways of rigging a sand worm for flounder are shown at left, and the normal set for hooking sand worms is shown at right. Stand by for strikes.

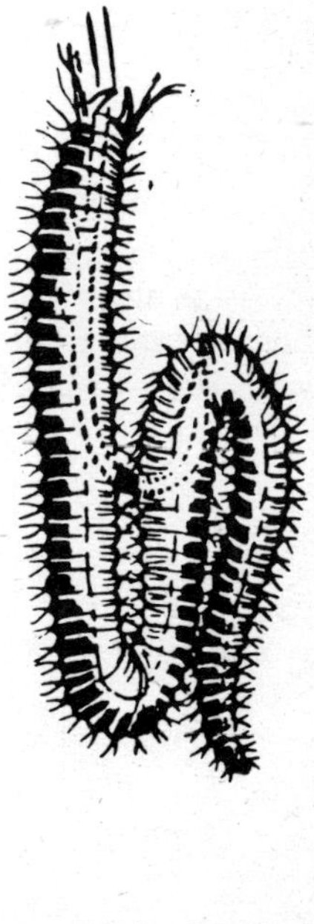

the oxygen lasts, so it follows that the smaller the container, the greater the need for the artificial oxygen supply.

Hook the shiner as gently as possible just under the skin and the dorsal fin — but not too deep or it will die. It's the lively bait that takes the fish! The dorsal method is the best for still fishing.

When trolling, hook the bait fish through both upper and lower lips. There are other methods, such as sewing-on, that are great for enticing landlocked salmon to strike. If you need to find out just how to prepare such a bait, I recommend a pow-wow with your tackle shop dealer.

Smallmouth bass have a craving for crickets that is insatiable. Trout, crappie, perch and most of the larger panfish find them just as desirable. These little black morsels usually are found hiding under old rotting boards, around woodpiles that have tall grass growing nearby, and under damp stones. Hook them gently under the collar just behind the head. You can fish a cricket dry or add a split shot sinker and let it sink and move with the flow if you're in a stream or river. Hook sizes No. 8 or No. 10 are large enough for anything but very big bass or trout.

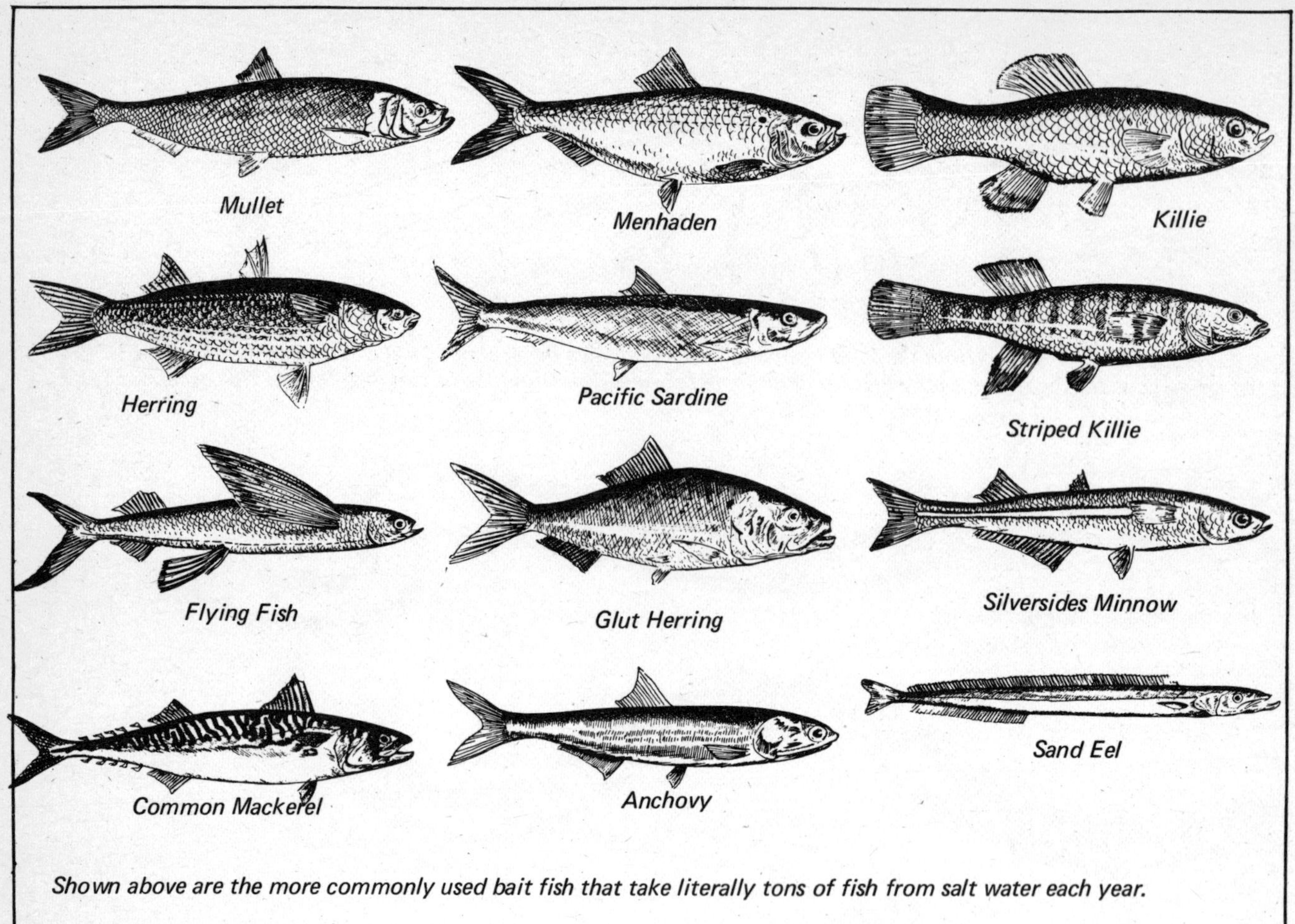

Shown above are the more commonly used bait fish that take literally tons of fish from salt water each year.

Looking like a dwarfed lobster, the crayfish is a good bait for many lake, stream and river fish. It ranges in size from about 1¾ to slightly over three inches. It frequents rocky sections of most shallow streams and also is found in the shallows of larger waters. Hook the crayfish through the tail section and when a braggin'-size bass picks it up, don't strike until the fish has had a chance to mouth it sufficiently.

Pickerel, northerns and both bass families are happy to see small frogs appear. The small, dark-backed frogs found along moist shorelines and in the wet grass are probably the liveliest of the breeds. They are called leapers around New England and are easily caught during the day, or at night with the help of a flashlight. It is best to hook a frog through the lips gently, then let it swim.

Check your state laws before you remove hellgrammites or nymphs from a stream bed. On some trout streams it just isn't allowed, as it removes a source of natural breeding stock and food supply for the fish that inhabit the waters. Neither hellgrammites nor crayfish are as easy to manage in the water as you might think. They are capable of getting under mossy rocks and getting your hook stuck pretty firmly. The helgies are best hooked as shallowly as possible under the collar just behind the head.

In a lake or pond it's best to fish them just off the bottom, and in rivers and streams keep them bouncing along the bottom by raising and lowering your rod tip.

If you don't want to hassle with catching and hooking fresh shrimp, try an imitation jig like one author uses at left.

This good-sized crappie sucked up a live minnow author presented in dark. Hooking minnows is tricky at first.

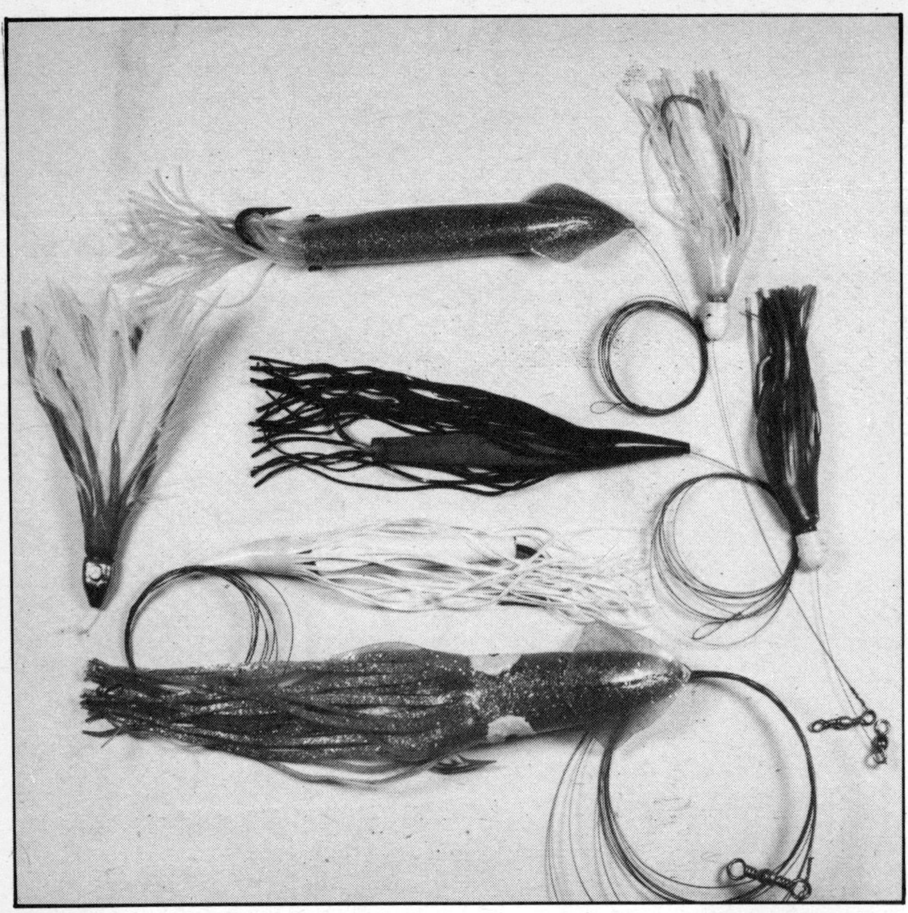

Squid and most natural saltwater baits can be successfully copied in look-alike models, as shown at left here.

An artificial for almost all bait fish can be found in the well-stocked tackle shop. These start at 1/8-ounce size.

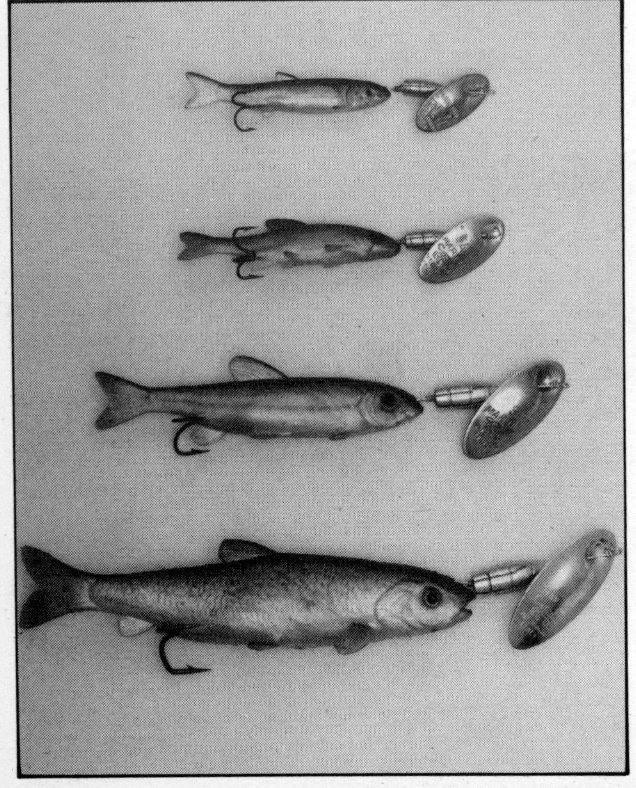

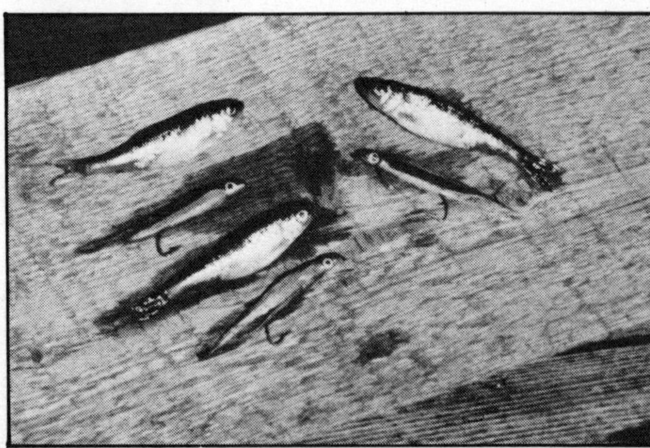

Zwirz' famous "Miracle Marabou Minnow" closely resembles real minnows and body flares out in water for even better resemblance. The streamer takes fish like the real thing!

Hellgrammites are excellent for both smallmouth and largemouth bass and big trout. Scent Baits is a specialized bait used essentially for catfish and other fish prone to locate food by smell or taste. It includes dough-type baits, blood baits and cheese baits, scented pork rind strips and soured clams. To increase their odoriferous quality, oil of anise or rhodium often are added to the concoction.

Leeches are found in leafy, brushy litter along the bottom of slow moving or still waters. You can use them like a worm and bass, trout, bullheads and cats will take them readily.

This is how live bait is rigged for float fishing after king mackerel at Cape Lookout, North Carolina (above).

Doughballs are the way to a carp's stomach, although I have known catfish to take them almost as well. This bait is made from cornmeal, flour, water and such attractors as honey, anise and special scent oils. Made correctly, they stay on the hook, slowly giving off the scent that attracts fish from amazing distances.

The saltwater specialist also has a number of deadly naturals available to him. Baits such as mullet, herring, menhaden, anchovies, ballyhoo, eels, killies, spearing, shrimp, sandbugs, squid, seaworms, crabs and various species of shellfish all account for some species of fish under appropriate circumstances.

The real McCoy is the top choice, when and where available. But nature and man being unreliable providers, several tackle firms have gone about the business of imitating and producing to minute detail insects and aquatic critters that can fool a fish when fished correctly.

The same is true on salt water, where squid and bait fish of all sizes have been copied in rubber or plastic even to the correct type of swimming action.

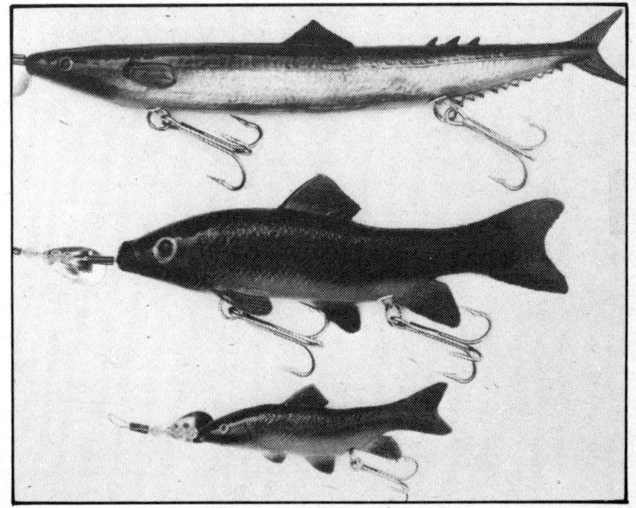

Years back, Leisure Lures, Inc., managed to copy all manner of live bait. These lures are but a few of them.

During an angling expedition to Tierra del Fuego, on the southernmost tip of South America, Zwirz caught one of the many record trout he's landed. This was a sea-run male brown. He used Miracle Marabou Minnow, 12-pound line.

TROUT: EAST & WEST

There Are Proven Methods For Filling Your Creel Despite Changing Seasons, Geographical Demands

NO MATTER how strongly you wish for all-season success with the several trout species, as water temperatures change and the days grow warmer, the wise fisherman's techniques and grass-roots thinking must alter accordingly, whether his primary stamping grounds are a New England river or one of the West's famed trout waters.

To enjoy an all-season approach to trout fishing – and to have your efforts bear fruit – it's a must that the subject be reduced to the basics that make each seasonal segment of the trout calendar something quite different from the rest.

To take on this subject intelligently, no matter where in this country an angler resides, he must comprehend exactly what happens to trout – or for that matter all fish – under specific water and air temperature conditions and how these and other variables affect both the natural food supply and feeding habits of trout.

Early Season Strategies

All species of trout are cold-water dwellers by choice, although this preference does not hold true when the water temperature drops below forty degrees Fahrenheit. The species is able to survive under such circumstances, but shows only a faint trace of their true aggressiveness. During those relatively short periods when they do feed, it is near impossible to tempt them to move any great distance for a lure or even a natural bait.

Big trout and salmon are taken not by luck, but by the angler who studies their position in rivers and streams.

Over many years it has become a fact that worms – any of the three major types – fished slowly along the bottom cover, produce more trout than any other method you might imagine. Using the worm fishing approach, it will be in the deeper pools and in the well defined deeper runs that the trout angler will locate most of his early-season fish.

This is no great surprise to those who have learned that these are the locations in any stream or river where trout tend to wait-out the hard, cold winter months. Keep in mind, however, that although I stated worms will produce best, there is no valid reason why the angler using deep-running lures cannot take trout, though possibly to a lesser degree. Specially designed lures such as Mepps, C.P. Swings, Panther Martins, Phoebes, Wob-L-Rites, plus weighted or long-lipped Rapala bait fish imitation plugs will definitely take their share of trout; particularly if the caster remembers that he must stick to the slowest retrieve possible, while still imparting a convincing, life-like action to his lure.

Casting to specific stations where trout are apt to be is another important way in which the fisherman who can read water will score consistently higher than those who cast without any serious consideration of where fish may lie.

One of the near insurmountable problems of fishing rivers and streams during the early seasons relates to the frustrating fact that waters often are excessively high, roiled and generally not ready for a normal approach; even though the rugged fraternity of opening-day anglers may consider it to be past time, having looked at their calendars. If high, roily waters are the norm in your area on opening day, it might not be a bad move to change tactics completely, and leave the high-flowing streams until they subdue and both air and water temperatures rise to at least forty-eight degrees.

Opposite page: This knowledgeable Kentucky lass prepares to net a trout taken on a fly. She read her water efficiently. Above: Michigan's Manistee River is great after dark for big brown trout. Here, Bing McClellan holds a six-pound brown taken around midnight on a Keel-Caddis fly. Fighting them is exciting in the dark!

While on this subject, have you ever seriously considered that it might well be a wise move to begin your trout season enjoying a few sessions on one of the more promising lakes or ponds that have been stocked with trout? In both the East and West, large trout of several species are taken during the opening weeks by anglers using spinning lures, plugs, bait and flies. It is a fact that ponds, lakes and impoundments are capable of yielding trout far earlier in the spring than usually is possible on fast-flowing waters subjected to heavy runoff from winter snows. High country in the Midwest and West can be notorious for this hindrance. It will be in the more stabilized waters, where one or more species are available, that you will find them accepting a wider assortment of natural or artificial baits.

From a practical standpoint, there are two basic approaches that have proven most productive for fishing large waters. Top technique calls for the use of bait, either trolled or still fished. The second method includes all aspects of trolling, regardless of whether spinning tackle, bait casting gear or fly rods are used to present the lure.

It is true that some small ponds and high-country lakes remain cold and basically unfishable until the days turn more springlike, but it's more prevalent to assume that a good percentage of waters holding both native and stocked trout will also have a share of deep holes, pockets and spring-fed areas. Keep in mind that water along the bottom strata normally is cooler than the surface water during the summer, but is just the opposite during a frigid winter. For this reason, trout will go deep during cold weather in order to find some moderation of water temperature. When medium depths and, finally, the surface water and air temperatures warm up, they gradually move into shallower areas, both as a place to live and a place to seek out food.

Based on years of experience on both eastern and western trout waters, chances are you will find water temperatures running anywhere from thirty-nine degrees to somewhere near a conceivable high of fifty degrees. If the lower reading is in evidence, you certainly will not

Match the tackle to the probable size of the trout you seek, and the size and flow of the stream or river for sport.

expect trout to be at all interested in any surface presentation of bait, lures or the general run of flies.

While mentioning flies, it might be helpful to know that there are few hatches of any great importance until the water reaches the forty-eight to fifty-degree mark. If there is any possibility, it will lie with an early mayfly known as the *Epeorus pleuralis.* This hatch, when present, is best matched with the popular Quill Gordon. Since this species sheds its skin while under the surface, the angler will have his best results when fishing the nymph pattern or the wet pattern in a size corresponding to the prevailing hatch. With this exception, the fly fisherman will do better if he limits himself to the top-producing patterns of either streamers or bucktails, which should be acceptable imitations of the bait fish common to the area.

Regarding the business of temperature and depth, there are numerous deep ponds, lakes and impoundments where both food and oxygen are present even at extreme depths; however, in many cases you will find the thermocline to be twenty-three or thirty-five feet in depth. Often the water below this strata is devoid of oxygen. On the other hand, there are lakes of unusual depth where the thermocline has been discovered as deep as seventy-five feet. The best way to be certain of such factors is to use a water thermometer and fish accordingly, unless reliable information is available concerning the lake you will fish. Local fish and game department biologists often have figures based on their own yearly surveys and maximum-comfort temperature readings for each species of fish inhabiting the watershed.

One other factor of great importance to spring anglers is the effect that wind and sun have on surface waters during the early season. Just following ice-out on many northern lakes, or in any area where temperature extremes are prevalent, there is a period when the surface water warms and the wave action, caused by wind, starts the warmer water sinking. At this time the cold water below mixes with the warmer water above, until it all comes close to a reading of 39.2 degrees. This particular phenomenon causes fish of the cold-water variety to begin feeding and move about just subsurface. This is the timing element involved with spring fishing for landlocked salmon; it works for the same period of time on mature trout.

Summer Fishing

Far too many anglers have the erroneous impression that once the hot, summer months take over, it's time to put

Nebraska's Nine Mile Creek offers particular challenges, with its undercut banks and deep, swirling pools.

their rods away or look for other forms of fishing besides trout.

Being the kind of angler who prefers solitude with his trout fishing, I have rarely in the past done much to change that opinion among my less persevering friends. Summer, especially in the East, has become an amazing time of sparsely fished stretches and favorite pools, with not a soul to bother the angler in search of peace. It does take some imagination and a change of pace to consistently take trout in the normally hotter days of late June through August.

If you have ever fished – hour after hour – in the broiling hot sun of August, chances are you wasted your time! Much of the discomfort you felt, as you cast and recast your lure, was being felt by the trout. Unless you had exceptional luck, you left the stream with an empty creel and perspiring brow.

But, you can take trout in the hot, summer months if you take into consideration the fact that trout feel pretty much the same way you do: uncomfortable and hot. That's why they are not showing. Now, when might angler and trout be most comfortable? During the sunless hours, the periods of comparative coolness. In the early morning, you'll find that water temperature is at its lowest. As the day progresses, the temperature will climb, then fall again in the evening and grow cooler through the night. It is possible to take trout during the heat of midday, but you'll do yourself a favor by working out a schedule that will put you in position when the fish are most active.

There are two such schedules. The first is for the man serious about catching big fish. He must alienate himself from those around him and catch up on his sleep. When darkness comes, this angler will be out on the waters presenting his offerings to the trout.

Where brown trout are present, the hours between dusk and dawn will produce the largest specimens. Browns are nocturnal fish, by and large, and this is especially true of the wise, old trophy fish who refuses to move from hiding until the protective shadows fall across the waters. As the sun begins to fall behind the hills, there is a definite upswing in trout activity. The fly caster usually can find a surface-feeding trout if there are any naturals at all on the surface, and the spin fisherman finds that he is casting to fish that have suddenly come to life. It will be this way all through the night and continue until the early morning sun sends the fish back to their places of hiding.

The fly fisherman should learn just what he may expect

An Alcedo Micron spinning outfit (bottom) and a fly rod shared honors for these three trophy trout.

in the way of hatches during these months and take advantage of the naturals that will show him the way. The last two weeks of June produce a good hatch during the day and again in the early evening. During the afternoon you can take fish with the Light Cahill in size No. 12. In the evening, the dry-fly man will be in his glory, and normally will find a No. 12 Ginger Quill to be his best bet.

July and August have hatches of interest to the angler. Mayflies are still on the scene and are best copied with patterns like the Pale Evening Dun. Usually you'll use these flies just about dark. You're also in position to fish the nymph pattern (Potamanthus nymph) with marked success, long before you have a similar chance with the dry. The Dun of this species offers the opportunity to fish one of the finest late-season dries, the Cream Variant, sparsely dressed on No. 12 hooks.

Later in July, a light-yellow mayfly makes its appearance just about an hour before dark. From late afternoon until I see definite dry-fly activity, I prefer fishing the nymph of this pattern (Ephemera). I've found it effective on a No. 10 hook. Once more the Cream Variant dry will outfish the usual patterns.

A few years ago I was given a bit of sage advice by a famous Catskill angler while we were fishing on the Beaverkill River. To take trout just before dark simply tie on a plain black and white bucktail and work it around the head of a run or the head of a pool. Fish have a tendency to move up into the head at this hour and just can't seem to leave a dace pattern alone. Once it is really dark, tie on a brace of wet flies. Many a large trout has been taken on a dark night with a big wet fly.

If spinning is your game, you have your favorite lures for average water conditions, as well as for low water. Most spin enthusiasts seem to have their best luck using lures like the Mepps, Panther Martins or C.P. Swings. I wouldn't hesitate to mimic a minnow as darkness descends; for this I'd recommend the Phoebe or some of the small, light, minnow-action plugs. Use either the ultralight or the lights. For the wise old heavyweights don't go afield without a selection of Ray Johnson's Real Minnow lures in several sizes and imitations; plus a copy of Ray's new and fantastic book, *Big Trout.*

If the streams you fish are small and shallow, you must practice stealth in your approach to the fish. Your tackle also should be lighter than you might normally expect; light-action, six-foot fly rods or ultralight spin outfits are the logical choices. Wherever you fish, you will take more and larger fish if willing to put in some nighttime hours.

Night fishing isn't going to please everyone. You have to be pretty devout to enjoy it and skilled with your equipment as well. Many fishermen prefer to concentrate on the peak periods from one hour before dawn until one hour after sunup and again from approximately four in the afternoon until an hour after dark.

A mountain stream in New Mexico's Vermejo Park produces a fine stringer of rainbow trout, and natural beauty.

Fishing with Zwirz in Patagonian lake in Argentina, two arm-weary anglers show what awaits South of the Border!

The second schedule is not such a sure thing, but it puts you on the river during the part of the day you choose. It is called white-water fishing and gives one a good chance to take fish about half of the time. The high content of oxygen present in heavy-pocket water has a tendency to keep trout more active. You will find that, although an occasional brown trout may live here, this sort of stretch is more often the home of the rainbow. The rainbow's personality has a tendency to keep him in a mood to hit a streamer, bucktail or even a surface fly as it swings by. And you may have equal luck if you run a spinning lure through his front door; I've watched many anglers pass up the real turbulent, difficult spots in favor of practically sterile stretches, especially when the water is warm and clear.

No matter where you fish, you can count on taking good rainbows from fast-water pockets. This is equally true in the East or in the big rivers of the West. It is a certainty that, with the right pace and schedule, you can take these warm-water trout.

Never forget that the best way to insure a successful fishing trip, at any time of the season, is to think out your strategy carefully before you make your first cast. Some careful analysis of present streamside conditions can go a long way toward increasing your scores on trout.

Though it is a proven fact that some sportsmen like to stack the odds in favor of the trophy, I am not a member of any such group. No way do I wish to have someone point out the toughest trout stream, river or impoundment, with the smallest population of trout in a given state, then urge me to be a hero. Show me trout water that has a winning record for producing potential trophy trout and my nature puts me into high gear. I want good reason to believe the trout population is high, the presence of heavyweights a known fact.

However, I'm aware of certain waters that are what many call "sleepers." Nearly every state – for that matter, every country – holding a trout population, will have a share of waters that hold trout that are true monsters. These same fishing areas are, strangely, unknown to native and visiting anglers alike. Difficult to catch with frequency, ofttimes these wise old hook-jaws end up breaking records for those who fish hard and wisely.

Not surprising, a great deal of what you will read here, relating to the quest for larger trout, will basically apply to each of our three most popular trout species: the rainbow, brown and brook trout. Though I personally consider a wise, heavyweight brown to represent the toughest-to-take of the trout species, in no way do I consider the rainbow or brookie to be inferior or less of a trophy catch.

It's hard to concentrate on the fishing amid the stunning scenery typical of British Columbia. Here you'll find an abundance of trout, salmon, bass, char and even pike, none of which have been pressured too hard.

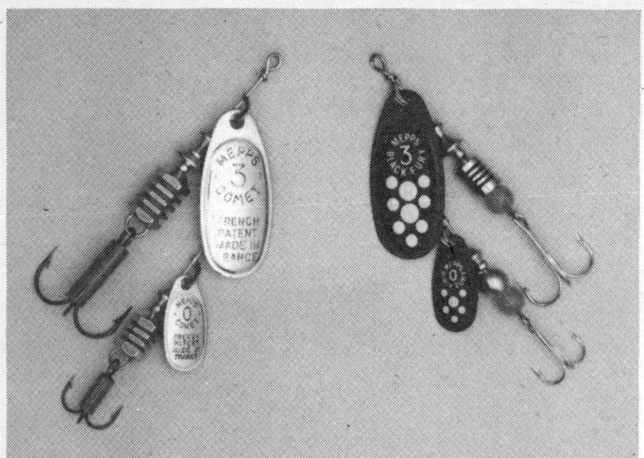

Mepps spinners, available in a dozen types and colors, take a heavy toll on trout when used with spinning outfit.

I do, however, classify them as being somewhat easier to creel under most seasonal water conditions than the fantastically clever, super-fussy German brown.

Up-front thinking, long before the angler actually casts an artificial or natural bait in the hope of creeling a truly worthwhile-size trout, he must first decide on which of our three friends he wishes to concentrate. Concentration on a specific species, you will discover – plus a knowledge of the habits of that species – will go a long way toward making the quest a successful one.

An unfortunate number of anglers fail to consider the unavoidable truth that trout, as a species, spend most of their hours feeding on aquatic insects well below the surface. This, I might add, is a fact that will play just as

Famous Argentine/German guide, Eric Gornik, shows why the author states trophy trout still await the skilled angler.

Like the Muddler Minnow at top left, all of the patterns of bait fish imitations can be deadly medicine.

High oxygen, unseen cover, a dappled worm or fly gently cast, and it's time for a big rainbow to strike. The real challenge comes when trying to hold him in this heavy flow!

important a role, whether the angler uses spinning gear, a plug-casting outfit, or traditional fly fishing equipment. And it is still of primary importance no matter whether that angler chooses to present the trout with natural or artificial baits.

Those who prefer to spend their streamside hours seeking either the rainbow or brookie must, as an example, base their techniques on proven data that shows these two trout take nearly ninety percent of their food underwater; such underwater feeding including all manner of aquatic life, such as nymphs and minnows. Brown trout, of all sizes, often indulge in feeding sprees that find them actively taking surface naturals, to a degree that it can easily represent more than twenty percent of their feeding within a given twenty-four-hour period.

There is one other highly important basic that must be considered if you wish to spend your time wisely, and that concerns itself with water conditions preferred by each of the species.

The brown trout strongly prefers deep, slow-moving runs, particularly where underwater rocks and boulders offer cover, and they will seek out the deep pools in rivers and streams. When present in a pool, a large brown will completely dominate it and, in an amazingly short span of time, either eat or chase away every other fish. On the other hand, you most often find trophy rainbows taking residence in cold, fast moving, clear waters that offer broken cover for protection from enemies, as well as respite from the primary flow. The brook trout shows similar preferences, though he rarely makes camp in flows offering a high oxygen supply. In fact, the brookie will take advantage of submerged brush piles, roots, log jams, and similar current breakers that offer him protection.

For large trout of these three species to be present, the areas of water they inhabit must be able to supply adequate feed, that all-important cover in one form or another is available, as well as relative comfort from the force of those excessive flows. Looking first at medium to fast-moving waters that so often hold a surprising number of the larger trout, the certain data will prove of definite help in locating areas containing those wise, old cannibal trout; trout that rarely position themselves in areas too easily reached or, for that matter, too easily fished due to the problems of presenting the bait in a reasonable manner for a long enough viewing period.

Unless natural or manmade obstructions are present, especially in the fast running sections, habitable water will be sought in another favorite area; the secondary flows, usually located to either side of the primary or central flow. But where available, they will move into the various depressions and behind those naturally placed barriers that are right in the primary flow itself. But only when adequate barriers are present!

Since this business of reading the water is so all-important, let's look at this subject a little more thoroughly. Every stream and river will comprise various complexities, inasmuch as the depth and flow are involved. You can be sure that the larger the stream or river, usually the more complex you can expect the flow to be. Small streams and brooks tend to reveal their mysteries with far less detective work.

Every variation of flow will require a specific technique for making your presentation, just as it dictates the best size and type of lure or bait; and whether you would score best by fishing deep, shallow or on or near the surface during special feeding periods.

Since trout of each species tend to have strong, personal preferences regarding the type of water they will inhabit, it also is important that you familiarize yourself with the various popular hybrids. This natural preference of each species holds true, regarding both areas and water temperatures, whether the fish are present in stream or river, lake or impoundment.

This matter of stream lore, or reading the water as most anglers know the art, is not one that anyone can learn overnight. Learning the important answers will be the result of the total hours of your own experience and actual time spent on the water, but one will amass knowledge once he begins observing the streams and other waters he fishes, mentally cataloging where, why, and how you catch the majority of trout over any given season.

Each of the popular trout species, and most certainly the larger specimens, have certain personality quirks that, when understood by the fisherman, will aid him in deciding how best to go about catching each. The rainbow will go to great lengths to locate those fast-water stretches in which to set up his home. You can bet that the larger the flow of water, the more it will suit his personal tastes.

Mann's new Piglet Rooter pulls big bass out of cover, and can do the same on trophy trout when properly directed.

Wherever big water is accessible to him, the rainbow will move in; it is fairly rare for the larger rainbows to be found in what might be classified as smaller brooks. If he is found in such small flows, chances are it will be due to the spawning season or during summer, because of the presence of cold spring holes that offer cooler, more comfortable water temperatures than exist in the larger river he would normally wish to inhabit.

Typically, he will be found in the faster of the white-water runs, in riffles, and under waterfalls offering an increased oxygen supply. Or, right out in the most turbulent fast water, just so long as there are those all-important depressions, rocks and boulders or other comfort spots in which he can find refuge from the force of the current.

In the case of brown trout, I have noted that an amazing number of trout fishermen fail to accept the fact that he can inhabit a broad range of water. While true that big browns often will take up residence in such places as slow-moving, deep-running meadow streams with their secret holes and undercut banks, it is just as true that these fish often will attempt to locate what can be classified as medium-fast runs.

They are more prone to settle in stretches that feature a flow broken by large boulders, rocky ledges, and such other obstructions. Where such an area lies close by a gliding run and one or more deep pools, you can expect to find trout of above average size simply because such a set-up is made to order for the wily brown's temperament. This is just as true of Western fish as it is of those found in the East.

You will discover the brown to be the wisest and moodiest of the trout family, at the same time the most unpredictable in feeding habits and periods of activity. In the case of the larger browns, it is not uncommon to have them lie quietly during the daylight hours, resisting even the best presentation of lure or bait that comes into their deep hideaway. But once the shadows of late afternoon begin to fall across the waters, this same fish will begin his most active period of feeding and, in most instances, continue to do so throughout the hours of darkness.

As stated earlier, the greatest mistake made by all of us is that we rarely fish deep enough for large trout. Even when we manage to keep our lure or bait in the stratum that holds these trout, it ends up being an all-too-brief presentation. Even worse, it is rarely a convincing presentation due to the difficulty of controlling the bait, naturally, in the swift-moving current.

The bigger and swifter the water, the more difficult the angler's problem. The fly fisherman most certainly requires an intermediate-sinking fly line if the stretch is unusually deep as well as fast. It is ofttimes a help if the flies are specially weighted when tied; the closer they come to scraping the bottom cover, the better the chances of hanging a really good trout.

Several anglers of my acquaintance who specialize in seeking out trophy trout, especially during the warmer days of summer, have found their success is dependent on the frequency with which they are able to present their lures or bait deep and slow. Unless a distinct hatch is in progress and the trout are actively feeding upon it, most large trout are taken from hot spots located right smack among the cover of the stream bed. Even when many of the average-size trout feed at various levels of depth during a hatch, larger trout (especially the browns) rarely join in the wild feeding.

The reason is simple: The larger trout have become more interested in eating other, smaller fish. Having grown to a size where they are primarily predaceous and cannibalistic, they feed in a completely different manner, and often at different times than the smaller inhabitants of the stream. However,the angler who works a bait-fish-type lure or a natural bait down where they live in a manner that is not suspect has a good chance of finding himself hooked to a better-than-average-size trout, even during nonpeak fishing periods. The Real Minnow brought out by the Ray Johnson Company is as deadly as any lure I've yet fished. Browns over five pounds simply engulf them.

Numerous rigs and methods can be used by the angler in such waters. Some are best for the spin fisherman, others for the bait caster or those who prefer the fly rod. Special lures that will run deep even in fast water, and sinker rigs such as the fish finder used with natural bait are but a couple of winning thoughts for such conditions. In fact, the fish finder is often the winning answer when spring water is high.

Few trout fishermen even bother to give the highly effective jigging-type lures a fair chance in these big-fish stretches. It is a shame, seeing as how they are so deadly! The weighted jig, often designed to resemble a bait fish, goes down to any depth the angler wishes, presenting little resistance to the flow. The fact that the hook on these lures faces up can be quite a bonus for casters who can concentrate on scraping the very bottom without fear of actually hanging up, I continually tout this lure for bass, as well as for many species in fresh and salt water.

When fishing for big trout in medium to fast water, nothing will teach the angler the dos and don'ts any faster than actually getting into the stream and experiencing the specific and often difficult problems regarding proper presentation of lures and bait.

But once the lessons are learned and you find yourself fishing deep, as well as convincingly enough to fool the wise fish population, you will quickly realize that you can take larger trout even at those times when the fish are not moving about during a peak feeding cycle.

Old, tried and true, these spinning lures have taken an unbelievable number of trout for the author world-wide.

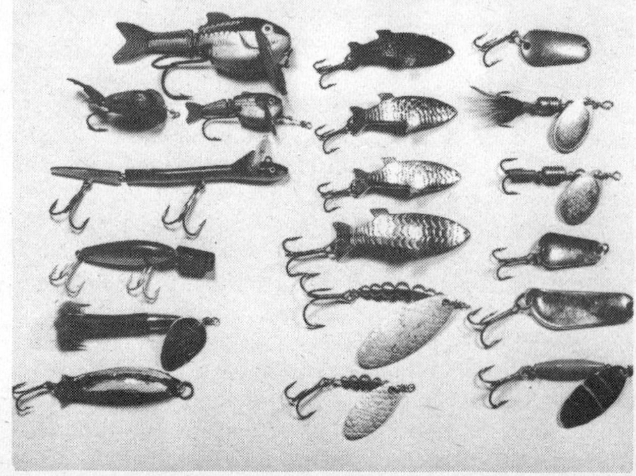

Never believe large saltwater bait fish imitations aren't great on the larger trout — they often produce tremendous strikes when standard offerings have failed (above). Large dry fly patterns (below), during periods of matching natural species, can provide fast and exciting action. Of course, the fly must be tied correctly, fished properly.

CHAPTER 11

THE ARROGANTS

Northern Pike And Muskellunge Are Among The Most Voracious Of Game Fish — And Act The Part!

Opposite page: A fighting-mad northern pike, taken on light spinning tackle at White Water Lake, Ontario. Their behavior can run from stand-offishness to voraciousness, and the spoons, plugs and spinners shown above have taken them.

IT IS LITTLE more than a conjecture, but I tend to subscribe to the opinion that the vast majority of northern pike are taken by casters, not by trollers. To take this crystal-balling a step further, a high percentage of the muskie hooked come as something of a surprise to the average angler who has been casting for bass!

The exception would be an experienced muskie fisherman, knowing prime holding areas of his favorite waters, who goes forth solely to coax the not always cooperative muskellunge. Such experts have the edge in taking trophies.

Northern pike also can be stand-offish, though normally they show such voraciousness that nearly anything that moves within their domain is certain to be pounced upon. To say they are one thousand percent more cooperative than a muskie is likely to be an understatement.

Where habitat makes it possible, the northern pike positions himself in among the cover, his keen eyes and senses checking the outer realm for an unwary prey. Often it is the same with the average-size muskie, which has a loner personality, craving cover under large deadfalls, logs or hidden in deep channels during warmer weather.

This brings us to the problem of what tackle is best under such specialized circumstances that almost guarantee snagged lures and hooks. An angler could use a light, sporty rod and correspondingly light line, from the viewpoint of pound-test against probable weight of the fish, but that is not the problem. Not only do you have to consider the problem of horsing-out a snagged lure from time to time, but also the mess of vegetation a hooked pike is liable to gather on your line during battle. Thus you are compelled

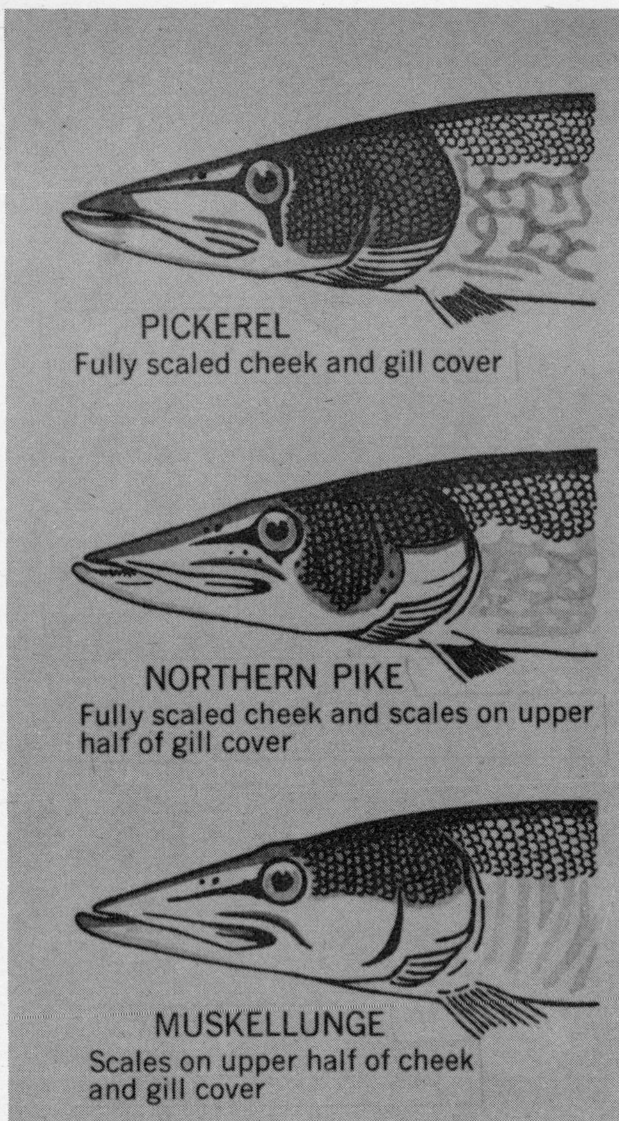

This chart can prove helpful in showing the differences between pickerel, northern pike and muskies you're after.

to use a stiffer-action rod and a line capable of taking the pressure when forced to lay into your fish.

During the first moments of hooking a trophy northern, put on the pressure immediatley to turn the fish and get him to the outer edge of yonder cabbage. This is where the rod and line with adequate built-in backbone help bring the pike into open water without breaking at the moment of peak action. There is one other consideration: lures, spoons, and even the larger Mepps spinner and bucktail combos are of a size to make typical bass spoons appear on the skimpy side.

The average length of a pike spoon runs from three to five inches in length. Because of their size, they frequently catch the wind to cast like a runaway saucer. Seventeen-pound-test mono is none too heavy and many skilled pike anglers use nothing lighter than 25-pound test. The heavier and bulkier the lure, the heavier the line needed to cast it. When line is too light for a given lure it will belly during the cast and control badly even on the retrieve.

In the United States we have northern pike fishing of only average quality generally in Michigan, Wisconsin, Minnesota, Nebraska and North Dakota. Of these, Minnesota offers the best fishing waters. Most suitable waters in our states have received heavy fishing pressure for an extended length of time.

For an action-guaranteed session on pike, I recommend the Canadian provinces of Saskatchewan, Manitoba or Ontario; northern pike fishing remains best in those waters that are remote and difficult to reach. The northern pike is so voracious he can practically be fished-out of an area when fishing pressure becomes too concentrated. This fish is that willing to strike a lure or bait.

A good deal of northwest Ontario is far enough from well traveled roads that you will find fair pike fishing in the general area of Oba, to the east and along a geographical line just below Hudson Bay. Many of the easier-to-reach areas in the more southerly tier of the province are fished throughout the open season.

Manitoba and Saskatchewan provide truly fast fishing, with larger fish not uncommon. In the area along the Manitoba-Ontario border and Lake Winnipeg are hundreds of fly-in lakes, many of them still virgin fishing waters. Another top possibility is the beautiful lakes lying in the northern part of the province near the town of Churchill. This area still has not been over-fished. Walleye, brookies

A muskie fresh from the cold waters of the Sioux Lookout, Ontario, tries desperately to throw the author's hook.

Really light tackle was used to hook a Manitoba northern pike that's being gilled here by a man who knows how to do it!

and lake trout help make up a pretty special kind of mixed bag in addition to record-size northerns.

If you are ready to rough it, utilize the services of a bush pilot. And if you really crave great fishing, the northernmost reaches of Saskatchewan contain the least-fished lakes in all of Canada. The Prince Albert area abounds in outfitters offering all kinds of packaged fishing deals, with guides and float planes available. Most areas within these provinces also have commercial camps adequate for a family that loves the outdoor scene.

In the business of actually catching northerns, oval spoons, heavy in weight, featuring a nickel finish on one side and red and white on the reverse side, usually spell success. A red bucktail tied into the tail hooks makes the lure that much more effective. Keep all spinners, spoons and similar lures glistening, as it is flash and erratic movement that goad a particularly lazy fish into a strike; this is especially true on overcast days or early in the morning and just before dusk.

In fishing for larger pike, it is a good idea to use a section of wire leader between the line and lure; it is exactly the same as if fishing for muskie. I have found that leaders running from six to twelve inches work fine. Most tackle dealers offer those covered with nylon to keep them from kinking; there also is the braided-wire type, which does not have the plastic covering. Both have built-in swivels as well as a snap swivel at the terminal end for fastening the lure or plug. The swivel is great but can bend or break.

It is not enough for you simply to cast your spoons, spinners or other favorite lures into likely looking hot spots. A simple retrieve is not enough, unless the fish are on a wild, feeding spree. It helps if you impart a little special, tantalizing action to the overall retrieve. I personally try to make the lure jump and twitch as it hits the water, just as an escaping baitfish would do when he breaks the surface in panic-induced flight. Always think of your lure as a live baitfish, not simply a hunk of inanimate metal.

You will locate most pike along the inshore waters, as

A northern pike will often put on that special burst of power when he feels hook. Don't lose fish with slack.

This is one fine pike for New Jersey and ice-fishing time. It's often cold and miserable out on the ice – and fun!

well as around cover that holds baitfish, frogs and similar big-fish fare. Pike will seek out deep holes if the weather turns extremely hot during daylight hours, but even these are accessible in the shore areas just prior to sunup to an hour or so after the sun has risen.

Some pike waters do not have all the types of cover described. In such cases, look for fish in channel waters, around drop-offs, and especially where brooks or streams empty into the main body of water. The big northerns will be lying in eight to twelve feet of water, possibly deeper in some parts of the country.

When you find this situation, use live bait. Suckers make excellent pike bait, but should be at least six to eight inches in length. Large pike prefer baits as long as twelve inches. Also try dogfish, yellow perch or bullheads; first clip the spines off the bullheads. All of these baits can be used for still-fishing or in the live-bait trolling harnesses used by many anglers who dredge up the lunkers from the deep runs, coves and deep dropoff areas while working from a boat.

Many rivers and creeks hold good-size pike. Such spots allow the caster to use slightly lighter, smaller lures. Fly and spinner combinations, large streamers and popping bugs often can be used on a typical bass-bugging rod, using a weight-forward line.

The best all-purpose, all-areas outfit for northern fishing is a conventional bait-casting rod and reel. This is almost a must if you will be spending a good deal of time on lakes that have a high percentage of weeded areas or an accumulation of underwater brush and deadfalls.

Rods known in the trade as Muskie Specials usually are around 5½ feet overall and are available in medium and heavy actions. Choose the lighter one for fishing the northern pike. It is best for casting or trolling the most practical weights in lures, plugs and baits. A quality reel is recommended along with at least 15-pound-test line, if the fishermen plans to concentrate on those heavily weeded areas or fears the loss of a trophy-size fish.

Spinning tackle is all right for the lighter lures and plugs and provides great sport, as does the fly rod. Just remember that you are going to be somewhat limited when it comes to handling a good fish in troublesome cover.

No matter how you go about fishing for the aggressive northern, you never should be disappointed in his strike or

Author's wife, Glad, readies the heavy gear and big plugs and lures for trophy-size muskellunge from the deep channels of the St. Lawrence River. Note plugs on camper door.

Wisconsin is famed for its muskie population, which has decreased by one monster (left). It was taken with a Muskie Special rod of 5½ feet.

An Alumacraft wide-beam boat and a trusty Evinrude 55hp engine provide the wherewithal to get out amongst those trophy northerns, and these fellows were rewarded with a lunker in the net. Knowledge of water is essential.

A large spinner provided the medicine to fool this whopper muskie at Wisconsin's Little Bass Lake.

in the knock-down brand of action he is capable of bringing to light-tackle anglers.

As already noted, the muskie not only resembles the northern pike closely, but has many of the same preferences in habitat and food. A sulky loner, its nasty streak is much more evident than that of its smaller cousin. Muskies come big and the fifty to sixty pounders are not uncommon, either to casters or trollers. You will find them in an assortment of sizes in Ontario, Wisconsin, Michigan, Ohio, New York, Tennessee, Kentucky, Minnesota and in several Pennsylvania lakes. Wisconsin has tremendous fish as does the St. Lawrence River.

I've done my share of muskie fishing in Ontario, Wisconsin and on the St. Lawrence, where trolling pays off big when the muskies crave large suckers. This remains true year after year in Wisconsin waters, although I'm not sure why. In any case, I prefer casting when it offers a remote possibility for success.

You should know about the king-size muskie fly-and-spinner combinations, the large muskie plugs, spoons and spoon-fly rigs. Large bucktails can be trolled or cast with a beefy fly rod, while some specialized surface disturbers can be cast with a powerful bait casting rod. There is quite a choice of so-called duck, sucker and mice plugs, among others. Large Jitterbug plugs from Arbogast always are great attractors and cast well.

With live bait you must use the utmost patience. As with other large game fish, there usually is an interim between seizing the bait, turning and engulfing it. So premature striking could result in a missed muskie.

When casting or trolling don't work well, try the old standbys: either still or drift-fishing. Suckers and other available baitfish or frogs and big crayfish, can spell the difference between success and failure. Work along likely looking weed beds, underwater logs, points of land and in the small bays and coves. They should prove the most worthwhile places for almost any method you choose.

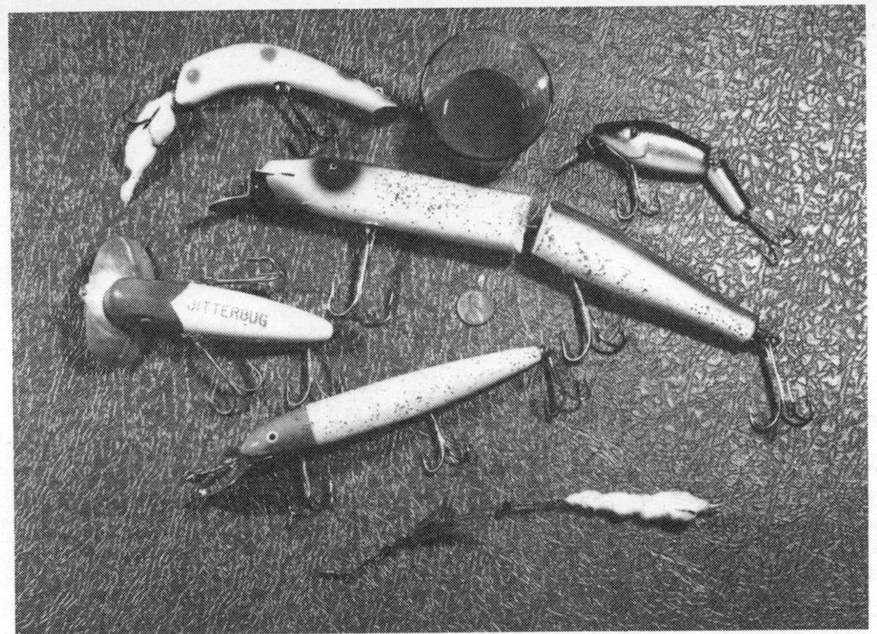

Here's a group of super-deadly muskie lures. At top left and bottom are shown blood-soaked cotton "tails" that really bring the big ones out of hiding. Don't overlook these predators' excellent sense of smell.

If you want to catch big fish, you must use big lures, says the author. Consequently, when he's after lunker muskie or northern pike, you will find big spoons and spinner along.

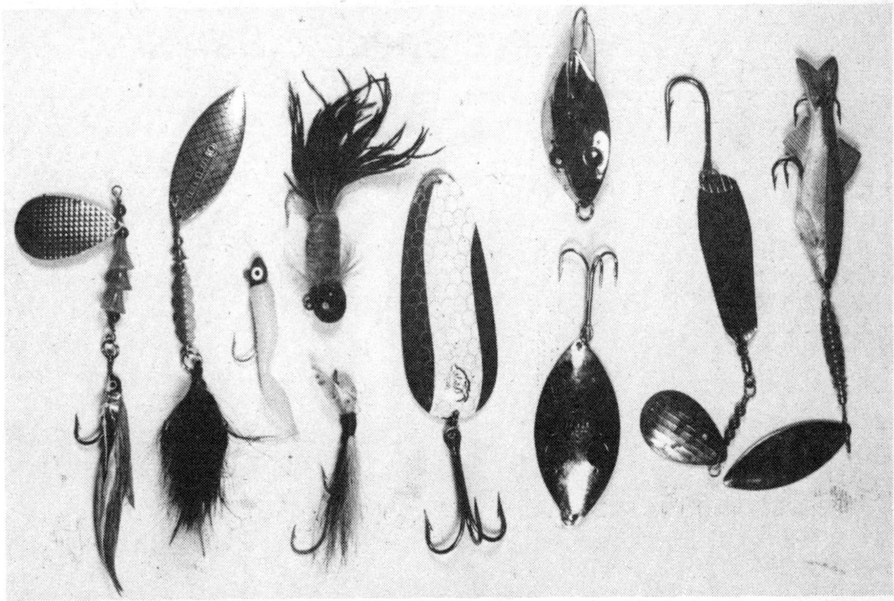

The variety of lures to which big pike and muskies respond is shown at left. Used imaginatively, each has put fish in the boat for Zwirz.

BUGGING MEANS SUSPENSE & ACTION

But, To Generate This Type Of Action, There Are Specific Required Techniques

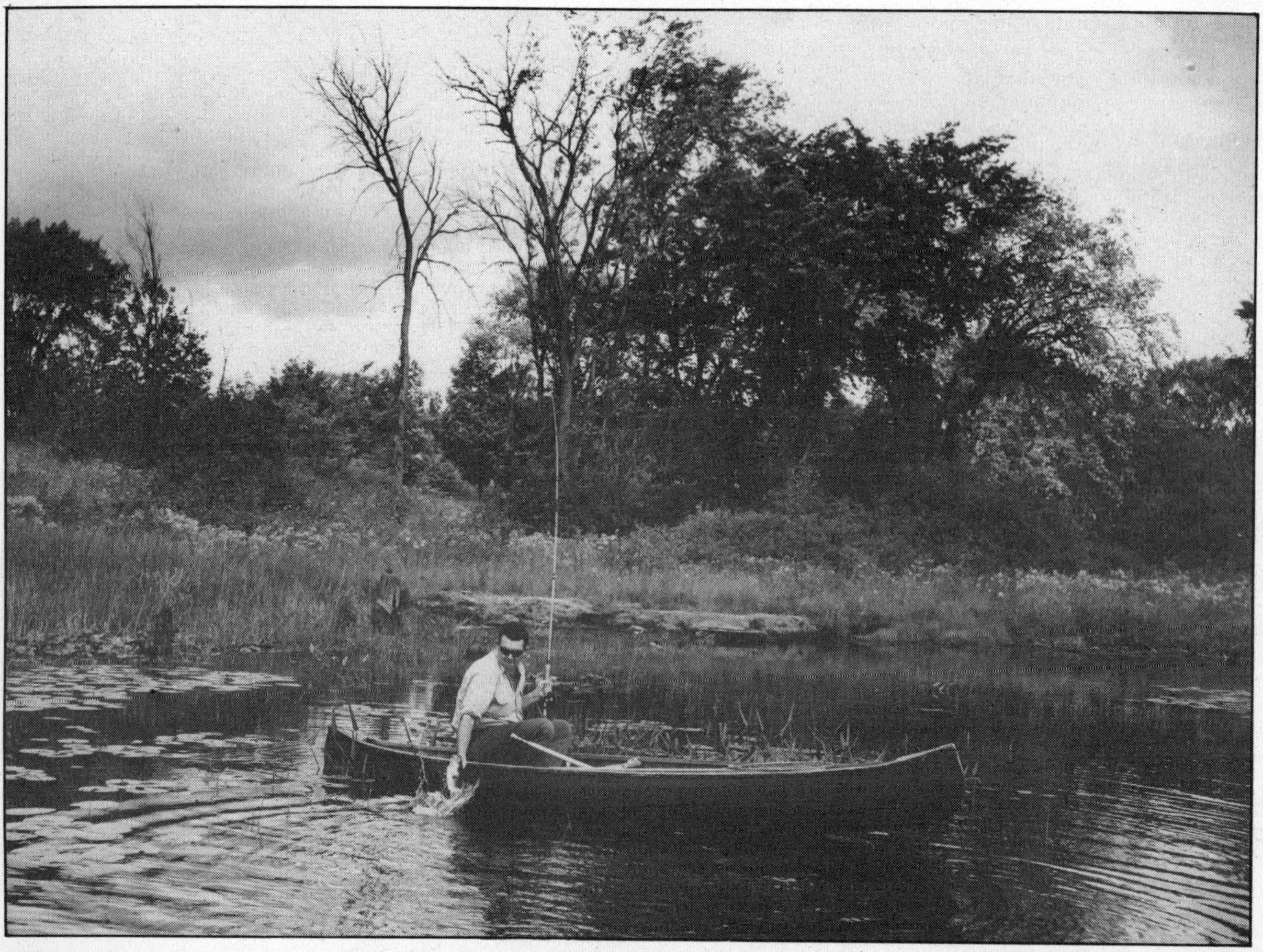

"Bass bugs" or streamers cast to drop off just outside of heavy cover and often right in the cover will often bring solid strikes from bass, northern pike and even a muskie. But you must work the bug with imagination, realism.

While angling in New Brunswick's Palfrey Lake, Glad Zwirz hooked a trophy-size smallmouth using fly rod and bass bug.

OF PRIMARY importance to any fly-rodder is what is best described as state of mind; a state that should guide his performance during the entire time spent casting.

His basic belief as he is about to cast a surface bug – or for that matter, any surface lure – is that it should resemble something tantalizing, edible and of special interest to the species of fish he is attempting to catch.

Since bugging no longer is limited to only largemouth and smallmouth bass, this will include the sizable lineup of popular gamefish that can be taken in either fresh or salt water.

One secret to consistent success with any type of surface disturber lies in the angler's ability to create the same performance the fish would expect from a crippled bait fish or one of the various critters, if that is the type of imitation he is using.

In addition to this art of putting on a realistic performance, the angler should gauge the speed of his retrieve carefully, as well as his specific retrieve action, based upon the conditions existing in the waters being fished.

Since we are dealing not only with the bass species in this report, but panfish, other surface-working freshwater game fish, plus a number of saltwater species, it is a necessity to point out that there are, at times, certain differences regarding the mode of acceptance of a surface bug, species to species.

But, before we go into this business of bugging in greater depth, let us first examine the selection of a rod and fly line. Possibly the simplest way of explaining the weight classes of the various fly rods will be to make some general recommendations in terms of the species to be fished, in relation to the angler's equipment.

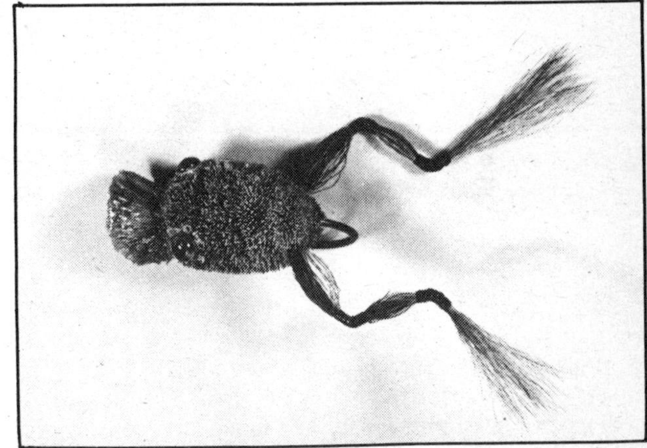

Of many bass bug designs, few provide better action than a deadly hair-bodied Sputter Frog offered on tapered line.

A satisfactory multi-purpose fly rod for general bugging should feature a medium action. You'll be casting weight-forward fly lines (also called bass-bugging tapers) along with air-resistant lures, ofttimes into the wind. Such a fly rod should have a progressive taper, progressive action.

For those fishermen ready to master the techniques, the fly rod offers the greatest sport possible no matter which of the popular species is sought. To a degree, other methods

Newfoundland's famed Gander River regularly produces fish averaging five to six pounds, and frequently the bank-casting angler will creel a twenty-pound Atlantic salmon. Many will rise to a pattern that's of bass bug type.

give the fishermen greater flexibility, but they just cannot surpass bugging when it comes to raising the hackle on the back of your neck. The greatest proportion of any angler's bugging will be spent fishing for the larger panfish species and for various members of the bass family.

There is little difference in overall equipment, techniques or fly and bugs whether the caster is seeking action with a striped bass feeding along an inshore tidal bank, or looks for his sport with a fresh or brackish-water bass or fish of similar size and temperament, along the shallows of a favorite freshwater lake.

Mode of acceptance applies to what a specific species looks for regarding the type of movement and retrieve speed of your surface lure more than any other factor. Whereas most bass are suckers for a slow, hesitant retrieve, a snook normally will demand a steadily moving bug, featuring constant fluttering and action.

Each of our popular fish species has some distinct personality trait that will render one type of lure action more attractive than another. The angler must come to know the changes in finesse that pay off, for each specific species. Once this is understood, you will find the overall approach of a bugging expert relates to casting ability coupled with a knowledge of reading water, along with other telltales that point out the probable presence of fish.

In the case of bass – the most popular of all fish taken on bugs – one obtains most consistent success, if careful to keep the tempo of fishing slowed down to a veritable crawl. This same basic approach succeeds in most cases and species – not just freshwater bass.

Have you ever noticed a grasshopper vibrating after falling on the surface? Or a big, juicy moth struggling along through the surface film? Their ruckus creates small rings on the water and the insect's legs and feelers move to and fro somewhat erratically. It's this action you should strive to simulate with your bass-bug offering.

Fly rod surface lures can be divided into several subdivisions. There are the traditional poppers, of course, while others, such as the hair-wing variety, are worked as surface teasers. Worked properly by the caster, each lure

Hip-deep in the Cacapon River in West Virginia, Zwirz lays out a ninety-foot cast with ease to present bass bug to wary smallmouth hugging far shore that's tangled with stickups. It takes practice and patience to learn casting.

causes some degree of surface disturbance that attracts fish by a combination of sound and motion. In addition to the poppers that imitate struggling bait fish or frogs, there are hair-wing feather surface-disturbers that are tied to closely imitate and resemble frogs, mice, large bugs, giant moths, birds and other critters that fish find appetizing.

Possibly the one most important factor, when relying on a surface presentation for most game fish, is the caster's accuracy in placing it on the spot where it will bring results. There are frequent times when a big bass, snook or pike will make a pass at a popper that lands within inches of its station, but will ignore the same lure if it lands only feet away. Those stories you hear about sliding a fly right in under overhanging branches, at the very edge of tangled roots or a rotting stump, are all true!

There are times when a big fish actually will chase a bug to get at it, but why gamble on the ifs and buts of a careless presentation? With a little practice and patience, one can become adept enough to drop his bug or other type of surface offering into any hot spot at sixty or more paces. The difference can be measured in more than one way: You will find extra enjoyment in becoming a skillful caster, while your stringers of fish will multiply porportionately.

During those times of the year when bass and other gamefish are in the shallows by choice, it isn't that great a trick to take them on any type of surface lure. Many species leave the shallower waters during the heat of the day, but you can bet they will return to the shallow waters as it begins cooling just before dusk; they often remain feeding until nearly an hour after sunup.

While fishing from an hour before dawn until an hour after, it is not unusual to hook a dozen bass, panfish or other fresh and saltwater surface feeders. The same usually is true late in the day, as a number of species move in to feed around the weed beds, shallow bars, or the shoreline itself. Fish actually have personality problems, in a manner of speaking, and can be counted on to react in specific ways to particular stimuli.

No greater example can be found than in the case of largemouth bass, although the smallmouth bass is much

During a fishing visit to Paraguay in South America, Zwirz hooked this panfish version using fly rod and small bass bug pattern. It's difficult to find an underwater species that won't take the bugs.

alike in temperament. Facts prove that bass actually can be irritated and excited into doing the kind of rash things that often result in their appearing on wall plaques over the family mantle. Always remember that advice about pinpoint accuracy in placing your cast where you feel a good-size fish may be lurking; under and over all deadfalls, close to stumps, gravel bars and weed beds, and under overhanging bushes, trees and foliage. These are but a few of their favorite hangouts.

If that favorite popper or bass bug suddenly races off, away from the quarry, one of three things will happen: The fish will figure that just one more character has cast a lure, like all the other lures before; the lure is in too much of a hurry, so let it go; or in one out of a couple of dozen cases,

Above: Optimal floating qualities, even in fast water, make these deer-hair-body bugs winners for the knowledgeable angler. Right: These surface-disturbing poppers are created to look like natural insects or animals, at least to the fish! This selection has been reliable.

Deadly on so many gamefish species, the Muddler Minnow made its reputation on big trout. It's now used with great success on bass, snook and other popular species. Variations in the hackle, tail are displayed below.

Glad Zwirz waded carefully into this boulder-strewn stream to present her bass bugs to surface-feeding bass during early morning session. This guy was fooled by floating bug that swirled into range with current drift.

The flat, broad expanse of Maine's Moose River provided superb casting platform as author sought lunker landlocked salmon. This guy was finessed by Muddler Minnow author presented, and is basis for sumptuous repast.

the fish figures it is just too tasty-looking to let get away, and the race is on! Experience on many of our better bass waters, however, has shown me that the bigger and smarter bass rarely fall victim to such a performance.

All it should take to improve your score is a little self-control and a large helping of patience, coupled with a few of those psychological tricks to which most fish are prone to react. When it comes to choosing bugs and poppers, I find those that incorporate a concave head, or some kind of fluttering tail or legs, work exceptionally well when concentrating on bass.

When using other surface lures which imitate everything from wounded minnows, bats, birds, swimming frogs and waterlogged insects, first analyze the habits and reactions of the natural under similar circumstances. This usually calls for motions and action a good deal slower than you might normally think.

When it comes to basics, all it takes to string a share of heavy fish, using surface lures, is a little casting skill and imagination, along with knowledge of each species' hangouts. A good deal of patience and faith in what you are doing and how you are doing it are added requirements.

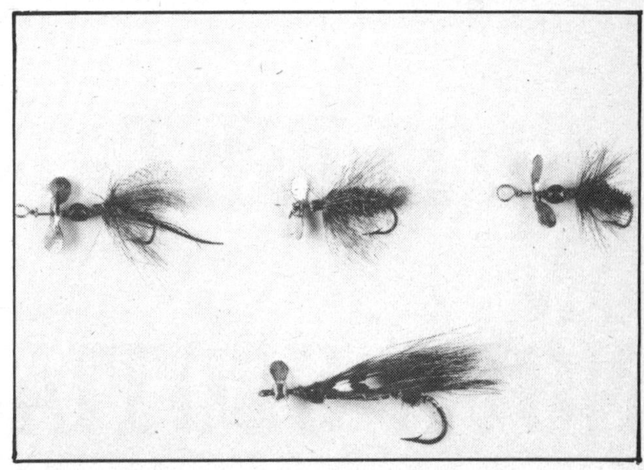

Innovations can pay off, providing they're not too radical...and then even radical ones can pay off at times! How about small spinners in front of bucktails or other patterns to add that little extra flash!

Nova Scotia regularly holds tournaments for such bruisers as the giant tuna going over the side. It was taken on conventional tackle of the super-heavy variety, shown right.

"Moment of truth" for angler and crew: Will the great fish snap line during last moments before the mate can grab for the leader? A giant tuna often does, to angler's dismay!

SPOTLIGHT ON NOVA SCOTIA

This Province Offers A Wide Variety Of Challenge To The Serious Fisherman

WITH MORE than 3000 freshwater lakes, a hundred rivers and brooks too numerous to count, sportfishermen flock to Nova Scotia from everywhere. They come to do battle with the royal salmon that make their homes in the rivers and pools; to breakfast on fresh-caught brook trout cooked over an open fire; or to contest the fighting shad in its home waters.

As the province has no leased waters, practically all of its lakes and streams are open to the visitor. However, in the interest of good fishing and conservation, certain regulations must be heeded. Visitors may obtain a non-resident fishing license at any of the Department of Lands and Forests offices located throughout the province, or from most sporting goods stores. Permits for residents of Nova Scotia also are essential. Fishing in the national parks requires a special permit issued by the park wardens. These may be purchased for only a few dollars by both residents and non-residents.

Any non-resident who enters any game area for the

Trout and salmon also are part of Nova Scotia's fishing scene. This tough fighter came out of St. Mary's River.

purpose of hunting or fishing must be accompanied by a licensed guide. Where angling is possible without entering any tract as mentioned, no guide is required. A guide will, however, save you valuable time in reaching the best places for hunting and fishing, will do the hard work along the way and will be responsible for camp chores. There are more than six hundred licensed guides in this province.

It's a good idea to take along a waterproof outfit and plenty of warm clothing on your Nova Scotia outdoor vacation. Early mornings and evenings sometimes bring on a chill. You'll find heavy and wet-weather gear at any Nova Scotia sporting goods or clothing store.

Atlantic salmon, plentiful in Nova Scotia, is one of the most closely studied species of game fish. A wealth of information is available on this species, but there is still more to be learned.

Life for the salmon begins in gravelly spawning grounds in a freshwater stream or drainage system. Here it remains until it begins its downstream swim to the ocean.

At each stage of its life, the salmon undergoes a physical change, as well as a change of name. For instance, until the egg yolk is fully absorbed, it is an alevin. As a small free-swimming fish, it is a fry for the first year, then it becomes a parr. After two to three years, when ready to head for salt water, it is known as a smolt. It undergoes a change after a year in the sea and is renamed grilse. Some of the grilse return to their native rivers and, in another year, become known as salmon.

As salmon, they return to the freshwater gravel beds to spawn. After fulfilling their reproductive duties, they do not die as do Pacific salmon, but return to the sea as slinks, black salmon or kelt. Catching or possession of slinks is prohibited in Nova Scotia.

The salmon angling season varies throughout the province, but most of June, July and August is open. Three in any one day is the limit, and salmon angling is restricted to fly fishing, although the fly preferred varies from stream to stream. Your guide can help in suggesting the correct fly for any particular river. Stock your tackle box with such wet flies as Silver Doctor, Jack Scott, Black Dose, Dusty Miller, Fiery Brown, Hackle and Silver Ranger.

Bucktail and squirrel-tail patterns like the Cosseboom and the Bomber also are good ideas, as are such dry flies as the Brown Hackle, Gray Hackle, White Hackle, Cinnamon Sedge, Pink Lady and Deadly MacIntosh (a native Nova Scotia creation).

Salmon rods in Nova Scotia normally measure from 8½ to ten feet and are equipped with a 2½ to four-inch reel and thirty yards of tapered line, spliced to one hundred yards of backing. Most salmon fisherman prefer nine-foot nylon leaders.

Landlocked Sebago salmon, on the other hand, spend their entire lives in fresh water and are not as large as sea-run salmon. (Details on season are included in trout fishing regulations.)

Not more than ten landlocked salmon may be taken in any one day, and they must measure not less than fourteen inches from the end of the nose to the center of the tail.

As landlocked salmon normally are deep feeders, a spinning rod and reel and a heavy lure that will sink, or a trolling rod with a fast sinking line – preferably a copper-type line – and lure are the most popular. The only water that produces the Sebago salmon in numbers is Shubenacadie Grand Lake, a few miles north of Halifax.

Speckled or brook trout (char) can provide the angler with an exciting contest on light tackle. Open season for trout varies by area, but all open in the spring and close in the fall, thus including the tourist season. This open season also applies to brown and gray trout and landlocked salmon, and is divided into four areas:

1. All waters of the province east of Highway 2 from

The frigid northern waters provide the top fishing grounds for cod, although this wide-ranging species can be taken farther south where the water is warmer...if you can find 'em!

Fine, clean-flowing stream offers fighting trout that can be taken on fly rod or spinning using natural baits or artificials. An extra bonus is the wild, unspoiled countryside.

Halifax to Truno, and all waters of Cumberland County, except the waters referred to in 2 below. April 15 to September 30.

2. In tidal and non-tidal waters of the Guysborough River, Guysborough County, but not including the tributaries of that river. May 1 to September 30.
3. All waters of the province west of Highway 2 from Halifax to Truno. April 1 to September 30.
4. All trout, including rainbow, in the following lakes: Sunken (Sumpter) Lake, Kings County; Rumsey Lake in Annapolis County; Levers Lake in Cape Breton County; Clearwater (Bright's) Lake in Digby County. May 15 to October 31. As these regulations are subject to minor changes, it is advised you write for revisions to the Department of Tourism, Box 130, Halifax, Nova Scotia.

Limits have been placed on trout so that not more than fifteen of any one species or combination of fifteen of two or more species in any one day may be taken, with a maximum possession limit of thirty.

During the early part of the trout season – until about May 10 – brook trout in Nova Scotia are most effectively taken with bait, lures, bucktails and streamers. For the rest of the season, either wet or dry artificial flies take preference. Ask your guide or outfitter for advice on the most effective use. The fly depends on a combination of conditions: the fish, water, available natural foods, kind and strength of daylight and other factors. This is when skill, experience and instinct come into play.

Flies for trout angling should be on hooks of from size 6 to 12 or even smaller, according to waters being fished. Some of these flies, in order of accepted merit, are:

Wet: Parmachene Belle, Silver Doctor, Stone fly, March Brown, Brown Hackle, Cowdung, Montreal, Scarlet Ibis, Yellow Sally, Professor, Queen of Waters, Black Gnat, Coachman, Jenny Lind, Nixion and Drummer. **Dry**: Brown Hackle, Gray Hackle, Parmachene Belle, Black Gnat, and a selection of duns and spinners are very effective.

Light rods of seven to nine feet length are preferred by most trout anglers. As speckled or brook trout often are subject to more fishing pressure than they sometimes support, the best trout fishing generally is off the beaten track in the seldom-fished waters of Nova Scotia's

This happy pair is preparing to build small cooking fire alongside this brook to enjoy evening meal of pan-sized trout. Can't you just taste it? These brookies came to creel after small flies were delicately presented.

backwoods. Once again, your guide is an invaluable asset. The highest yields of brook trout to date have come from Guysborough, Halifax, Inverness, Cape Breton, Victoria, Lunenburg and Cumberland counties.

Sea trout are brook trout which make their way to the sea for a period of time, where they change their appearance. Sea trout customarily re-enter streams in two annual migrations or runs, the first in April or May, while a later run occurs in late June and early July.

The total annual catch of speckled trout in Nova Scotia in recent years is reported as 394,000 fish, weighing almost one hundred tons.

Anglers seeking good sea-trout angling should be familiar with the following:

Stream	Early Run	Summer Run
Musquodoboit River Halifax Co.	May 1-20	June 20-July 10
Moser's River Halifax Co.		July 1-15
Salmon River (Port Dufferin), Hfx. Co.		July 1-15
Ecum Secum River Hfx. & Guysborough Cos.		July 1-15
Gaspereaux Brook Guysborough Co.		July 1-15
St. Mary's River Guysborough Co.	Apr. 15-May 1	July 20-July 15
Margaree River Inverness Co.		June 15-July 15
Clyburn Brook Victoria Co.	May 15-30	July 1-15
North River Victoria Co.	May 15-30	July 1-15

Rainbow trout have been successfully introduced into Nova Scotian waters from the West Coast and have gained the reputation of being furious-fighting sport fish. Open season for rainbow stretches from May 15 to October 31. Not more than fifteen fish per day, with a maximum of thirty in possession, is the limit.

For summer fishing, deep trolling with artificial spinners at depths of fifteen to thirty feet or more is recommended. Sunken (Sumpter) Lake, Kings County; Rumsey Lake, Annapolis County; Lever's Lake in Cape Breton County; and Clearwater (Bright's) Lake in Digby County are best locations.

Brown trout may be found in several of the rivers. It took ten years – until 1933 – for these famous European game fish to establish themselves in Nova Scotia waters. These trout are more tolerant than speckled trout of high temperature, mild pollution and a variety of spawning conditions and therefore provide trout fishing in waters that otherwise would lack it; but they are inclined to be very shy.

Season and limits for brown trout angling fall under the same rulings as speckled and gray trout. Brown trout are taken throughout the angling season with small dry flies, bait and spinning lures. Late evening usually is the best time to fish for this species.

Substantial populations of brown trout may be found in the Milford Haven and Salmon Rivers, Guysborough County; Cornwallis River, Kings County; East River (Sheet Harbor), Halifax County; Mersey River, Queens County; Salmon River, Yarmouth County; Kilkenny Lake, Cape Breton County; and Waugh River, Colchester County.

Lake or gray trout or togue are larger than the other trout, but not as plentiful. On the average, they weigh three

Even though level of stream is down, it still holds heavy fish. This fine catch accepted a sparsely tied "Spider."

to six pounds and occasionally twice that. July and August offer the best lake trout fishing at a time when speckled trout fishing is falling off. However, in the early spring, when they come up from the depths to feed in shallow water, they also provide good sport to the angler. Limits and open season are the same as those for trout.

In the spring, as they feed in shallow waters, they may be caught on trout fly tackle or by bait-casting. Later in the season, lake trout swim deeper in search of preferred temperatures and may be taken with deep-running spoons and spinners. These native Nova Scotian fish are caught chiefly in Pockwock Lake, Halifax and Hants counties; and in Sherbrooke Lake, Lunenburg County.

Shad is the largest member of the herring family and provides the freshwater fisherman with excellent game fishing. This "poor man's salmon," as it is known, is found in many rivers along the coast of Nova Scotia, some of which never are fished when the run is on. A schooling fish, the shad spends most of its life at sea, but runs up freshwater streams to spawn. They may be seen in schools just beneath the surface of these streams shortly before dusk, waking or boiling, as their movements are termed by shad fishermen. Because they are constant movers and migrate upstream in a circular movement, it is not necessary for the sportfishermen to seek lies or holding spots.

In Atlantic coastal rivers, the mature shad run upstream in late spring or early summer, depending on whether the water has reached a temperature of fifty to fifty-five degrees. They gradually travel into streams from south to north as the water warms. The season usually opens in mid-May and continues into July; June being the most bountiful month. Shad can be taken in all waters during the legal trout fishing season, with no bag or size limit.

Shad will take artificial flies or lures readily during their spawning runs upriver. Most popular are the darts, beads and weighted streamer flies, practically all bright in color. These flies and lures will vary in the different rivers, as sportsmen continue to experiment with new ways and means of catching this sporting fish.

When taken on light tackle using small artificial lures and bright flies, the shad produces amazing resistance. Shad have delicate mouths and cheek membranes and, if not handled with extreme care, the hook often will tear out.

Light fly rods and spinning outfits are ideal tackle and with light gear one can enjoy the battling tactics of this game fish.

Rivers with large numbers of fish entering to spawn are: Mersey River, Queens County; Medway River, Queens County; LaHave River, Lunenburg County; Musquodoboit River, Halifax County; St. Mary's River, Guysborough County; Annapolis River, Annapolis County; Stewiacke River, Colchester County; Shubenacadie River, Halifax and Hants counties.

A number of rivers in this Canadian province are listed for fly fishing only, whether you're catching salmon, trout, shad or striped bass. Visiting anglers fishing a listed river for the first time should watch for notices describing the area restricted.

Nova Scotia is located strategically in the mid-Atlantic, joined to the mainland only by the Isthmus of Chignecto. Atlantic tides driven by tangy ocean breezes wash over 4625 miles of coastline, bringing visitors to rugged shores dotted with rustic fishing villages, and saltwater sportfishermen to meet the challenges of the sea.

In many of the fishing villages – nestled in the lee of protective headlands – a boat and crew, equipped and experienced in saltwater sport, may be hired at a reasonable cost for a local fishing or sightseeing trip. Many will even provide tackle. For these men the sea is home, their way of life. They know the waters, moods and harvest and are more than delighted to share this knowledge of the sea with those who share their love of the sport.

Nature calls for seasons for the saltwater angler. When the fish are running, it's fair game for all. No licenses are necessary for this ocean sport, except when fishing sea trout, salmon and striped bass.

Pollock are great game to the saltwater angler. They're abundant, streamlined, powerful, and put up a great fight. On the average, pollock weigh four or five pounds, but have run as high as thirty-five pounds. Pollock fishing is one of the most rewarding experiences for the angler. Parties have been known to bring in five hundred to six hundred pounds from just a half-day's fishing; not one is wasted, as there is a good market for pollock.

Small pollock provide great fun for the kids who dangle their lines from local wharves and their three-pound prizes make delicious eating. Larger pollock may be caught from a boat not far from land and sometimes even by casting from the shore. For larger pollock, be sure your tackle is heavy. Pollock strike hard at any lure and also take such bait as herring, clams, seaworms and cut squid. Nova Scotia fishermen sometimes use white feathers to make pollock lures more conspicuous.

Pollock are caught from various depths and may be taken by jigging a deep-sinking lure or, at the beginning of the season, by trolling. Likely locations include Long and Brier islands, Digby County; Tusket Islands, Yarmouth County; Cape Sable, Shelburne County; all of Halifax County; Chedabucto Bay, Guysborough County; Big Bras d'Or, Victory County; or find your own spot.

Mackerel grow to an average of fifteen inches in length, three pounds in weight but are often larger. Smaller mackerel are popular table fare and are called tinkers.

For their size, mackerel are exceptionally muscular and active. Their black bodies, with green and bluish belly tinges, will be found in deep water some distance from land in the winter. In May, schools swim closer to the shore. When a school of mackerel is in pursuit of bait fish near the surface, you can see the dark stir of ripples on the water.

When mackerel first come into shallow water they do not take bait or lures, but in August and September strike eagerly at them along inshore saltwater areas. Chumming – repeatedly throwing handfuls of such food as chopped-up herring or other baitfish overboard – attracts the fish and conditions them to strike at the bait or lure. Shiny metal lures are recommended, the diamond jig being the most popular. Small bait such as minnows, clam bits or seaworms also is effective. When mackerel feed close to the surface they often may be taken with artificial flies, especially streamer patterns with conspicuous white markings.

A boat is the usual method for mackerel fishing, but often one can bring in a few by casting from shore. Rising or high tides offer the best mackerel fishing. Best locations are near shore in salt waters all around Nova Scotia, particularly in harbor approaches.

Striped bass, a real challenge to the game fisherman, prefer certain areas over others: estuaries of rivers entering Bay of Fundy waters; the Northumberland Strait; southwestern shore; and open waters beside certain sandy beaches. Large stripers can go to forty pounds, but fifteen pounds is considered a good catch in Nova Scotia. These bass usually feed on small fish, eels and the like.

Spinning gear and lures, trolling and bait fishing are most effective, using minnows, seaworms, clams, crabs or cut bait. Eelskin rigs are great favorites in some places, but gear and methods vary from place to place, depending on the habits and preferences of the bass locally. Seek the advice of a guide.

Under favorable conditions, good striper fishing is enjoyed in the lower reaches of the Bear, Annapolis, Gaspereau, Shubenacadie, Stewaicke, Avon, Waugh, Tusket, Mersey and Tidnish rivers. Surf casting and wharf fishing for stripers provides good sport along the shores of the Minas Basin, Cobequid Bay, the south shore and the Nova Scotia shore of Northumberland Strait.

Even freshwater fishing for striped bass is rewarding in

A young salmon begins to tire as the "long rod" takes its toll of his fresh-from-the-sea strength after long battle.

Nova Scotia. Many fish for them from boat or shore at Shubenacadie, Grand Lake, just a few miles from Halifax.

Deep feeders such as haddock, cod and halibut go for bait on a hand line and provide good fun for the whole family. Charter boat operators will arrange an excursion, provide suitable gear and bait, plan the day to include saltwater fishing, a picnic on an island and perhaps a visit to a seabird colony.

Tautog fishing is something quite new in Nova Scotia. The fish were discovered in 1951 at Eel Brook in Yarmouth County and the tidal river at Argyle, a few miles away.

Spring and fall are the best seasons for Tautog and fresh bait – seaworms, mussels or diced crabs – suspended a few inches from the bottom are the most popular bait. A tug and haul species, tautog offers the saltwater sportsman excellent game.

The giant bluefin is a huge kind of mackerel, which pits its tremendous speed and power against the skill of the angler. The battle is long and hard and, after a struggle of as long as eight hours, the angler may give in and cut his line.

Special tackle is required for tuna fishing, heavy to medium, according to individual taste. Boats must be specially equipped with swivel chairs and footwells, with guides or experienced boatmen a must to direct and complete the operation skillfully. Tuna up to eight hundred pounds are caught frequently in Nova Scotian waters.

Chumming at dawn with fresh herring is a sure way to attract the giant bluefin. The bait is strung out, sewn to the hook and allowed to sink a few feet. The tuna rushes the bait like a torpedo, causing a terrific tug on the line. Then he's off at terrific speeds on a long run, with the angler's boat following as quickly as possible to avoid excessive strain or emptying of the reel. Run after run eventually is checked as the fight goes on for hours. Finally, the tuna breaks the surface and begins to circle the boat. To end the contest, the angler must maintain a continual strain on the line, preventing the tuna from getting his second wind.

Suitable boats and boatmen with tackle to rent are available in most all ports. Lists are available from the Department of Tourism, Halifax, Nova Scotia. The best places for tuna fishing have been Cape St. Mary, Digby County; Wedgeport, Yarmouth County; Chester, Lunenburg County; Halifax and the Strait of Canso area (St. George's Bay). Schools have been reported on the North Coast of Cape Breton Island to Cheticamp, Shelburne County; and Ingonish, Victoria County, as well.

These giants of the sea move in from their deep water playgrounds to shallower, offshore feeding grounds providing good fishing in July, August, September and October.

Each September, the Olympics of tuna fishing are held in the Cape St. Mary and Wedgeport areas of Nova Scotia.

These neophyte anglers, holding the reels upside-down, had fun and success while jigging black tin squid lures for cod.

Two knowledgeable anglers work together to make sure this scrappy cod makes it to the fish-box (left).

The International Tuna Cup Matches, begun in 1937, include teams from all over the world. Scandinavian, Australian, New Zealand, Italian, Mexican, British, Caribbean and American anglers battle the bluefin in hopes of carrying the coveted Alton B. Sharpe Trophy home to their native countries. As many as seventy-two tuna have been taken in only three days of competition.

Another deep sea competition held in the area is the Intercollegiate Game Fish Seminar and Fishing Match, which also has gained international recognition.

When brook trout follow their native streams to salt water, as they frequently do, they become known as sea trout. When they arrive in the estuaries of brooks and rivers they are spent and of poor quality. They seldom venture far from native brooks, but feed on the shoreline until they become sleek and powerful. After two or three months at sea, they become a silvery color and begin their long, difficult migration to the spawning grounds.

During June and July, trolling with light spinning tackle and small lures near or in the estuaries is a preferred method. From mid-July until late September, some of the finest fly fishing in Nova Scotia can be found in the rivers and brooks these fish ascend. Small, dry flies of the upright wing type are the best for sea trout.

The majority of rivers which sea trout ascend are scheduled for fly fishing only; the law prohibits bait-fishing except in tributaries of these rivers. Angling for sea trout is subject to special regulations only on posted salmon rivers and is prohibited from October to April.

When the brown trout lives in water that has access to the sea, it has the sea-running habit. When it hits salt water, it loses all its colored markings and turns silvery. Five to seven pounds is the average weight of these fish; however, they do reach weights of twenty-five pounds.

Lures and streamer-type flies are used commonly when angling for sea-run trout. This sport is subject to special regulations only when fished on posted salmon rivers. The season for sea-run brown trout is the same as speckled, brown and gray trout, except in tidal and non-tidal waters of Guysborough River, Guysborough County, but not including the tributaries of that river. The season runs May through September.

You'll find sea-run brown trout in the estuaries of rivers at Guysborough Harbor, Tatamagouche Harbor and Merigomish Harbor.

Nova Scotia is a delightful change of pace. The people have something of a robust, salty tang about them and, most important, they seem glad that you came to their area.

JUST CASTS APART

There Are Great Similarities Of Technique In Taking Blackfish And Atlantic/Pacific Mackerel

WHETHER YOU, as a fisherman, pursue the Atlantic or Pacific mackerel, light tackle is the key to peak sport. The same could apply to bottom fishing for blackfish except for one inescapable problem: Blacks feed among the rockiest areas they can find and are experts at using those rocks when hooked; a black between or under rocks – particularly a shelf rock – all too often can result in a frayed and snapped line or, more simply, a neatly dislodged hook. Blackfish seem to know what leverage can do for them!

Add to these items the matter of a strong running tide and you often require a fairly heavy sinker, all of which tends to move you into heavier tackle than the fish demands. Thus, when you think it over, it's the natural conditions that force the use of conventional tackle rather than the lighter outfits suitable for most types of mackerel fishing.

Though mackerel and blackfish can be located and caught close to land – at times, even from shore – the tackle, bait and proven techniques differ just enough that it will be wise to treat each species separately.

Starting with the mysterious business of names, let us clarify that the Atlantic mackerel may also be referred to as the common mackerel, Boston mackerel or cavalla, a cousin to the king mackerel, cero, chub mackerel or the Spanish mackerel. In turn, all of these are related to larger species such as tuna, bonito and wahoo.

When it comes down to the basics of fishing for either the Atlantic or Pacific mackerel, both favor a diet of smaller fishes, crustaceans, squid and shrimp. As for distribution, the Atlantic variety can be found north from Cape Hatteras, North Carolina, in great numbers.

Opposite page: Lightweight, open-face spinning tackle and a Spanish mackerel that grabbed a bucktail jig in the Ten Thousand Islands, Florida. This is top action!

Vinny Cuilla of Milford, Connecticut, takes a chance and lifts a fine-eating blackfish over the side of his boat in Long Island Sound. Finding proper depths is a problem.

Creatures of habit, they always move in large schools, often mixed with schools of chub mackerel. As a rule of thumb, they approach the coasts in spring, then move offshore into deeper waters in the fall. They frequently are taken offshore at the edges of bars. As to migratory schedules, they appear off Hatteras in mid-March and April and in New England waters during May.

The average mackerel we catch in New England runs from one to two pounds (sixteen inches average), but have been reported as large as seven pounds and twenty-six inches in length. This is a rarity.

On the West Coast, the Pacific variety averages around two pounds and three-pound fish are not rare. Off California, they are present in quantity from July through November. As for distribution, they make the scene all the way from Alaska to lower California. Both Atlantic and Pacific varieties take small baits, plus those lures that simulate bait fish, as well as those other items in their diet.

Light tackle for fishing mackerel allows one to choose a light-action boat rod and a 1/0 reel or a correspondingly light spinning rig; either opens the door to peak enjoyment. Monofilament should be your choice of line, no matter what the type of tackle, as this material is nearly invisible in the water.

To round out your mackerel gear, you'll need a small number of mackerel jigs or small chrome-plated squids. Hooks must be small, as the species simply doesn't have a mouth styled after a snook or largemouth bass. Also include a dozen or more snelled hooks with bright-colored plastic sleeves covering their shanks. Without any bait on these hooks, mackerel will strike readily at the bright, worm-looking plastic sleeves as they undulate along just ahead of the brightly hued jig.

When you sight a large school of mackerel, move in close to its edges, but never into the actual school. Once you've found the school, it's wise to set up a chum line, as you would for working on bluefish. It'll hold them close for long periods.

It's almost impossible to tell where mackerel will be in greatest number; there are times when you will jig at forty feet and find your best action of the day. At other times, they are no deeper than ten feet. If you do not sight an actual school of fish, chumming is still the tried method for

Above: Here is a group of boats and anglers who know exactly what to look for when fishing for blacks. The cagey fish remain near the protection of rocky outcrops, and will either sever your line or dislodge a hook quickly.
Right: Chumming with crushed crabs is pure magic when blacks see a free meal settling among their rocky haunts!

This typical-sized blackfish was taken near the rocky bottom after author's party had chummed green and fiddler crabs to hold school close. The rig this angler is using is a basic bottom setup, using sinker, three-way swivel and hook and leader. The requirement of heavy sinker prevents most from using the lightweight tackle fish deserves.

attracting them from afar. Such chums as mossbunker, mullet or other oily bait fish will do well.

It's no trick to jig-up more mackerel than an angler really needs. When mackerel are plentiful in an area, there is simply no way of shutting off the action, unless you just refuse to drop a hook over the side.

But there are times when mackerel suddenly will stop striking your jig or tube hooks. This is the time to bait up with natural baits. Strips of squid are excellent, as are small V-sections cut from the undersides of mackerel already caught. Even small baits cut from bunker will do under most circumstances.

Many fishermen believe mackerel are too oily to eat, but they are no more so than a bluefish. To reduce the oily taste, cut out the dark meat while dressing out the fish for broiling.

As for blackfish *(Tautoga onitis)*, the habits of one species of bottom feeder often will apply to others in the same general category. Once you have mastered the subtle business of dealing with the sneaky blackfish, you are pretty well fortified to win out with other less finicky bait-nippers.

Depending on where you plan to wet a line, old *Tautoga onitis* has managed to assume more than one alias; the farther you push into New England waters, the better the chances that you will find him referred to as a tautog. Around New York, New Jersey and Connecticut, rarely will you hear anything but the term blackfish. In some regions, he is referred to as oyster fish, black porgy, saltwater chub, white chin or black bergall.

One should locate him from the provinces of Nova Scotia and New Brunswick in Canada, to the upper reaches of coastal South Carolina. The hotspots usually are along rocky shorelines, around sunken wrecks and pilings and among rocky patches of inshore waters.

The most productive method of fishing for blackfish calls for the use of such baits as green or fiddler crabs, seaworms, grass shrimp, clams, even baby lobsters.

As for size, they usually will weigh from one to four pounds, but it is not uncommon to find yourself fighting a stubborn fellow of eight or ten pounds. While not common, blackfish have weighed around twenty pounds.

As far as season is concerned, blackfish are present in good number from May through November. Once the first effects of winter are sensed, they move to offshore waters. When found in bays and inshore waters, look for them at depths of four to eight fathoms. The majority of my own catches have been at just above six fathoms, always in areas that offer some type of parasitic shell life.

One of the more frustrating things about fishing for blackfish concerns the need to know where proper bottom cover exists. For example, near the Norwalk Islands in Long Island Sound, a huge rocky mass sits atop a gentle knoll. At high tide, it's 6½ fathoms down to those rocks and among them always lies a sizeable school of blackfish. If you are not right over these home grounds, forget it. If your baited hooks are even fifteen or twenty feet shy of the correct spot, nothing happens.

When it becomes this much of a necessity to pinpoint rocky points, reefs and other hotspots, you can see the

Using a jig and mackerel rig featuring colorful plastic sleeves or dropper-tied hooks, you often catch three or four fish at a time. Note the arrows pointing to plastic sleeves that must resemble small sea worms, sand eels.

Four at a time! This is typical of action you can expect when mackerel are feeding. Ron Fine, V.P., Marketing/Sales of O.F. Mossberg & Sons, is the angler who offered the plastic-adorned mackerel rig over the side in Atlantic.

When the action for blackfish dropped off suddenly, Ron Fine hooked up a small chunk of squid and went back down. He's shown unhooking the results here, taken on light tackle. He was lucky to horse blackie out of the rocks!

Vinny Cuilla and angling mates moved their boat right near underwater rockpile, then anchored securely to stay where the fish are. A depth-finder or experience on the waters can help you determine those black hotspots!

And into the live well goes another blackfish. These bait-nippers must be handled delicately, and usually test the offering before deciding whether it's fit for consumption. Don't jerk too soon, or you'll come up empty.

Spanish mackerel, as they're called on the West Coast, may be found schooling at depths varying from ten to forty feet. Once you get the right amount of line into the water, you can stand by for action like three at a time!

necessity of knowing for certain where a specific fishing area is located in reference to landmarks – or of utilizing the assist of a reliable depth-finder. Being close doesn't make any points in blackfishing.

Blackfish are equipped by nature to handle all manner of tough shellfish. A combination of thick, hard lips and powerful teeth/jaws are designed to collect and masticate every bait we've named, plus mussels, barnacles and most other crustaceans. This preference for shellfish doesn't stop the species from feeding on such other delicacies as spearing, small sand eels, squid and even cut-up periwinkles.

As for bait-nipping, you are not about to catch many blackfish by accident. Blacks do not blunder onto your hook. Instead, they approach your baited hook like a bonefish, standing on their nose to look it over. When they decide it looks good enough to try, they will rap and tap at the bait, nibbling at your offering. At this point, the fisherman tends to try to hook him prematurely. They only problem is that the hook is not inside his mouth.

This is a nice-sized blackfish that wolfed down two chunks of crab before finally being hooked by Gary Dillon. With his tough mouth and finicky method of mouthing your baits, it's easy to reel in an empty hook. Patience is required.

The time to strike is when you feel a somewhat more positive tug on the line, a signal that the fish actually is mouthing the bait. The time is now!

If lucky, you'll find yourself fighting a scrappy black, not that all-time nuisance, the bergall. If you find yourself constantly losing bait to the bergall population, try switching to small, soft clams with the shells left on. Crack the shell so its succulent juices make themselves known to the blackfish. A blackfish will go after such a delightful morsel immediately; the bergall, with no crunching apparatus at his disposal, will not bother.

If you don't find action in a specific spot, try to bring the blacks within reach by way of a little chumming. Either crushed clams or mussels are excellent. Assuming you choose crab for your primary offering to blackfish, take a second look at the better ways of serving up this bait. If your choice – or availability – calls for a blueclaw crab, remember this bait is used during its shedding period. When using any species of crab, make certain you bury the point of the hook so that it is well hidden in the meat.

Anchor your boat when fishing for blackfish to stay on the hotspot, not drift away from it. This does not preclude the fact that they are taken by jetty fishermen and those working piers, bulkheads and inshore rock piles. Even surf casters can connect in rocky concentrations and holes within reach of a cast.

With the exception of the surf caster, who requires his own special equipment, bottom fishermen should choose tackle that has adequate backbone to handle the problems of bottom terrain. The blackfish instantly runs down between those rocky clefts when he feels the sting of the hook. He will try for the sanctuary of a coral reef once he knows he's in trouble.

For conventional tackle anglers often spool monofilament of at least 30-pound test on a 1/0 or 2/0 reel. Spin fishermen must pick a rod with a tip adequate to the problems: If the fish turns out to be a heavyweight, the abrasions of rocks and a fair tide will require a fairly heavy sinker, usually a bank-type. Make sure you carry enough sinkers to allow for occasional hangups in the rocks and that you carry various weights to match requirements dictated by the strength of the tide.

Most tackle shops offer a standard blackfish hook, which comes snelled to a tarred line. You also will find Virginia hooks with gut snells or loose hooks you can rig yourself in a number of sizes. Number 2 or 3 hooks would be a choice for the largest blacks. Number 6 is a good choice for fish in the six or seven-pound class and a Number 8 is sufficient for the smaller bay fish.

As for the blackfish rig, a two-hook setup is most practical. The first should be positioned about two inches above the sinker, the top hook up just far enough to keep the two from catching each other and tangling.

Pound for pound, blackfish are much like the warm-water grouper in choice of habitat and in the brand of fight they provide. They are gutsy when hooked, cagey when it comes to nibbling away your baits and clever about leaving overly suspicious hooks well alone.

Zwirz used light spinning tackle and 6-pound-test mono to land this excellent shad. Yellow-and-white shad dart brought strike, and is more effective than most lures.

THE SHAD IS essentially a saltwater fish, though they condescend to allow freshwater fishermen an excellent opportunity to join action with them each year as they school-up, then enter and move up our rivers in great number. This run signals the start of their spawning cycle.

This so-called silver flash is a member of the herring family and, of interest to the seafood gourmet, shad has been a highly desirable table delicacy for generations. Depending on your palate, it may grace your plate filleted or as the highly touted shad roe. It was not really until several years following World War II that its potential as an extraordinary game fish was realized.

SIZING UP THE SILVER FLASH

The Shad Is A Relatively New Challenge Among Game Fish And Requires Special Considerations

If light tackle has gone hand in hand with a sportsman's introduction to shad fishing, you will find agreement that a fresh-from-the-sea shad qualifies for a top rating among aggressive game fish. Pound for pound, a shad makes a black bass seem to be standing in concrete. Shad often reach a length of thirty inches, adult males averaging two to five pounds, while the female can tip the scales at three to six pounds. However, the species frequently reaches twelve pounds on the Atlantic and all of fourteen pounds along its Pacific fishery.

Shad are found along the Atlantic Coast from as far north as the Nova Scotia/St. Lawrence area, down to the St. Johns River in Florida. It also is found in numbers on the Pacific Coast from the southerly reaches of California to southwestern Alaska.

The female – or hen, as it is called – is sought more than the buck for several reasons. First is that delicious roe which she carries and is so welcome in the gourmet's skillet. Second is the matter of size, the female being heavier and feistier than the male.

Spring is when the main run begins, slowly, as the water reaches 50 to 55 F. It reaches a peak when water temperature hits the sixty-degree mark. The shad is a schooling fish often seen in vast numbers just beneath the surface of their waters, normally just before dusk, working or boiling. These are terms used by many anglers I've listened to over the years, particularly along the northernmost distribution of the species. Because they are constant movers and migrate upstream in a circular movement, it is not necessary for the sportfisherman to seek lies or holding spots as is common when fishing the Atlantic salmon.

Like the Atlantic salmon on its upstream spawning journey, the shad does not take food, but strikes out of a reflex motion. It's based on the old, built-in urge to take a crack at anything that seems to resemble its natural saltwater foods. This reflex makes it possible for the angler to take his fish. There are as many ways to fish for the shad as there are rivers that beckon the species.

Until about 1932, shad were not recognized as game fish of any importance and no one had figured how to catch them on fishing tackle. The only way they made it to the table was by way of the seine nets or by an enterprising soul here or there who kicked an occasional one onto the bank.

Today numerous lures are employed by shad fishermen, but perhaps the most prevalent is the lead-head Dart. Possibly the best style of Dart features the polar bear or bucktail tails. They almost always are referred to as Shad Darts and are manufactured by the Pequea Tackle Company among others.

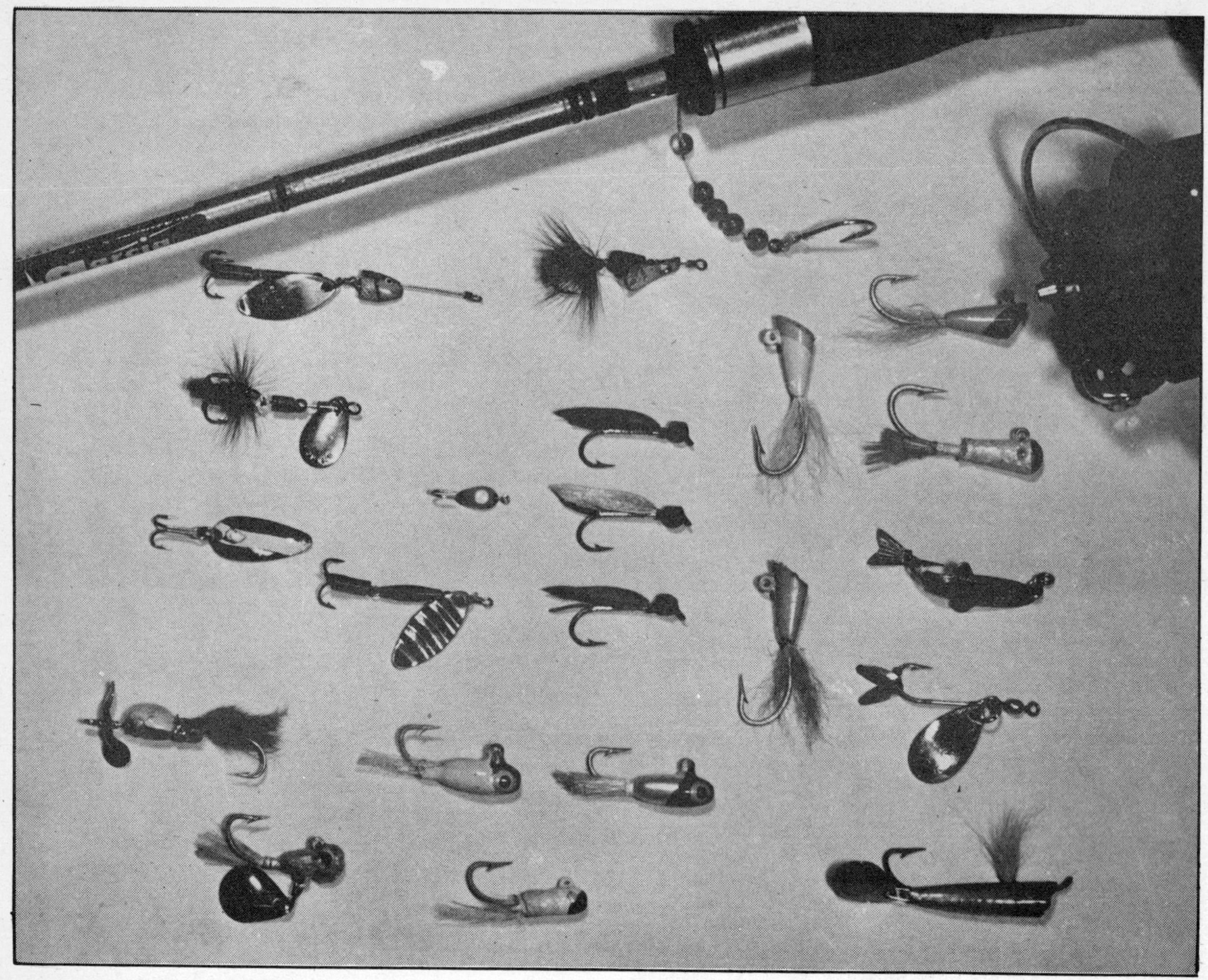

Shad darts and small spinner-type lures found in author's tackle box when the shad begin schooling in preparation for their spawning runs. The "silver flash" is a real challenge when using lightweight spinning tackle on them.

This art of taking shad started when a group of locals were of the opinion that these fish could be caught, but how? Experimentation, over a period of time, proved they would not accept bait, plugs or any of the standard large items one might expect a five-pounder to crave.

Through trial and error, folks learned that, like the Atlantic salmon, they would strike at a small lure, apparently out of the same reflex action. The first success came when a gaudy, sparse wet fly was used in conjunction with a small gold spinner. It also was noted that when these fish congregated in fast water channeled by boulders, islands or dams, they were prone to strike a lure with some consistency.

Most of us who have fished these runs have found that shad are choosy concerning the paths they use. Each year, there is little difference in the channels used, but their depths vary little so long as the river is in average flow. However, if the river is in flood or has been subjected to winter re-channeling, the fish tend to reroute from previous seasons or to spread out a little more where high water still exists. Even then, they are found in the fast current areas ready to run up into the next pool.

On the larger rivers, fishermen pursue two distinct methods. We have the rugged individualist who shuns the use of a boat to get within range of the main run of fish. He wades the shoreline, fights the white water and braves the cold. He also has an armful of Darts or flies or what-have-you, because he is going to lose a passel of them.

At Connecticut's Enfield, as an example, this type stands hip-deep, balancing precariously on rocks shaped much like coconuts. He casts across the current and slightly downstream. The fishermen generally use spinning tackle, though some do manage to try their hand with the fly rod, to put out a good cast and carry the lure to the desired depth in the fast current. If they use a larger Dart, weight often is not necessary.

As luck will have it, a man does not always feel the lure just right or his retrieve with the reel sometimes is a bit too slow. Next thing, he is playing a rock fish and he must break loose and tie on another lure for the shad.

The more one fishes a given area, the easier it becomes to judge things just right. Then suddenly you find yourself into four or five pounds of silver dynamite fresh from the salt. At this point, it's worth all the effort you've put into your quest.

Then there are those other fishermen. They sit back, firmly ensconsed in comfortable boats anchored fore and aft amid the fast current tongues. They swap lies, drink beer and complain about the cushions not being soft enough. They continually suggest that the boat be moved a few feet, because the fellow to the right or left seems to have snagged an extra fish or two. All they really have to do

Returning shad anglers have learned that the silver-sided fish will use the same channels and depths as in the previous years, if stream-bed conditions are unchanged. If rechanneling or flooding has occurred, it's harder to find the fighting-mad quarry that offer such spectacular action, as Zwirz proves trying to net a three-pounder.

Using a fly rod with favorite shad patterns and spinners offered from outfit designed for them, Zwirz and his state fisheries' guide both filled out a legal limit on the toothsome, palate-pleasing shad. Stand by for action!

about casting is to let a finger off the spool so anywhere from ten to eighty feet of line slips slowly off the reel.

The lure, usually a Dart, finds its way down among the milling fish. Sooner or later, a heavy hen or a vicious buck clobbers the lure and the battle is joined. Smashing runs, surface slashes and plain old bulldogging are all part of shad strategy. After several minutes of savage play, the tired shad comes to net and ends up in the fish box or on a stringer.

The boat approach does offer a fine opportunity for using the fly rod and the weighted flies for utilizing something akin to the fastest sinking line, as available from Scientific Anglers/3M, Cortland, et al. Hanging there in the current, such flies are quite deadly and once the fish is on, you can almost envision that you are onto a fine grilse or junior-grade salmon. The long rod is nothing short of great fun.

Recent years have brought the shad into many rivers that were devoid of them before the last big war. Only a few years ago, we discovered that the Delaware River and its tributaries were running rich with this tough silver flash. Fishing weighted nymphs with a bottom scraping motion has brought me as many shad as brown trout, the species I was after primarily.

"Always a grandstander," says Zwirz of his wife, Glad, who plays and nets her own trophy shad while the guide looks on in amazement. Perhaps her catch exceeded his???

Ultralight spinning tackle is just about tops, too, if it is a fair scrap you are seeking; just make certain water levels are down close to normal. Rule of thumb is to use the duller lures on bright, clear days and the brilliantly hued or flashy lures when the day is dull and cloudy or wherever the water is especially high or milky.

Down on Florida's St. Johns River, I've watched a technique that paid off in a limit of big fish. These anglers, in a boat, zigzagged back and forth across a slow current

Could be, since here she is netting another shad that struck the feathered shad dart she presented to feeding fish.

Glad gets some assistance from guide in hoisting heavy stringer of soon-to-become-supper shad. They're delicious!

Most anglers would avoid the fly rod in such fast-moving currents, but Glad Zwirz is a seasoned angler and hunter who's gone all over the world. Get the net ready, boys!

that ran over a rocky area. All they did was allow the speed of the boat and of the current to hang the lure somewhere between bottom and surface. Their boat, by the way, was heading into the current and they never were moving ahead any faster than two knots, maybe even less. They did fill a stringer or two!

Color is important with those Darts and it would seem there are favorites which hold true around the country. White with a yellow head is excellent. So too is white with a red head and many times an all-yellow is favored.

Obviously this is only possible if you inquire of those states that are geographically coastal. My most recent survey lists a few areas with some top-quality fishing and the approximate seasons.

California: Anglers will find action on the Russian River,

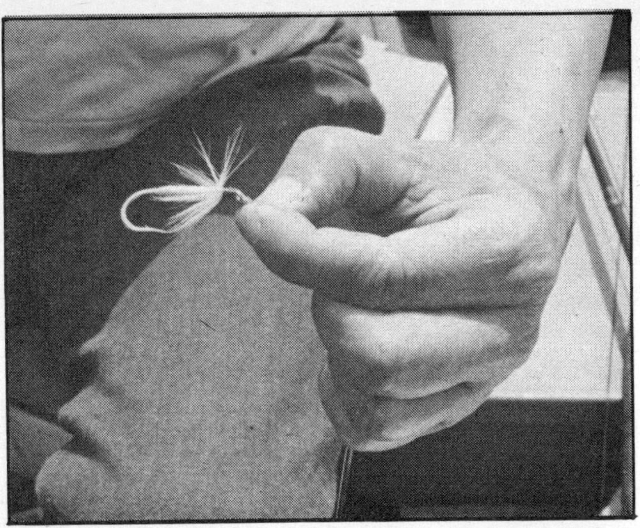

Although Cole Wilde hasn't yet named his winning fly pattern, according to Zwirz it drove shad to distraction!

near Guerneville; the American River, near the city of Sacramento; or on the Feather near Live Oak. One other good producer is the Yuba River, a short hop east of Marysville.

Connecticut: The Connecticut River, in the vicinity of Enfield Dam; also well worth looking into are the Eight Mile River and the Salmon River. (May 15-June 15)

District of Columbia: Potomac River. (April 12-June 10)

Maine: The Narraguagus River in Washington County is a fairly good producer. (July-August)

Maryland: The Susquehanna River is tops, but the following also are well worth your efforts: Gun Powder, Winters River, Patuxent, and Middle Rivers. Octarro Creek, north of Conowingo Dam, is fair. (April-June 15)

Fishing at Enfield Dam on the Connecticut River provides some of the best action in the country during the peak of the shad run. Once you can locate the schooling fish, you'll likely get some action. Set the hook hard!

If you're serious about trophy-size shad, consult the state listing and then go and get 'em!

After a hard fight up to the boat, this silver flash almost escapes as he makes a desperate gyration up and out.

Massachusetts: Connecticut River. (Mid-state area, late May-June 15)

New Jersey: Delaware River, from Raven Rock upriver. (April 15-June)

New York: Delaware River. (Southeastern New York, April 15-June 15)

North Carolina: Cape Fear River at Navigation Rocks, the Tar River at Rocky Mount, and the Neuse River at Pitch Kettle. (Spring)

Oregon: Try the Willamette, Columbia or Sandy Rivers, all near Portland.

Virginia: The Chickahominy River (Kent County), Cat Point Creek (Richmond County), Totusky Creek (Richmond County), James River and tributaries (near the city of Richmond) and possibly the best bet in the state, the Rappahannock River at Fredericksburg. (Starting in mid-April)

Washington: Columbia River, Washougal River, lower stretches. (June-July season)

It would be well worth your while to check with your own state conservation department to learn where your best rivers for shad are located, the top waters around the country.

GO DEEP FOR TARPON AND SNOOK

These Fighting Fish Call The Signals And The Fisherman Better Know Them!

RATHER THAN kid ourselves that even the most accomplished of fishermen can take tarpon or snook practically at will, using artificial lures only, let's face facts. It is the fish that call the signals.

But if we are willing to put aside our plugs, spoons and flies, when a change in strategy is indicated, there is a nearly foolproof method of producing nothing less than pure action. Without this basic technique of finessing both tarpon and snook, a number of my sessions along Florida's coastal waters might well have been total washouts.

Opposite page: In 1969, Zwirz set a deep water record for fly rod presentation using weighted fly line down 23 feet and drifted pinfish. The author is 6 feet 4 inches, so judge the length of this giant tarpon taken on 12-pound-test leader. To prepare deep baits that'll catch monsters like this one, you first align sharp knife at an angle (above). The photo lesson continues on the following pages.

Cut off body of topsail catfish from behind dorsal fin.

Make a coat-hanger tool using a 12-inch length of coat-hanger wire. Bend one end into a small hook. Now place swivel and leader into the hooked end of the wire.

During the spring months of '76, '78 and '79, I timed my trips to coincide with what experience has suggested to be the beginning of mass activity by both tarpon and snook. The tarpon had as usual worked their way down from wintering grounds and already were present in numbers among the Ten Thousand Islands. But, by the end of the second day, it was obvious that none of my many plugs would hang a tarpon or snook.

My favorite tool, the fly rod, did no better. The final coup de grace for artificial lures came as four of us made the long outside run from Goodland to the mouth of the Shark River, sixty miles away. The Shark River area always has spelled big tarpon and while the fish were present, we fished plugs among them to no avail.

One big silver king of about 140 pounds followed my Creek Chub Darter to the side of the boat, then spun away in such haste after spotting me that he splashed a gallon of water into the boat with his broad tail. We never saw him again.

That night we held a council of war. It finally was decided we would swallow our collective pride and admit that a basic change of fishing strategy was needed. The solution to our problem was an old-fashioned brand of deep and dirty fishing that in the past never had failed to put tarpon into the air.

The method was bait fishing and the bait par excellence was that improbable creature, the gaff-topsail catfish. Right

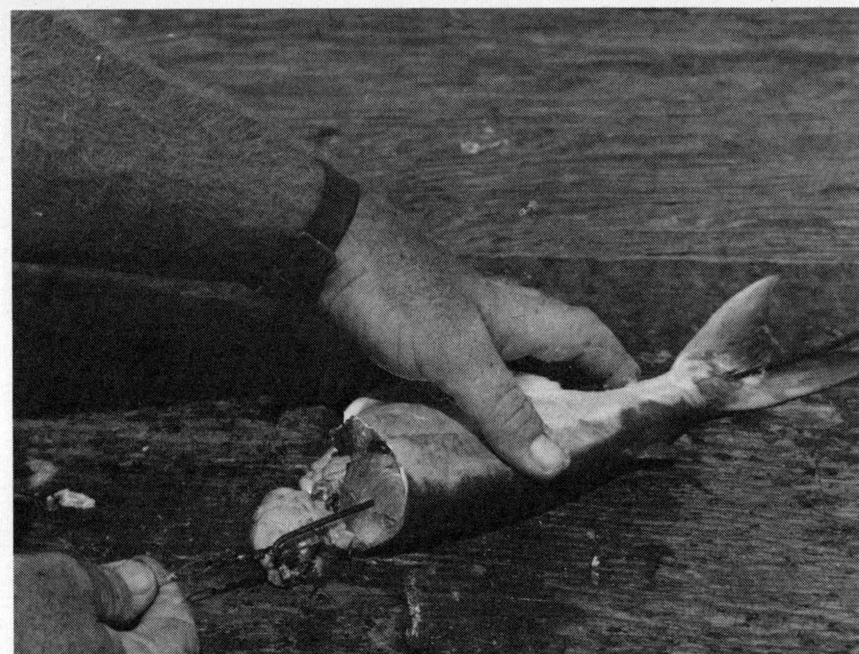

Insert the wire into the meaty part of the cut bait, and run it out the tail as shown in illustration at the left.

Pull the swivel and leader through the body to the tail. Imagine trying to do this without using a chunk of coat hanger!

away I sense readers asking, "What about shrimp, crab, pinfish or mullet?"

The topsail catfish probably is the most easily procured, durable and easily kept of the natural baits you can catch or buy in southern Florida waters. These cats also attract tarpon and trophy snook like crazy and the switch saved our day. I would rather fish for snook and tarpon with light tackle and artificials any day, but when the fish won't cooperate on my terms, I'm not too proud to fish for them on their terms.

The fishing system I'm about to describe has spelled the difference between failure and success for thousands of visiting fishermen with limited time and for local gentlemen who have been denied big fish action for too long. It works wonders in hot weather and will hook tarpon and big snook at noon as well as at night.

If there is any secret to this simple method, it relates to the fact that many of these game fish remain for long periods in specific areas that become home. Most tarpon/snook specialists are familiar with locations where fish will be present during predictable hours. The degree of fishing success depends on such predictable constants as location, phases of tide and moon, general abundance of fish and on such variables as the weather and clarity and temperature of the water.

To a great degree, action will depend on knowledge of just where and how a natural bait should be presented to be seen by the greatest number of hungry fish.

This photo shows your cut bait rig with hook attached. It'll take you a few sessions to learn to fashion this rig with speed and dexterity.

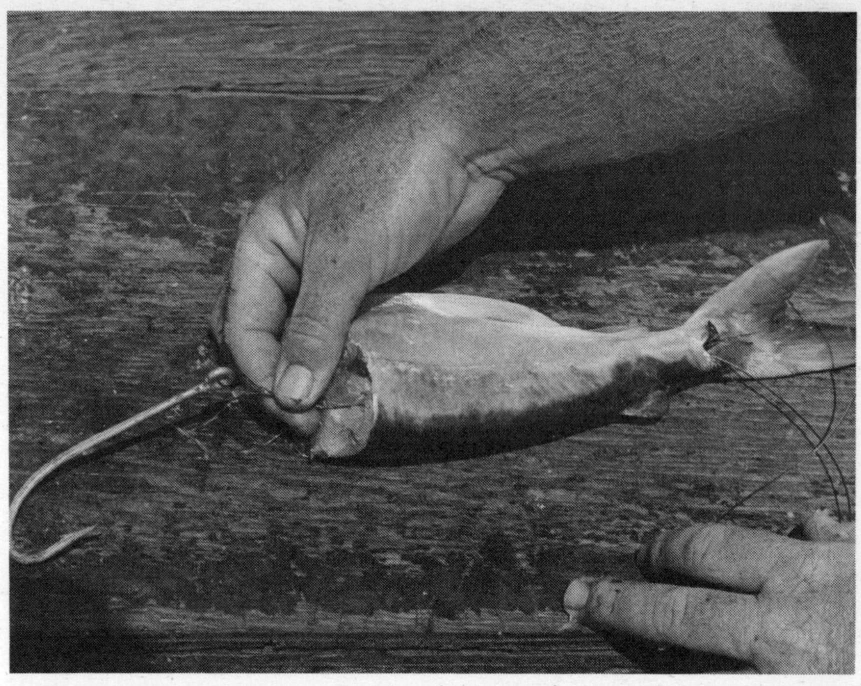

Now draw the leader up tight so the hook is snug against the body and you're ready to head for deep water!

One of the best examples of such a spot lies only a few moments from the dock where my boat is kept on the lower Caloosahatchee River. The presence of this well of plenty had something to do with my choice of the area as a favorite fishing hideaway. Coupled with this hot spot is a fishing buddy, Denny Bero, a year-round resident. Our choice of tackle is as follows:

Rod: A stout boat rod model capable of standing up to 60-pound test line. Select a model that will enable you to cast a dead natural bait a reasonable distance, for when live bait is not available, dead bait is better than no bait at all.

Reel: A good star-drag model of 2/0 or 3/0 size, such as manufactured by Penn, filled with 40, 50 or 60-pound-test monofilament.

Line: Some anglers balk at line as heavy as that mentioned, but they lose plenty of hooked fish to coral, sunken logs and other underwater obstructions. I prefer mono over braided dacron for such fishing, but some fishermen do well with dacron.

Hooks: 9/0 or 10/0 O'Shaughnessy.

Leaders: Four feet of 80 or 86-pound-test Sevenstrand braided wire, preferably dark-stained rather than bright. Some anglers use heavy mono of 80 to 120-pound test. Either type will work, but you lose fewer fish to leaders cut by sharp gill covers and other hazards when you use wire.

Sinkers: Two-ounce to four-ounce barrel sinkers and barrel swivels large enough so they will not pass through the eyes of the sinkers.

Rigged topsail catfish is best presented using a conventional bait-casting outfit with a boat rod or stout spinning gear. You'll need heavier equipment, since the fish you'll take will go from 30 to up to 100 pounds. That strains tackle!

The weight of a rigged topsail catfish makes for long-distance casting, enabling anglers to remain discreet distances from the known tarpon hole. No tail-walking tarpon is against cleaning up a free and easy meal lying on the bottom, so keep alert!

If you can't procure topsail catfish, mullet or pinfish will work quite well, but the brackish-water catfish is caught so easily and so firm-fleshed that I prefer it over other baits. If you have to use mullet, it should not be over sixteen inches long.

Rig the catfish exactly as you would a dead or live mullet. For rigging dead baits, you'll need a pair of pliers, a sharp knife and a length of coat hanger wire about a foot long. Bend a small, tight hook into one end of the coat hanger wire. This is used to pull the swivel and leader through the length of the bait's body.

With live catfish, mullet or pinfish, hook the bait lightly through the flesh of the back just forward of or under the dorsal fin, not deep enough to injure the bait's spine. Live bait often can be used without a running sinker. Dead bait, on the other hand, often has to be cast out away from the boat and this is where the barrel sinker pays off.

After rigging up the dead bait, pass your fishing line through the eye of the sinker before attaching the line to the barrel swivel of the leader. Thus rigged, the line is free to slide through the eye of the sinker with little friction. This is a variation of the old faithful fish-finder bait-fishing rig favored by Yankee surf fishermen after blues, stripers and big drum in the ocean surf.

The tarpon is not adverse to performing the job of scavenger. Both he and the snook spend considerable time cruising and sniffing around in deep holes and channels. Either will take an easy meal when it's available. Once the bait is on the bottom, it's anyone's guess as to how long you may have to wait for a pickup. If patience is not your strong point, then bait fishing may not be for you. But, if you can relax and play the waiting game, bait fishing really pays off.

More than a dozen times I've been surprised by the suddenness of the pickup. On one occasion, I had hardly set down the rod after engaging the click and putting the reel on free-spool before line began to pay out. This is where timing and the free-sliding sinker work to advantage. When a tarpon or trophy snook picks up the bait, it must not feel the weight of the sinker. With the sinker rigged above the leader swivel, any amount of line can slide through the sinker eye as the fish moves off with the bait in its mouth. This is where you must hold in check your desire to strike.

At the first indication of a pickup, disengage the reel's click (which is only an alarm in case you fall asleep) and let the line pay out on free spool. Thumb the reel spool lightly, applying only enough pressure to prevent a possible backlash. If you can avoid thumbing entirely, so much the better.

After the pickup, let the fish take out line, until he stops to turn the bait in his mouth and swallow it. You'll know when this happens, because the line will stop paying out. Don't strike at this point! Instead, wait patiently for the line to start moving swiftly, then sock it to him as strongly as you dare without danger of breaking the line. Give him at least one heavy strike, preferably two, to set the hook deeply in his gullet.

Don't worry about the sliding sinker. As soon as you

have a tight line and start bringing in the fish, the sinker will work down the line by gravity and the water friction until it fetches up on the leader swivel. The sinker, incidentally, should only be heavy enough to hold the bait on the bottom in the existing current.

The simplest way of describing the tarpon is to state that it is one of our most magnificent game fish, thus worth full attention. It not only performs the greatest aerial show known to anglers, but will smash lure or bait and seems to care little if you challenge it with heavy tackle or attempt to bring it to a standstill on the lightest possible rod and reel.

It is the angler's choice as to whether he wishes to try for the larger battlers weighing in excess of a hundred pounds, or for sheer enjoyment and more relaxed moments those fresh or brackish water lightweights that are so well suited to catching and releasing on light trout or bass tackle.

Tarpon can be found as far north as Nova Scotia, though rare in this extreme region. They are present in great number along the east and west coasts of Florida, as well as off the coasts of Texas, Alabama and Louisiana. Mexico, Central America, several South American countries, the West Indies, the Gold Coast, Nigeria and the Cameroons all have tarpon in all sizes.

For many moons, I have extolled taking tarpon on light bait-casting, spinning or fly tackle, but many sportsmen don't have the leisure time necessary to become really

And here he comes! This tarpon picked up the rigged topsail catfish just moments earlier, and angler restrained the urge to set the hook until the giant was in position. This is the first surface jump after the hook was set, and bait's sliding on line!

Late afternoon action at yet another favorite hole of deep tarpon. This is a typical jump when hooked, and you can expect 15 or 20 during the course of your arm-wearying battle. To get one on the line, you've got to present the proper bait to him.

proficient with light tackle on big fish. Therefore, let's concentrate on how to take large tarpon with conventional tackle, using methods almost guaranteed to produce action.

Fortunately, the tarpon is present along inshore waters, on the flats as well as in the bays, inlets and rivers. His diet consists chiefly of small fish such as mullet, but he finds squirrelfish, pinfish and crabs – as stated earlier – to his taste, often taking these baits when nothing else will tempt him.

In Florida tarpon spots around Boca Grande, Cape Coral and Naples the waters are extensive and deep. Here charter boat skippers feel that changes for a good day's fishing are enhanced if the angler is willing to use conventional saltwater tackle and fish the appropriate baits for the time of season. With this approach, success is likely even for fishermen who never before have had a chance to fish for tarpon.

Saltwater anglers who have had some experience trolling, drifting or still fishing for large game fish will find no problem handling tarpon that go seventy-five pounds or more on a regulation trolling rod with a nine-ounce tip. This standard rig calls for 54-pound-test line or monofilament line of 50 or 60-pound test. The reel should be a 4/0, though a 3/0 can suffice. Whatever reel you choose, it should spool at least 250 yards of line.

For those who feel their saltwater experience justifies the use of sportier gear, I'd suggest rigging a lighter rod with a 3/0 reel. It should be spooled with three hundred yards of 30-pound-test Dacron (or monofilament if desired, though it has a great deal of stretch).

Wire leaders should be used to withstand the razor-sharp gill covers of the tarpon, which has the disconcerting habit of rolling onto the line. The extremely large scales of this fish are, in themselves, capable of parting a line. Most pro skippers use at least six feet of number 9 stainless steel wire. A barrel swivel also is a must with the 2/0 the recommended size.

Whether you plan to still-fish or troll live or strip bait, the best hook will be a short-shanked O'Shaughnessy. Depending on the probable size of fish in the waters you're exploring, you normally will use hooks in sizes 5/0 to 9/0. Make certain they are top quality, well honed and feature a tinned finish. The Martu, Sobey (opened eye) and Octopus hooks are also fine.

You can use the tackle I've described for trolling with some of the large tarpon lures that will take big tarpon from big waters under the right conditions. There are spoons, Jap feathers, artificial eels and surgical-tube lures that can be used with appropriate weights to bring strikes from bottom-feeding tarpon.

The boat must be kept at slow trolling speed, no faster than four or five miles per hour. Even slower speeds are indicated for trolling live bait or rigged bait fish. Keep in mind that tarpon are not fast strikers; they generally roll sideways toward the bait, then engulf it rather than smash it with a lightning move.

You often can have a wonderful day trolling deep-running saltwater lures such as Creek Chubs, Cisco Kids, Rapalas or Rebels (especially the DR-2300 and DR-2400, or the 2026 that swims and looks like a panicking pinfish). I've often used these plugs off the coast of Mexico with a 6/9 trolling outfit employing a 2/0 reel and 27-pound-test line. In a single morning, I had seven tarpon in the air, their weights ranging from sixty to 115 pounds.

Of the seven, only three let me work them to the side of the boat for release. The others either threw the plug during the first few jumps or managed a similar maneuver at some point in the contest. Sure, I lost the fish, but I would have released them anyway; you always release tarpon unless you're collecting a mounting trophy. But the point is that those lures attracted fish.

Do not hesitate to try plugs, spoons or any of the other artificials, trolling just subsurface. The same goes for strip bait. You never know for sure where the action may start when tarpon are herding bait fish close to the surface, rather than scrounging along the bottom. There are days when a long line seems the only answer; other days they prefer to stalk your spoon or bait just aft of your wake within a mere forty feet of the boat's transom.

Specific conditions of an area will dictate how you should rig when you're fishing baits. Most skippers prefer their clients to use wire (invariably the case around Boca Grande), but others who work relatively shallow or clear waters feel wire and swivels may spook a wise old tarpon.

Using a freshwater bait-casting combo you'd employ for black bass, author hooked, fought and boated a 120-pound tarpon that grabbed a cast plug. This calls for real rod finesse, knowledge of equipment.

Snook, like the mighty tarpon, are fierce battlers when hooked. On light tackle like that shown here, the action is simply incomparable.

Casting bucktails on a saltwater fly rod, Zwirz took the wind out of this tarpon that grabbed a perfectly offered fly. Here he's about to slip gaff out of fish's jaw and release him to fight another day. There's no finer angling sport.

These skippers splice in nothing more than a five-foot section of fifty-pound nylon leader to which the hook is joined. You may lose some fish, but perhaps you'll entice an extra number of tarpon, because of the unadorned monofilament rig.

The bait can be rigged for presentation to fish near the surface by the simple expedient of attaching a plastic bubble and adjusting its position for the depth at which you want your bait. If the bait tends to swim above the depth you wish, or if the wind or current angles it out too far, the addition of the appropriate weight of clinch-sinker usually will remedy the problem.

There are times when tarpon are moving along the surface and will take a swimming bait that's drifted or cast to a spot they will pass. In such cases, no weight of any kind should be attached. This situation is handled nicely with a pinfish for bait, hooked through the forward portion of the eye sockets. In this fashion, they stay active and move in a fairly natural manner.

However, you will find mates and skippers in Florida and Mexican waters, who prefer to hook all bait fish through the back just below the dorsal. Either procedure works well. Once the bait is among the moving tarpon, there is little you need to do, except to strip out some slack line so the bait can move naturally.

Movement, whether just below the surface or down ten to twelve feet, will be noted quickly by the tarpon, many of which may be cruising well below those you've seen cutting through the surface waters.

When you feel the take or note the slack being pulled up fast, do not strike immediately. Chances are the bait has just been mouthed by the tarpon. If you strike now, you may pull away or fail to find a purchase for the hook. Remember that a tarpon's mouth and jaws are bony. Wait it out. Count to three, then sock the muscle to him.

A good-sized snook and the popular plug he couldn't resist. Pin-point accuracy when presenting lures is a must, or wary fish will pass you by.

Below: A fabulous morning's work, admired by author and friends. Not only are snook great on the line, they are also great on the table!

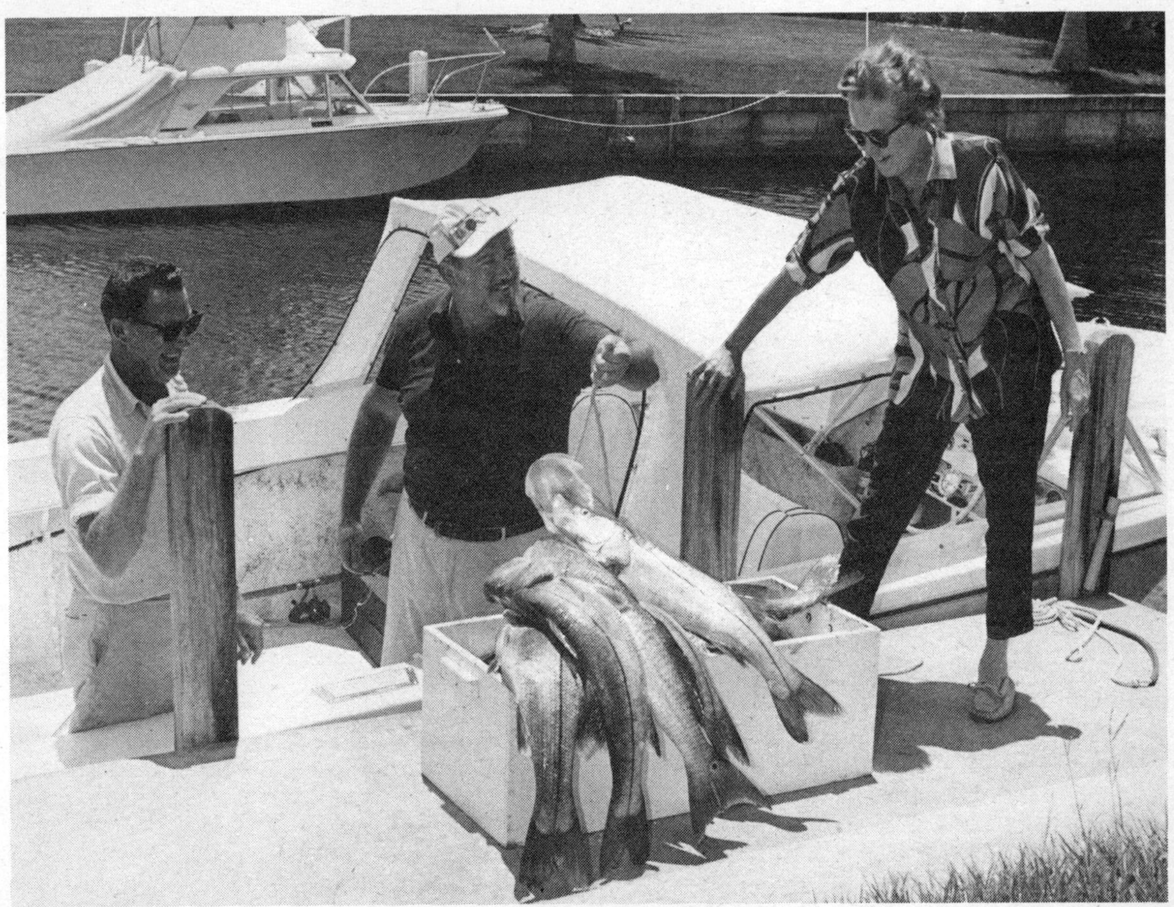

Cast accurately, an Arbogast Dasher can hook you up with a trophy-sized snook or tarpon – or any of several other fresh and salt water trophies that find it remarkably like a bait fish. Dick Kotis (left), is Arbogast president.

Tarpon rolling in school formation near Boca Grande, on Florida's west coast, provide the challenge: Can fishermen accurately cast a bait that the fish will take? If so, expect the sea to explode as the mighty battler tries to escape.

Though I've fished blue crabs for tarpon, their use represents less than twenty percent of my bait-fishing sessions. However, lately I have revised the crab's position in the order of things. While fishing out of Boca Grande with a Florida Keys guide, I learned a good deal about the effectiveness of this bait when the silver king is feeling moody.

It's a bait that can be fished at any depth you wish. It can be cast or worked like a squirrelfish or pinfish, though top results seem to be guaranteed with rigs and weights to take it to the bottom. In many passes, cuts and holes, this requires you to get it down sixty to seventy feet and it must be worked slowly.

Using a six or eight-ounce break-away sinker, you bait up with a blue crab (or pinfish or squirrelfish, if crabs are not available) and get it to the bottom. Then reel in three to five feet of line so it can move and not constantly hang up on the bottom during the drift.

Quite a few of the Florida pros use the engine to "mooch" the bait, constantly sliding it along with a slow, stop-and-go forward motion. Often, as the bait is seized, the skipper will gun the boat forward, using the power surge to sink the hook deep. From this point on, the angler is on his own.

Upon feeling the hook strike home, your silvery giant is going to make an express train lunge for the surface; in one magnificent, spraying leap he is in the air, viciously trying to shake free of the hook.

If he is still hooked after three or four furious leaps, chances are you are in for a battle ranging from fifteen minutes to more than an hour. The trophy tarpon that do battle on the surface tire themselves far faster with their aerial gymnastics than fish that bore deep and confine their efforts to controlled bursts of power.

Once you've mastered the art with conventional tackle, you're almost sure to try tarpon on ultralight gear; maybe even a fly rod. More fish than ever will throw the hook, but it's great to battle the silver king – even when you lose.

YOUR BAG OF TRICKS FOR STRIPED BASS

Determining The Right Tackle Combo Is The Greatest Plus For This Type Of Fishing

FOR THE STRIPER fishing fraternity, whether the angler wets a line along the East or West Coast, there are better than a baker's dozen similarities, especially good examples being the bluefish and the striped bass. When we examine proven methods of catching either species in the surf or by trolling, these parallels run deeper than many suspect – both species can be coaxed in close by way of the chum line; they can be jigged or taken while drifting or still-fishing. When we consider the range of both species, we find wide areas where both are present in vast numbers during the same seasons.

While striped bass are found along both coasts, they also are a popular species found in a number of large landlocked impoundments. Several regional names for the striper include rockfish and linesides.

Along the Atlantic Coast, this great game fish ranges from Florida all the way north to Nova Scotia. They appear in greatest profusion in the waters between Cape Cod and Cape May, New Jersey. During May and June, the bass are abundant in the Chesapeake Bay area; at about the same season they make a first showing around Cape Cod and Cuttyhunk. This run of fish stays with us through the summer months, reaching a peak in number and in size of the fish by September or October.

Left: Surf casting at Outer Banks, North Carolina, proved rewarding for this spin fisherman. This striper fell for a baitfish look-alike. Note wire leader used.

Normally, for the best brand of bass angling, you can depend on the fall months as the big schools work their way back to home waters. This, of course, means they will

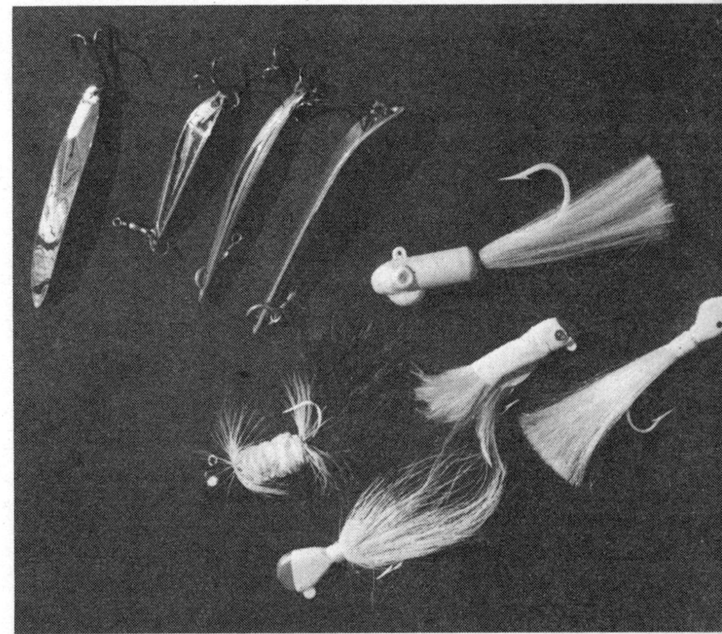

This is just a small sampling of the lures, spoons and jigs the author mentions in the text. Fished near the bottom, each resembles a bait fish and has produced fish.

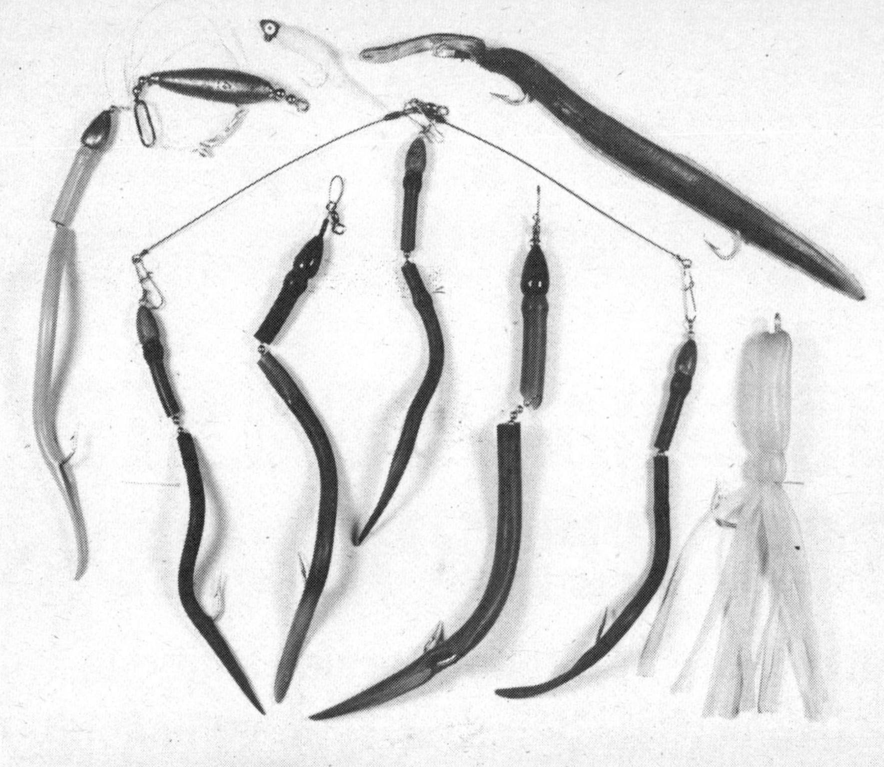

The umbrella rig displayed in the center is deadly on large blues as well as striped bass, when trolled at appropriate depth and speed. Artificial eels and squid take a big share of fish, too, when presented down deep.

be on a southerly route. Action can be fantastic, as the fish move through during this pre-winter period.

The striper also is known in the Gulf of Mexico, but offers itself as a target only in the coastal rivers. They are at their best here from June to mid-January.

For West Coast sportsmen, there is ever-growing interest in the striper as an important game fish. Even though the striper now found in Pacific coastal waters is a transplant, he has made giant strides in the ninety-odd years since being planted in San Francisco Bay. Gathered from New Jersey waters for the experiment, they have taken hold from well up around the Columbia River in the state of Washington, clear on down to Monterey, California. Spring and fall offer the most consistent action in West Coast waters.

Wherever the angler fishes for this game fish, he is going to find that ol' linesides is predominately what we refer to as an inshore fish. Probably the most exciting way to fish for stripers is in the surf, but it doesn't produce nearly as many or as large a fish as can be caught by trolling methods.

Let's take a look at methods that put stripers in the boat from early season right through October and November on the East Coast.

First, many rod and reel combinations make sense for fishing stripers. The choice depends upon whether you will fish in the bays, rivers, beyond the surf or in the school areas which often hold schools of large fish. As a prime example, there is Romer Shoals lying between the Rockaways and Sandy Hook, Long Island. During recent falls, literally thousands of stripers have schooled up in several miles of water; some have weighed fifty pounds or more.

Two years ago, trolling and casting to these fish with just the right lure earned several of us over a hundred stripers during late October and in the first week of November. Several fish in the twenty to thirty-pound class and three of forty-six pounds made the late season extra-special that year despite the limited number of days we could get to that particular striper area.

In the early season, many fish are found in bays, rivers, in Long Island Sound and in similar spots within the overall range of the striper. Medium-weight spinning rods are fine for smaller fish that will take a cast lure or a spinner and worm rig. A spinner that revolves well at slow trolling speeds, followed by a couple of neatly baited bloodworms, is sure to have some takers.

Bloodworms, by the way, are not a bad idea for the fish-finder rig when used on the bottom wherever stripers are present during the early season. Smaller saltwater plugs and lures will work well, and the small edition of the Hopkins lure is a natural for imitating the small natural bait fish on which stripers feed. Small plugs such as Pflueger's Mustang, Atoms, and Pflueger's Pal-O-Mine will take a share of fish whether cast or trolled. This calls for light outfits and light line, as average weight of the smaller lures runs seven-eighths-ounce or less. Weighted bucktails also are worthwhile, with the half-ounce models about right.

Once you find the best fishing in the close-to-shore areas or in the actual surf, you must start to use tackle with slightly more power. The surf fisherman can use the same basic kind of tackle as for bluefish in the surf. The requirements, lures and general conditions are not all that dissimilar. However, the troller/caster has several options, each requiring a different kind of rod. One should have a standard trolling outfit, say a 3/6, or possibly make do with

Anglers trying the cold autumn waters along the North Carolina coast could find themselves ferociously attached to bluefish, striped bass, or drum. Depending upon peculiar local idiosyncrasies, surf casting is most productive in the period one hour before and through one hour after flood. Flexibility, author says, is required for stripers.

a regulation boat rod and reel holding at least 250 yards of twelve or fifteen-thread line. As the small boat angler can get within casting distance of jetties and the beach, he should have a rod/reel combination aboard that will allow him to drop a spoon, eel or similar bait-of-the-moment among the rocks close to the beach.

I lean toward two outfits for this kind of precision work. The first is a fairly long popping rod used with the dependable Ambassadeur 6000 reel and fifteen-pound-test monofilament. The second is a Fenwick eight-foot three-inch spinning rod saddled with Zebco's Omega 840L; this also is filled with fifteen-pound-test monofilament. With one or the other on hand, I'm always ready to try a session when tide and general conditions look promising.

While trolling around a school of stripers, one often will see a good fish boiling right on the surface. In a split second you can whip a Rapala of the right size into the fish's path for a good chance of getting a strike.

For much of your trolling, it will be necessary to spool a section of wire between your leader and the main section of mono or dacron, depending on which you use. The section of wire is a necessity at times to get your spoon, eel, or plug down to feeding fish that your lure normally would pass over.

There is also the possibility that the fish could be working just under the surface. You must decide these things for yourself, unless you happen to be on a charter boat and are receiving top advice from the skipper. If this is the particular case, a second reel should be available with just the monofilament – no wire line. You have to be ready for conditions as the fish present them, not as you might wish them. You should find any of several types of weighted lines superior to drails or planers. These accessories work, theoretically, but are a nuisance to handle or when working a good fish. Wire takes care in handling,

Nice striper, visible underwater to the right of splash, strains to make deep water during night fishing excursion. They can be taken in shallow water during dark hours, and this guy grabbed a mouthful of bloodworms.

but is superior for the depths in which you normally troll for stripers.

In July and August, colored surgical tubing starts to pay off, as does the series of latex eels available. These imitation eels produce like magic for striper fishermen in eastern waters.

The bait fish look-alike plugs have been my top producers for teasing a striper into action. Last fall, between the small saltwater plugs and a spoon or two, it wasn't necessary to look deeper in the tackle box to score. Certain days would call for the spoon at one depth or another, that night it might call for an eel presented right along the shoals or just off the beach. That's the way striper fishing goes and only those who stay flexible and study the conditions of the moment are going to be really successful. Haphazard casting or trolling with just any lure isn't going to keep you in action with any consistency.

I know of few thrills that compare with hooking a good striper off the North Bar of Montauk, New York, or of an evening on a well cast plug, but there is a greater challenge! For many, there is nothing that beats the satisfaction found by sportsmen who have made up their minds that fish like the striper can be taken successfully with the saltwater fly rod. Their primary lure is the specially tied bucktail; occasionally they get in their licks with surface fly-rod poppers. I've even known them to drift shrimp just to finesse particularly slow fish into hitting. The resulting action was worth it, even though they had lost a little of the purist's outlook.

The rod is a well used Fenwick F109, a nine-foot rod of amazing power, yet as light as a feather in the hand. The reel is a Fin-Nor No. 3, boasting a drag second to none. The largest Pflueger's No. 1498 or Orvis' FCO V and VI saltwater fly reels are other excellent choices. Fly lines from Scientific Anglers round out this well balanced outfit. The line to correctly balance that particular Fenwick is the special saltwater WF9F. It also will handle the WF10F, in capable hands. Scientific Anglers also has a floating saltwater line with a sinking tip. I used this line for test purposes in Nicaragua on large tarpon and found it handles

No wonder author rates Montauk Point, Long Island, so highly! He's seen here struggling with a heavy stringer pulled from the surf by a Blue Atom.

Left: This fisherman, with his partners, kept only the best stripers for the freezer and palate, releasing more than 200 in the course of a few days. Much of this success was credited to their superior preparations and the ability to experiment on the water.

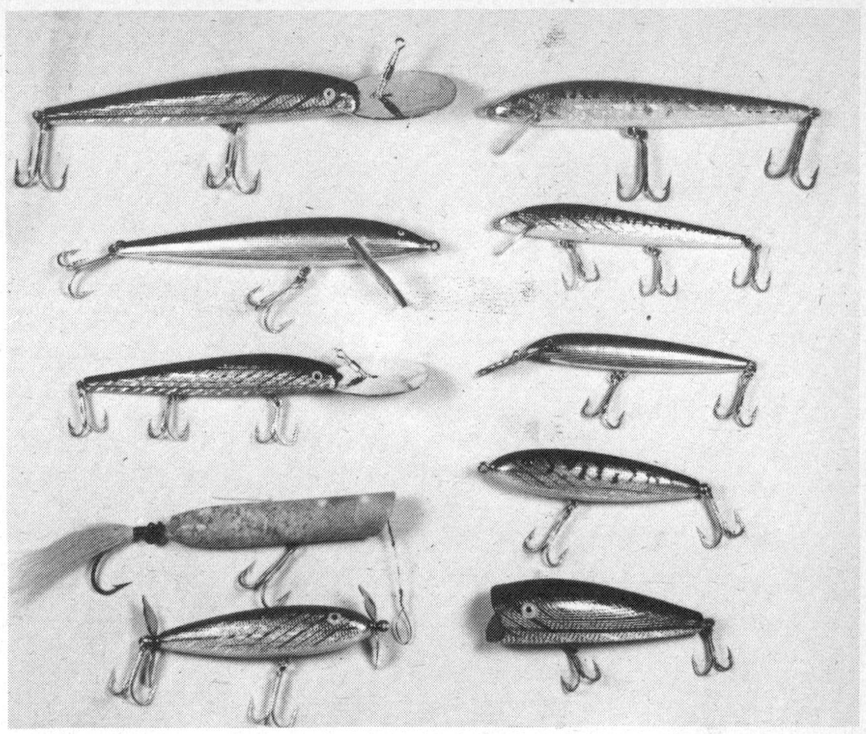

Right: Deep-running (top), mid-depth (center) and surface plugs (bottom) are all you need to take fish on the East or West Coasts. Western striper is a transplant and has wide range.

streamers well and at proper depth for cruising fish.

The West Coast striper is available to anglers throughout the entire year. Anywhere from the general region of Coos Bay along the coast to Monterey, this man-planted game fish is growing in popularity among western fishermen. It offers trollers, casters and bait fishermen a chance to sample the kind of angling made to order for the small boat owner; or, for the caster who frequents the coastal areas from close to San Francisco, to Coos Bay up in Oregon.

West Coast trolling methods differ little from those used in the East; bloodworms working behind a Cape Cod spinner or the Northern produce well. A slow troll is best for larger stripers. While spring is the best season for the bloodworm tactics, rigged eels, utilizing a two-hook setup, also are excellent, most effective along the bottom and fished as slowly as possible without hanging up. Eel skins are good, but even better are the remarkably effective eels and worms as produced by Alou. These artificials score well on both coasts for trollers and casters, but Barracuda jigs, Rapalas, and Mirro-lures are deadly when baitfish are in the area and tops on the striper's menu.

Topwater plugs – for both coasts – include the Atom, Striper Swiper, Sylvester Blue Mullet, Rapala Surface Popper, and Heddon Flaptail. Jigs such as the Hopkins, Montauk and Sand Eel also are excellent. Tipped with a strip of pork rind, cut bait or squid, they have even better fish appeal. A Drone spoon or two comprise a good idea for trolling the big fish.

For dredging up those trophy fish consistently, my top producers have been long-lip, deep-running plugs. Creek Chub's Striper, the weighted Alou eels and the weighted eel-skin rigs also are musts in the angler's tackle box.

Bait fishermen will find a whole squid just right for large fish; it works well in surf or on any sandy bottom. Bloodworms, seaworms, small shrimp, live eels or whole small crabs are considered choice by the stripers of either coast. Shrimp, used in conjunction with ground shrimp in a chum line, is a top baiting method in California waters. Strip mullet, another good bait, usually is not difficult to obtain. Trolling seems to pay off best, especially in the quiet bays and backwaters of the West Coast, between dusk and dawn. Calm weather also helps anglers using artificials or natural baits.

Trolling Techniques And Your Tackle

Unfortunately a sadly high percentage of anglers who have laid out heavy bread for some type of small fishing boat eventually find themselves disappointed and frustrated. This is due to the fact that they hook into far fewer fish than they expect.

However, an astonishingly small number of anglers catch the highest percentage of fish; this is as true on the saltwater scene as in freshwater fishing. Simply putting in time with a rod and reel, or keeping a lure or bait in the water longer than the next fellow, will not guarantee the fisherman a successful day. If such an angler can convince himself that it really doesn't matter, and that with a little luck he'll slaughter them on the next trip, be certain that he will not be a high-scorer.

When you take paying customers aboard, the sport who pays a substantial sum to be taken fishing rightfully looks forward to tangling with some fish. Whether the boat is chartered for stripers, blues, albacore, tuna, marlin or swordfish, that man expects more than a boat ride for his money.

Fully aware of all this, the charter boat pros normally try unstintingly to put fish in the box. This is not always possible, but certain tried and true methods give the pro a far better chance for success than the weekend skipper. It

Using fly rod and saltwater streamer, Zwirz hooked this and fourteen other stripers in six hours. Here he tails it rather than using a gaff or hand-gilling. Tailing is an old Atlantic salmon trick — for the deft! For most situations, author prefers Fenwick's F109, a nine-footer.

would be an impossibility to touch on the countless proven trolling methods used by the country's head boat captains, to charter-boat skippers, inshore guides and other knowledgeable professional fishermen, but most of the methods we will discuss apply in many instances to other game fish as well.

Until the close of World War II professional methods of trolling were rarely practiced by anyone save charter boat captains and owners of well-equipped sportfishermen. Now it's not uncommon to see seaworthy outboard runabouts as well as inboard-outboard types, rigged with fantail rod holders and lightweight fiberglass outriggers. Even light aluminum foldaway fighting chairs are available for the slightly less committed.

One of the best saltwater fishermen on our Atlantic Coast is a man who, years back, asked me to teach him to fly cast; it turned out to be an even trade. He taught me tricks about saltwater trolling, drifting, rigging baits and bottom techniques.

This pro has worked at most jobs around saltwater, has been a mate on other men's boats, but is now strictly his own man working, most recently, out of the Florida Keys. He not only fishes nearly every day, but spends any free days looking over new areas, testing his imaginative techniques and the special baits he has hand made for his own use for years.

The rest of this report is the result of fishing with him for years in Long Island Sound, as well as off the New England Atlantic coast. As fast as I learn his latest method, he is perfecting something even newer.

Trolling success for stripers leans heavily on experimentation, but with pretested and proven ingredients: depth, speed and lures or bait used. The troller normally uses wire. You should have several boat rods of different lengths, each equipped with a good trolling reel that will spoon both the required amount — one hundred feet — of Monel, along with sufficient monofilament backing. The exception is the short rod at center-stern with only sixty feet of Monel on the spool.

The accompanying line drawing illustrates the setup for trolling with five rods. Depending on specific situations, fewer rods can be fished when desired. The center of the stern rod should have a minimum bead chain drail of six ounces; it can require up to a twelve-ounce drail. The long rods should carry a minimum of from two- to six-ounce drails. The two 7½-foot outside rods should carry a minimum of four or six ounces of drails.

Forty-pound-test leaders generally are used on this type boat. Under certain conditions, such as fish breaking on top, one fishes just three rods, including the two long rods with no weights attached. They are trolled with one hundred feet of Monel, plus anywhere from fifteen to thirty feet of mono. The short, center rod carries either two- or four-ounce drails, with the wire about fifteen feet out of the water.

When bass are noted on top, trolling speed should be slow enough not to create excessive wash at the stern of the boat. Six hundred rpm is about right on inboard motors from 115 up to 175 horsepower. If this speed does not produce strikes, try running at 750 rpm; finally, go to 850 rpm if necessary. However, if you do, first let the long rods out until wire is in water. Also, use a two-ounce drail on one of these long-rod setups. If the center rod is not producing, try it with a six-ounce drail, twenty feet of leader and all the wire in the water.

When fish are really up, particularly bluefish, the best deal calls for five feet past the wire, running at approximately 800 rpm, using no extra weights. Eight hundred fifty rpm is about as high as I've seen this expert

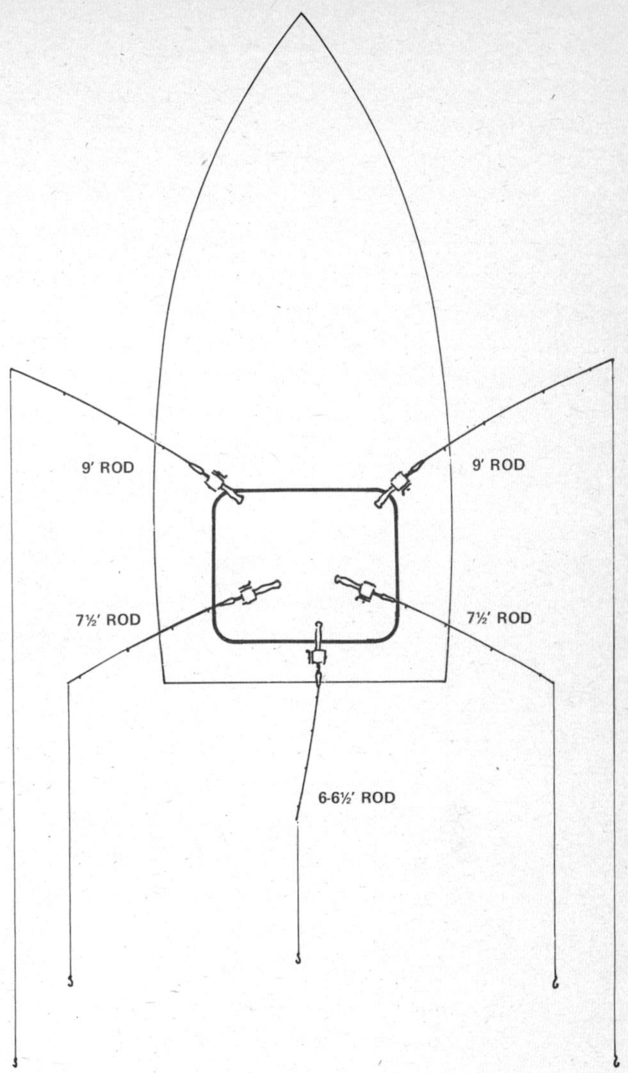

Several local pros insist on using lines of differing lengths and weights, stating that it causes less tangles and enables the testing of a wider range of depths. Other New England/Florida charter boat skippers may well dispute this, claiming line of equal length lays parallel without crossing on turns and offers baits or lures in "school" effect. As with most things, professionals rarely agree!

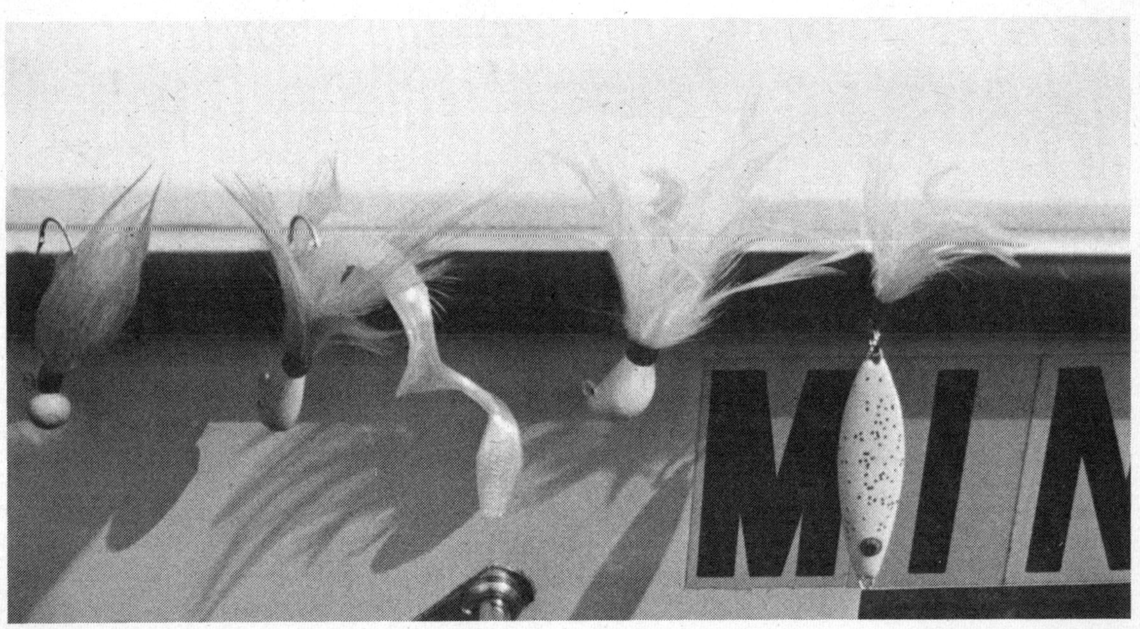

Top producers on landlocked stripers, particularly in the midwestern and southern impoundments. You've got to learn proper presentation, however, and the services of an older, more experienced guide could be worthwhile.

By virtually any fishing standard, this has to be considered a prize rockfish, which was taken off the Cape Cod coast.

move when blues are around. Occasionally, when small stripers are feeding actively he has worked around them as fast as 900 to 950 rpm – and pulled them in by the dozens. It is all a matter of experimentation, but give the effort half an hour to an hour.

Even though you may actually see fish breaking, don't be surprised if the center rod with the six-ounce drail takes the fish. For every bass breaking, there probably are five nearer the bottom. When nothing is showing on the surface, it is time to start scraping the bottom. The best way of knowing if you are actually close to bottom calls for you to let out line until wire and drail hit the bottom cover, then simply take a few turns on the reel until it stops bouncing bottom.

I can't emphasize enough the importance of not having all your lines out at the same distance or at the same depths. Equal length can only result in tangles beyond description. Also remember the rule: longer lines out first, shorter lines taken in first.

Of all the tried and true methods of taking trophy bass, one that beats them all calls for a lot of patience and trolling with tubes running sixteen to eighteen inches in length, with a quarter-inch outside diameter by 3/16-inch. The best all-purpose tube, for most all bass, is 13/16-inch interior diameter with a 3/32-inch wall. This size is great in fourteen, twelve and ten-inch lengths. Most fish over the past couple of years have preferred the fourteen-inch length in my home waters.

As for colors, natural amber is fine for early morning until about 10:30 a.m. After that hour, on a bright day, amber becomes least visible in the water. Between midmorning and late afternoon, a darker brown tube is an excellent choice. The idea is to offer bass or blues a contrast; a bass near the bottom cannot see amber overhead readily when the light is bright; a dark shade shows up vividly.

Slow, deep trolling is the ticket for big stripers, especially between 8 a.m. and 6 p.m. From dusk until daybreak many of us fish the two long rods with no weights; one out at 170 feet from the boat. With the other,

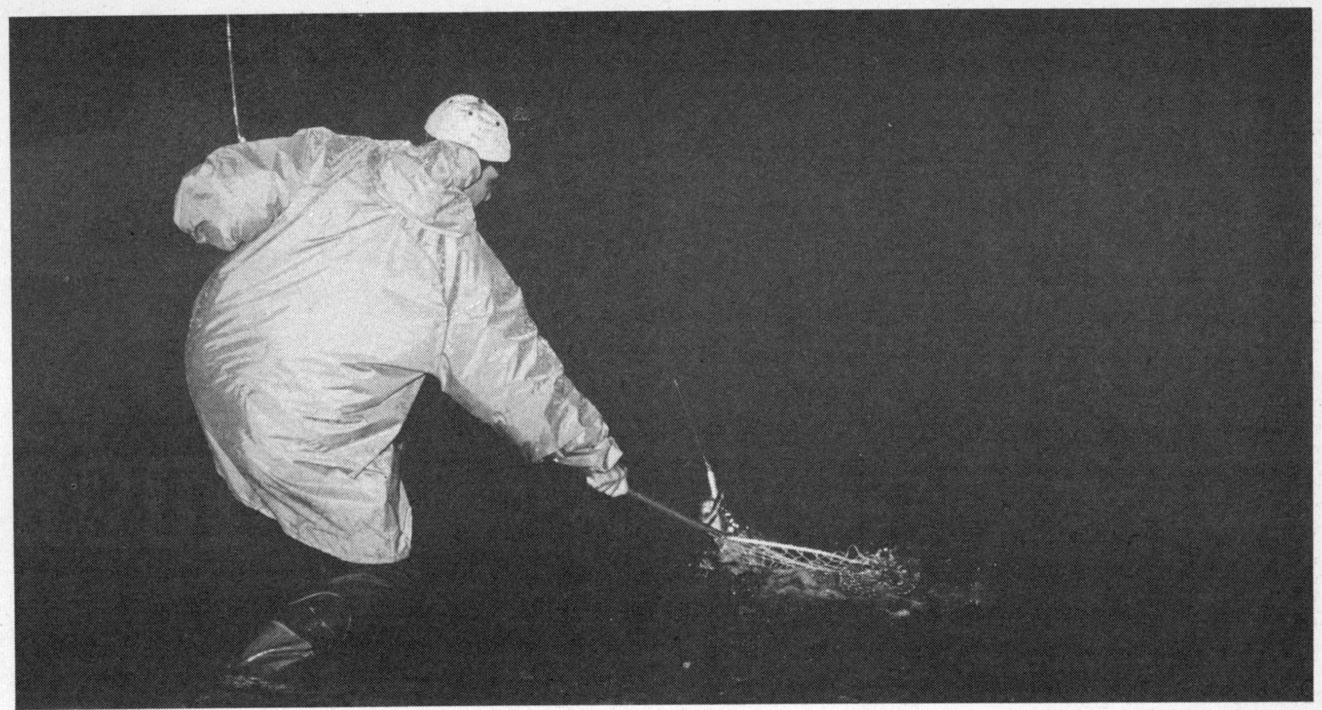

Joel Arrington nets a 12-pound striper off North Carolina, using a bait-casting reel, which is coupled with medium-action plug. (Below) Drails on rods enable bait fish imitation plugs to get down where school of stripers was feeding on mossbanks. The result inhabits this gaff.

let the end of your wire touch the water, then bring in twenty feet. Quite often, early in the morning, we fish a line of 195 feet, including leader.

As an example: starting out at 4:30 a.m. with the tide about one hour before flood, we will troll sixteen- or eighteen-inch tubes on the two long rods and on the center-stern rod. Trolling at a snail's pace close to the beach, we have amber tubes on the outside rods, a black or light blue on the stern outfit. When a bass strikes a particular color, all are changed over to that color. One other effective eelskin rig calls for using a fourteen-inch skin, with the light side out. This same beach-rig eel can be fished with no drail or with two or four-ounce drails if fish are deep.

Tubing has long been a magic word around New England waters. The hottest color is bright red, a killer for many of us on both bass and blues. To get the color you must start with a bright natural amber tube, then dye it with a Tintex color coded as Pagoda Red.

First, bring four quarts of water to a boil, put in the dye and let it work for about four minutes. Add your tubes to the boiling water while stirring the pot. After two minutes, the tubes should have the correct reddish glow. Occasionally it takes a few seconds less, as you do not want this lure to become too dark a shade of red. The brighter the red, the better.

Another top winning tube, the medium brown, can be obtained with the same tinting, using Tintex Rust. One minute of this produces a rich orange tube – another winner. To come up with black tubes, use a full packet of black Tintex. For light blue shades, simply keep checking the effects while stirring this company's dark blue dye.

For those who have heard about effectiveness of a white tube – not readily obtained, except in plastic – you can attain good results by using commercial whitewall tire paint. It outlasts conventional paint of any kind and stays supple, drying in about twelve minutes. Sears' Allstate

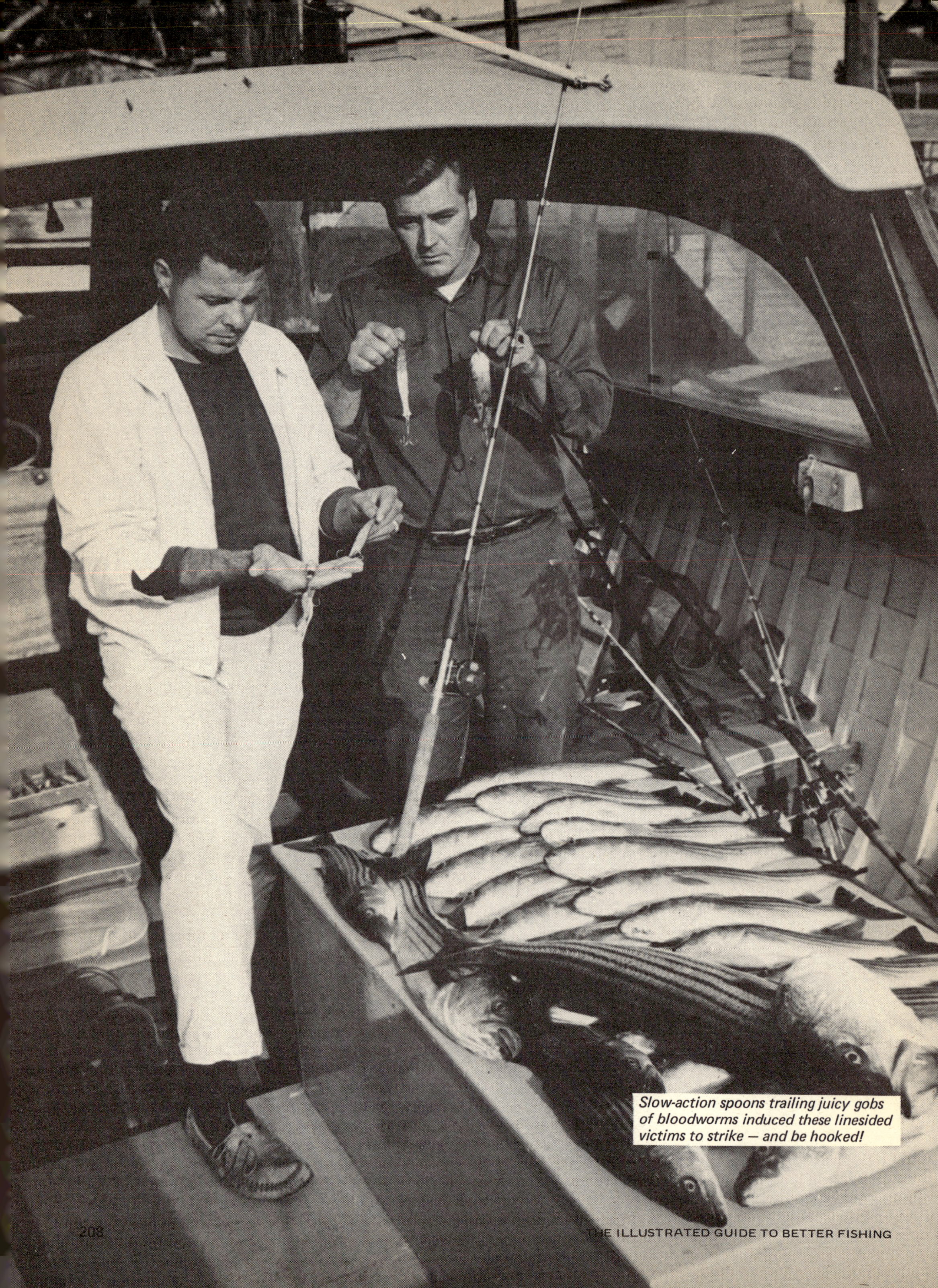
Slow-action spoons trailing juicy gobs of bloodworms induced these linesided victims to strike — and be hooked!

Many an eel, natural or imitation, brings powerful strikes from all sizes of stripers, particularly during eel season. This famous lure is the Alou.

whitewall has proved cheapest and best under heavy use.

My angling associate never could emphasize this next piece of information too often: The less the angle of bend in a tube, the slower the action. This is the answer for trophy bass. Fish weighing over thirty-five pounds are slow and lazy, will rarely go far out of their way to chase a lure that is moving or working too fast. Remember, slow-action lures for big bass, coupled with a slow, deep troll.

Using a light-action fly rod, Zwirz hooked and boated these four "eating-size" stripers on saltwater bucktail flies. The time was just as the tide was changing.

This expert's tubes for smaller fish are almost horseshoe in shape, while the long 7/0 and 8/0 tubes feature nothing more than a slow, graceful curve. Also, cutting a split in the tail of tubing is an added inducement for most game species. An eight-inch tube with split tail, colored either black or red, is of special interest to big bluefish.

An oversimplified rule of thumb for trollers specifies top conditions for taking fish as one hour before flood tide, during flood, and for the first hour of the ebb. Strangely enough, many areas have particular idiosyncrasies that change these basic rules. The only way to find out about the exceptions is to fish the areas on a research basis until you come up with specific answers.

Trolling against the tide can be effective, but considerably more weight will be needed; as the tide lets up less weight can be experimented with for effect. Cross-tide trolling can be effective when there is a strong moon-tide.

Two days before, until three days after a full moon and during the full moon is the time to be out after big fish. Deep and slow again is the pro's ticket to big fish and lots of them. Heavy weights are a necessity, as tides run strongest during these periods.

Creek Chub, Worth and Rapala plugs are my own favorites. I spool no wire on the reels used for plugs, just wire leader material for blues and similar sharp-tooth species. I tend to troll them out around 150 feet from the boat while using two-ounce drails and the twenty-foot wire leaders. Plugs are best at sunset or daybreak, or when bunkers or mullet are in the area. The Creek Chub Pikie in red and white is an excellent choice, while their Silver flash is also good. Atoms, Rapalas and similar plugs work well, too. Rebel has saltwater models in every conceivable finish, length and action, with designs for fishing near all depths.

This is also a good time to use the big, flat-white or plain finish bunker spoons; keel weight can be painted bright red. A particularly good rig for bunker spoons is one hundred feet of Monel and the twenty-foot leader. When these spoons are working right, you can feel a slow, rhythmic beat through the rod. Again, slow trolling speed is the secret to success with these large spoons. As for smaller spoons, try Squid spoons in sizes 1 to 4, the Pflueger Record spoon, the Tony Accetta spoon in sizes 17 to 21, Worth, Wilson and Seadevle – all plain or with pork rind tail. The Clark, sizes 1 to 4, is one of the best all-around striper spoons.

Use one hundred feet of wire, a six-foot leader and a six-ounce drail for jigging bucktail while trolling. Fish just along the bottom and work the rod with an action like that of sweeping with a broom; slowly, but with a decisive sweeping motion. Usually 130 to 160 feet out from the boat, you'll hit bottom, then reel in a few turns. The Bridgeport is a killer!

Fishing live eels is an effective way of taking bass, especially around beaches, shoals and rocks. Use a Siwash hook (6/0 to 8/0) run right through the eel's lips. It is best cast on mono toward the beach or jetty and as close as possible. Reel in slowly. Or, you can run a dependable boat close to shore, cast the eel shoreward, then run your boat out some three hundred feet while the reel is on free spool. Stop the boat, reel back slowly, and when the bass picks it up, let him have enough time to work it over, then strike. Live tinker-mackerel, hooked through the hump between the eyes and fished the same way, can add up to big fish.

The angler who fishes deep is going to come home, most consistently, with more trophy bass. Experimentation is any angler's first big step toward day-to-day success in his particular area; try various depths to find your fish, and vary trolling speeds depending on the size of fish in your area at any given time. And don't forget that the multi-eel umbrella rigs, used with wire line, are deadly!

A good deal of this know-how can be applied to other game fish; lures like the spoons, Rapalas and Creek Chubs, or squid, eels such as the justly famous Alou, and the big dark tubes take far more than any one species of fish.

115
115
Johns
SeaCraft

CHAPTER 18

CATCHING COHO IN COMFORT

Catching This Big Water Denizen Requires Big Water Equipment

MOST SERIOUS fishermen know that the Great Lakes offer some of the greatest fishing in our country. Thanks to the people at Johnson Motors in Waukegan, Illinois, I've had ample opportunity to learn about the techniques put to use by Lake Michigan fishermen who have had plenty of practice.

Recently, I revisited the scene with John Leak, vice-president of Sterling Arms, as my highly knowledgeable guide. Based in Lockport, New York, Leak keeps his highly sophisticated fishing machine where he and Tommy Lee, his arms designer/chief engineer, can cast off and be into big fish in record time.

Left: This is the brand of action Zwirz enjoyed while fishing with the Johnson Motors staff for coho. Boat is a super fishing machine, properly outfitted for any type of game fish. His guides are Johnson executives, pros. (Above) This take of coho reflects why Lake Michigan once again is finding favor with fishermen for salmon species.

This is not a coho, but a king salmon that was taken on a fly with the most basic type of boat, minimum equipment.

The Sea Nymph with twin outboards by Evinrude is the type of boat that the author favors for salmon on the big water.

For the first time since Pacific salmon were planted in the Great Lakes more than eleven years ago, chinook salmon are running in southern Lake Michigan, while coho salmon and steelhead are bigger and more plentiful than ever.

Well equipped salmon sportfishing boats on Lake Michigan are the rule now, and one of the best-equipped rigs has been launched by Johnson Outboards for use by visiting sportswriters.

This twenty-three-footer from Sea Craft of Miami, Florida, is their Tsunami model, twin Johnson 115s with power trim and tilt mounted on her transom. She speeds out to the hot spots at better than forty miles per hour, then can troll at super-slow speeds for hours without missing a beat. Her deep-vee hull configuration can take just about everything the weather throws at her. A little luck still is a necessity, but this boat's modern fishing gear goes a long way toward pushing the odds in the fisherman's favor.

Lowrance Electronics of Tulsa, Oklahoma, has supplied quite a bit of her fish-locating gear. Four new downriggers, including two with built-in temperature sensors monitor the water temperature at any depth you select. This, I learned, is critical on Lake Michigan, because coho prefer 50 to 55-degree water; these temperature downriggers can find it without your having to stop trolling.

The downriggers are capable of taking the fisherman's lures down to any water level desired. When the fish hits, it pulls the fishing line out of a clip and the fisherman plays the fish, not heavy lead weights. The use of heavy tackle with wire line or super-heavy monofilament – typical of deep trolling in the past – has been eliminated.

There are two Lowrance electronic fish Lo-K-Tors aboard. One is a flasher/sounder model. When the boat passes over a fish or school of fish, it flashes on the dial and beeps an alert. On the stern end is mounted the new Lowrance flasher-graph; this unit literally draws a picture of the lake bottom, the surface and any and all fish that pass between. It will even show a diagram of a fish approaching a lure for a look-see.

A surface temperature meter, mounted in the dashboard area, gives the pilot a continual readout of the surface water temperature, important in locating pockets of warmer or cooler water more likely to hold fish. The golden glow of the line helps the guide keep six to eight lines trolling straight and reduces the possibility of fouled lines behind

PICTURE KEY TO IDENTIFY ADULT COHO SALMON, CHINOOK SALMON AND RAINBOW TROUT

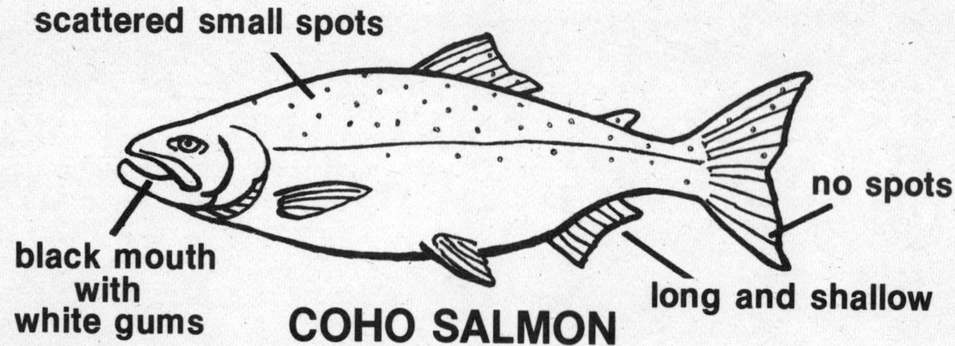

COHO SALMON

(spawning condition: reddish with enlarged jaw)

CHINOOK SALMON

(spawning condition: dark coloring and enlarged jaw)

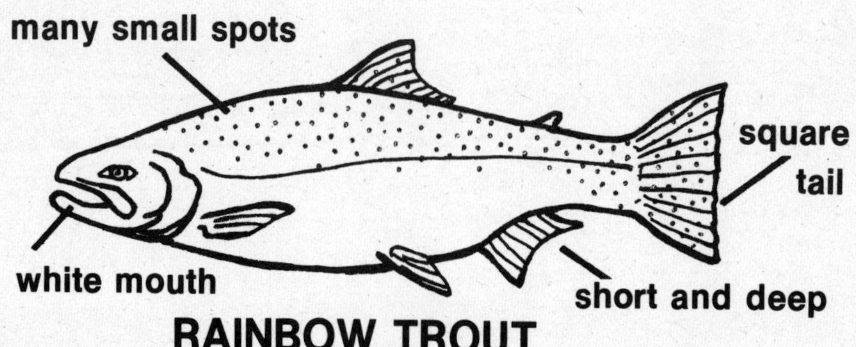

RAINBOW TROUT

(spawning condition: reddish side stripe and somewhat enlarged jaw)

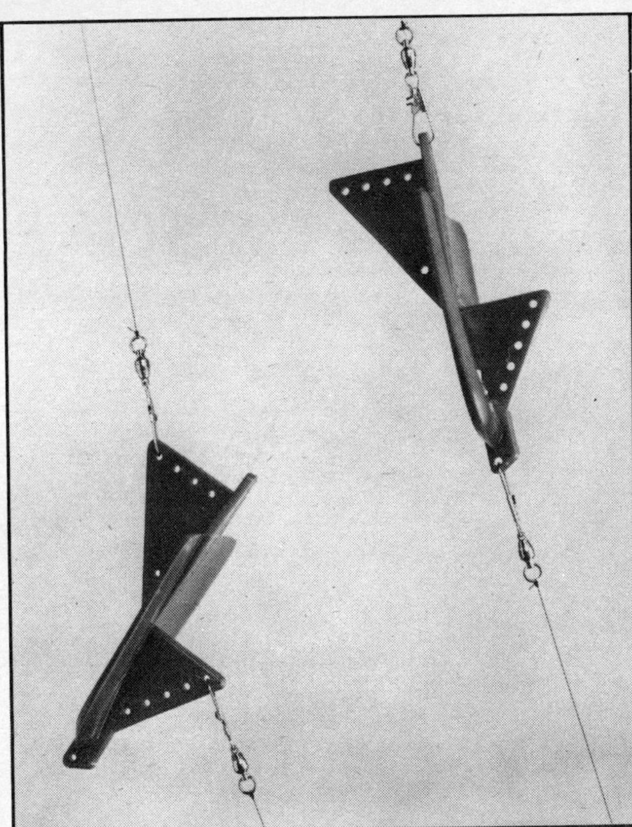

This inexpensive fish seeker made by Doelcher Products of Mission Hills, California, permits trolling at depth range of three to eighty feet. When fish strikes, the device flips over and surfaces. Author says it works.

the boat. This line glows only above the water so the fish do not see it.

For trolling flat lines, the Johnson boat has two outriggers and two planing boards, which pull the trolling line off to the side of the boat much like a water skier pulling against the boat. Again, with both the outriggers and planing boards, the fish pulls the fishing line out of a clothespin or quick-drop clip and the angler fights the fish unfettered by any hardware.

She holds eight balanced rods and reels. The reels are Penns, both the free-spooling and open-face spin-cast types, filled with fluorescent 17-pound-test Stren line from DuPont.

A big Plano 747 tackle box has more lures and fish attractors than some tackle stores. There are enough Rapalas, Rebels and pixie spoons and many others, of all colors and shapes, to do the job. There are even a couple of sharp Normark fillet knives in there which also have seen better than their share of duty. Naturally, this is all a result of having all those fishing authorities aboard!

This Sea Craft carries many of the amenities that can make fishing mighty comfortable. She has a galley, sink, stove, table, cutting board and even a mini-bar. Up front, there's a marine head and, beyond that, a cozy bedroom or two.

But out back, it's all strictly fishing machine. Two huge, matching insulated ice chests come with the boat. One is mounted under the reclining back-to-back seats on the port side; another is located in the transom area and when the skipper says, "Put it in the box," it means throw another freshly caught coho on the ice.

The canvas that comes with this boat can turn her from a sunny-day fishing machine into a foul-weather fishing machine, or even a secure floating camper for pretty luxurious over-nighting.

The toggles and dials in front of the pilot look as though they belong on an aircraft, but all have their logical uses. Tachometers and synchronizers from OMC, lighted

The Active Pass area near Victoria, British Columbia, is considered an excellent sector for big West Coast salmon.

Michigan seems an unlikely area for coho, but they are being taken from a fleet of charter boats in that area available for singles or parties.

compass, alternator gauges for both engines, bilge pumps, running lights, interior lights, fuel gauge, blower, thermometer, barometer, humidity gauge and trim and tilt buttons all are there.

While I fished with Johnson Motors, conditions were right for close-in trolling well within clear sight of the several miles of shoreline running on both sides of the city of Waukegan. Although the hot coho/chinook fishery covers roughly a forty-mile area, we never found it a necessity to troll more than a few miles in either direction; we always were within sight of either the Waukegan skyline or the neighboring towns that snuggle against the lake's shoreline.

As for gear, lures and methods, a good deal of my data was established as a result of many hours spent with Ron Pederson and Bill AuCoin or due to keeping an ear open to the local guides and skippers.

In Michigan, salmon fishermen start taking big coho and chinook as early as the first week in July by using big boats and special trolling tackle and techniques. Any well made electronic fish locator or depth finder should show blips of salmon schools or even larger individual fish. Maturing coho and chinook feed actively in water ranging from a low of 44 degrees to a high of approximately 58. Experience has shown that 54 degrees is best for peak activity. During late August and throughout September, deep-water trolling should produce tremendous salmon fishing; in late September and through November, weather permitting, you

The chinook salmon found in Michigan's Muskegon River is worth the effort even to fighting a crowded river bank.

A guest angler on a Johnson Motors research boat allows Ron Pederson to handle his netting chore. This firm does a great amount of research not only on its own products, but in determining top fishing areas for benefit of others.

will find plenty of salmon close to shore, especially near the mouths of tributary streams.

All of these species can be caught with ultralight spinning gear or even fly rods, but they are not the ideal rig for such fish. For the most part, these are big, hard-fighting fish and the average angler is advised to use somewhat heavier equipment. A reasonably stiff trolling, spinning or bait-casting rod is a good choice. In fact, you'll find a fair number of anglers using tackle that might best be described as light saltwater. Level-wind reels should have a smooth drag feature. Choose a reel line capacity of at least two hundred yards. Any good-quality monofilament or braided trolling line is suitable for fishing salmon. Line weight is a matter of personal choice and skill, but eight or ten-pound test would be a minimum; fifteen-pound test is recommended for most conditions.

Although many coho and chinook are caught by casting from a shoreline, most anglers prefer trolling from a boat. The reason is simple: Fishermen can cover much more water and present lures or bait down at the 54 to 55 degree water temperature level.

Once you have located the depth of this layer of water, the problem becomes one of how to get your lure down to that level and keep it there. West Coast and a fair number of Great Lakes' salmon anglers have developed techniques to almost a science, but secrets of their success usually involve two items of specialized equipment.

The newest of these is the downrigger. Many are homemade, but commercial models are available from around \$30 to \$150 (as examples: Lowrance, Riviera, Big John). These are large (six to twelve-inch diameter, holding up to two hundred feet of strong cord or wire line) reel devices which are attached to the stern area of the boat. A four to eight-pound lead is attached to the end of the line. About four feet above the lead, a breakaway rig is attached, usually a three-way. The swivel is tied firmly to the trolling line, then attached with a light line (two or four-pound test) to the downrigger cord so that, when a fish strikes, the light line breaks and the angler can play the fish.

Basic purpose of this rig is to get the trolling line down to the desired depth without having to run out 150 feet of line. Using a downrigger, the angler can troll the lure thirty

Zwirz' goal for the day is accomplished as he takes a coho with the help of Ron Pederson, his fishing companion for the day on the Great Lakes.

to forty feet in back of the boat, permitting sharper turns and avoiding foul-ups with trolling lines from other boats in the fishing fleet.

The second piece of equipment is the trolling plane. This is a plastic or metal plane or fin designed to pull a lure downward in the reverse manner that a kite pulls upward. This handy device usually is rigged with a slip-swivel so that the trolling line can be retrieved with a minimum of resistance by the plane.

Coho and chinook salmon, like steelhead and lakers, go for such a wide variety of lures that it is possible to mention only a few personal favorites. The most popular lures with experienced fishermen, however, fall into the following general categories:

Plugs – Heddon Tadpolly, Rapalas, Helin Flatfish, Deep Diving Rebels, Burke's Big Dig and Little Big Dig, Spoon Plug. Colors are silver, blue, white, fluorescent red, and yellow with red spots.

Spoons – Williams Wobblers, Dardevles, Johnson, Flutter Spoons, Nepco Pixie spoons; in silver, gold, white, fluorescent red and white, black and white, yellow, red and blue.

Spinners – Large (No. 2, 3) Mepps, C.P. Swing in silver and gold.

Bait – Large Minnows and nightcrawlers.

Flies – Streamer flies in bright or hot colors, or solid white, yellow, red.

You'll find that firms like Luhr Jenson of Oregon offer an unusually large selection of specialized tackle and lures for both Great Lakes and West Coast fishing of this type. Also, you will soon find need of becoming familiar with such everyday names as Flash Flies (Manistee), Herring Dodgers, Popes Fishback, Big-B, Arbogasts Razorback, plus Pink Lady, Deep-6 and dozens more items that can nicely be added to a tackle box of the in-crowd of coholand.

Nothing can be more of a circus of frustration than when more than one angler hooks a salmon at the same time. As one can imagine, the slightest miscalculation in technique can result in a tangle of lines that means loss of the fish.

How To Care For Coho

1. Keep dressed fish packed in crushed ice until it can be refrigerated. Fish spoil easily.
2. When received, wrap in moisture-proof paper or place in a tightly covered dish and store immediately in a refrigerator.
3. Keep coho in coolest part of refrigerator.
4. Fish may be cooked in frozen or thawed state. Thaw

frozen fish slowly in refrigerator, not in hot water. Never refreeze thawed coho.

5. Fish cooked frozen will take about twenty-five percent longer to cook than fish thawed.

6. Do not allow fish to stand in water or be exposed to air.

Cleaning Coho

1. Wash and clean fish thoroughly, then dry.

2. Using a stiff knife, scrape scales off, working from tail to head. A scaler may be used instead of a knife. Coho may be cooked unscaled.

3. Remove head and pectoral fins by cutting above collarbone. Remove the dorsal or large back fin by cutting both sides of fin with sharp knife. Give a quick pull toward head to remove fin with root bones. Remove other fins the same way. Never cut off with shears or knife, since bones at base will be left in fish.

4. Cut full length of abdomen, remove entrails. Liver and roe may be separated if desired. Plan to cook these separately from fish as they take longer. Wash cavity in clean, cold water. Be sure cavity is clean, especially along backbone.

5. Recommend cutting off strip about one-half-inch wide along belly sections to remove fat. This strip could include pelvic fins plus anal or ventral fin. Scrape along backbone with dull spoon to remove any other fat deposits.

6. To fillet, slit the flesh along the back from tail to just behind the head with sharp, thin knife and then cut down to backbone. At base of head, turn knife flat and cut flesh along backbone, continue to run knife over rib bones until tail is reached. Lift off whole side of fillet in one piece.

To skin, one method is to place fillet skin-side down on cutting board. Hold tail end tightly and with sharp, thin knife cut flesh through to the skin. Flatten knife on skin and slide or push knife forward while holding free end of skin firmly.

7. Wash thoroughly in cold water. Rinse in cold water.

8. Refrigerate, freeze or cook immediately.

For preparing coho or silver salmon, handle with special care to bring out the distinctive and delicate flavor. There should be the shortest time from catch to use. Keep coho chilled and cold. Cook just until it flakes apart when tested with fork. Do not overcook.

Baking – Whole, Fillets or Steaks

Season and brush coho with melted butter or lemon butter; place fish on greased pan.

If whole fish is stuffed, stuff loosely; slivers of garlic, herbs, etc., can be placed in fish cavity for seasoning if not stuffed with dressing.

Bake slowly in preheated oven at 325 to 350 degrees F. until flesh breaks apart or flakes. Fish can be basted occasionally with salted butter, lemon juice, lemon butter, milk or cream. Flour or bread crumbs can be sprinkled over top of fillets or steaks.

Left: Bing McClellan, president of Burke, hefts 21-pound coho which he caught on his firm's Little Dig flex plug.

Fish fillets or steaks can be partially covered, at least for part of cooking, with greased paper or aluminum foil to keep in moisture. Bake about ten minutes depending on thickness of fillets or steaks or until fish easily flakes apart. (Excellent results obtained when fish fillets are partially covered for full cooking period of ten minutes.)

Sprinkle with lemon juice or lemon butter.

Broiling – Fillets or Steaks

Brush coho with melted butter. A little lemon juice gives flavor. Dill may be desired. Try a lemon butter sauce with dill, which has been stored in refrigerator for several days.

Preheat broiler to 450 degrees F. Place coho on greased broiler pan, skin-side down, four to six inches from flame. Broil slowly. Fillets or steaks need not be turned if not too thick. Cook only until flesh is delicately brown and it flakes apart. Season before serving.

This big coho was taken on spinning tackle from river in British Columbia. It is large enough either to cut into steaks or to fillet for broiling or frying pan.

Pan Frying – Fillets or Steaks

Season and prepare fish according to method desired. May be coated with:

Flour (paprika can also be added), beaten egg and bread, cracker crumbs, crushed corn flakes, a mixture of half cornmeal and flour, pancake flour, or prepared batter.

Heat fat, about one-eighth-inch deep, in heavy frying pan; place fish in hot, but not smoking fat.

Fry coho slowly in moderate heat. When golden brown on one side, turn carefully, then brown on other side. Reduce heat and cook until done.

CHAPTER 19

TAKING SEA TROUT

This Many-Named Species Responds Well To The Light Tackle Challenge

AS A CONNECTICUT Yankee versed in New England fishing jargon, I'm duty-bound to state for the official record that the species discussed in this chapter, *Cynoscion regalis,* is correctly named: weakfish. However, this exceptionally popular species wanders the sea under so many aliases it is a necessity to identify this scrappy fighter – with all facts in order.

All of the fish we'll talk about here are called weakfish, but there are several subspecies that further fill out the family tree, namely: the spotted weakfish and the silver weakfish. In southern waters, the weakfish almost always is referred to as a sea trout or gray trout, the spotted weakfish becoming known as either a spotted sea trout or speckled sea trout. This same weakfish also is known as a white trout, while the silver weakfish for some unknown reason answers to the moniker of sand trout or – pardon the expression – bastard trout below the Mason-Dixon line. Many New Englanders and several of the Long Island commercial crews refer to this fine eating fish as a squeteague.

Sea trout – or weakfish – appear from Massachusetts

Left: Although termed a weakfish, the sea trout is a scrappy adversary even as far north as Nova Scotia. (Right) Light spinning tackle of the saltwater breed can guarantee fishermen top flight sport with this species.

A dressy bucktail fly was cast to a nearby dropoff, the fisherman thus locating not one, but a school of feeding fish. The result was that this particular fisherman ended up with four fruitful casts in a matter of minutes.

speckled sea trout may be caught anywhere from New York's coastal waters to Texas. In recent years, it has been somewhat scarce north of Virginia, a condition that has shown promising signs of correcting itself. South of Virginia, the species is thriving. The sand weakfish is limited mostly to the Gulf Coast, while the silver is well distributed from Chesapeake Bay to Florida, with a fair share found on the gulf side of Florida, especially near the Ten Thousand Islands and in the vicinity of the Caloosahatchee River.

All of the species rely heavily on shrimp, herring, seaworms, squid, menhaden, scup, butterfish and mummechogs for food. Thus, they are prone to accept bait-fish-imitation lures and plugs, streamer and bucktail flies and shrimp-pattern flies. It is equally true that they are easy marks for hooks baited with any of these natural baits.

The average weakfish/sea trout generally weighs in the vicinity of two to five pounds, but seven to ten pounds is not at all uncommon and specimens close to twenty pounds have been taken in commercial nets. Back in 1967, I managed to hook and land a rare beauty in a favorite New Jersey hotspot; it tipped the scales at fourteen pounds five ounces. I was using a fly rod on this particular drift and had baited an Eagle Claw hook with a double serving of shrimp.

On light tackle, any member of this species will give you an honest run for your money. Do not, however, go after these fish with gear that is unsporting or overly heavy; all you will do is ruin your own sport.

There is nothing really weak about a weakfish except the tissue around its mouth, which explains the name of the breed. Weaks are treated with kid gloves by knowledgeable fishermen, because of their tender mouths; it doesn't take all that much horsing to tear a hook or lure free.

This is a simple fly pattern, but it looked enough like a natural bait to coax sea trout into a savage strike.

Off the coast of North Carolina, a trio of fishermen jig their Hopkins lures at dusk to take many sea trout. This particular species is located in widely separated climes and can be taken on a number of baits and lures.

There is a great spot for jigging or trolling or still-fishing sea trout just off the coast of North Carolina, easily accessible via the charter boats operating out of Carolina Beach. It's well within the shoreline of Fort Fisher, just a short run south of the Carolina Beach inlet. Here you will find excellent sea trout fishing well into the fall months, in the inshore waters, the protected bays and creeks, and in specific open-water spots known to the local fisherman.

These hotspots hold big fish. Kings and stripers also are present in quantity and actually seem to be sorely neglected by visiting sportsmen. I can only assume that word on this fine fishing potential has just not gotten around to enough engineers.

No matter how you add up the figures, the sea trout/weakfish clan is one of the most important groups of game fish available. In southerly waters, it accounts for an outstandingly high proportion of fishing man-hours, and rightfully so. It is a handsome-looking fish, one that is welcome on the table, and simple to clean and dress-out once caught. But, undoubtedly, it finds greatest favor simply because it is available in so many types of water and can be caught by so many methods. I personally have little doubt that the greatest number are caught by still-fishing and trolling, but catches are made when the tide is coming in or during high slack, as well. Live shrimp, as previously mentioned, will produce heavier stringers than most any other bait you could name.

It should be emphasized, however, that this game fish is made to order for the fly fisherman, bait caster and spin fisherman. He doesn't hesitate to slam a surface-popper or streamer for members of the long rod fraternity; small plugs and spinning lures work well and, of course, we have his aforementioned natural bait preferences for those who crave the peace, quiet and tranquility of simply dunking bait.

In Florida gulf waters you'll find sea trout mostly in bays, on grass beds and around inlets and passes. In the last two spots mentioned, look for them along edges of eddies, not too often in the primary flows. Winter and spring tend to be the best seasons on both the east and west Florida coasts. The spotted sea trout, for the benefit of surf casters, is no stranger at all to their favorite waters.

Within ten minutes of the dock I use on Florida's Caloosahatchee River, I've been able to spend casting sessions lasting less than two hours that provided as many as sixteen silvers and sands, running from three to over six pounds. With the use of typical freshwater bass tackle, this is enjoyable fishing in any man's book. A number of plugs

Using the same sporty bait-casting combos on which they had taken largemouth bass, Zwirz (in background) and a friend found them more than adequate for taking sea trout. They took forty-three such fish in two hours.

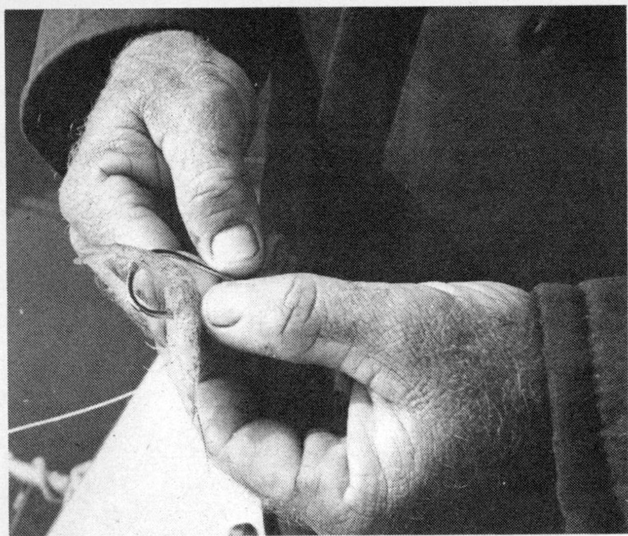

A wide variety of natural baits can be used for the sea trout, but author has found shrimp to be an almost sure winner. Care must be taken in placing it on the hook.

used successfully on bass, snook and small tarpon work just as well on a fair-size weakfish. The South Bend Bass-Oreno is just great as is a 4½-inch Rapala or Rebel. In the case of the Rebel lures, several models are working well. So too is the Sea Hawk and copies of the needlefish. Another old standby for many southern casters is the Creek Chub Darter.

My old friend, Connie Mack, Jr., who lived year-round at Cape Coral, Florida, first showed me the hundreds of mangrove-lined acres of shoreline that offered as much chance for the seatrout as it did for either snook or tarpon. This region abounds with all the tarpon, snook, kings, channel bass, jack crevalle, mangrove snapper, pompano, cobia, sea bass and mackerel any angler could hope to handle in a lifetime of fishing. Hot spots around Useppa Island, Josslyn Island and the general area of Pine Island Sound still hold plenty of trout. The same is essentially true around the inner side of Cayo Costa and not far from Captiva and Sanibel.

The secret to top-flight enjoyment when fishing for seatrout is to keep your tackle light and sporty. On six or eight-pound-test monofilament, or on a fly rod, he is a surprisingly exciting fish.

However, it was not always like this, though wise old coastal fishermen did use everything from fly rods to the long, special-purpose surf rods. Only during the days following World War II did we see the new-to-the-scene magic wand appear – the spinning outfit with its threadline connection.

Remembering my own father's choice of gear, I'd be safe to say he craved that fly rod for handling a chum slick, a plug-casting rig for tossing artificial lures. Only rarely did I note him going to a light squidding combo for those not common happenings when the heavy tiderunners made their way into the hefty currents of the surf. Speaking personally, I'd have to say that with today's superb tackle my most popular choice for all-purpose work would be a spinning stick of six or seven-feet capable of tossing lures or baits in the one-half to one-ounce group. With an open-face spinning reel spooling 6- or 8-pound-test mono, as previously stated, you are mighty close to being master of all the weakfish action you'll encounter. Live baits will not present a problem, nor will live-lining a chum line. Further, with the drag set so as to give line on a strike, trolling is not beyond your scope.

Keep in mind that in no way am I ruling out any of the other types of tackle, as long as the combos are kept light and sporty. Often, in Florida waters, I will stay with a favorite plug-casting outfit (as used for black bass in fresh water), or with a popping rod and Ambassadeur reel – not much different than I like for school tarpon or snook in

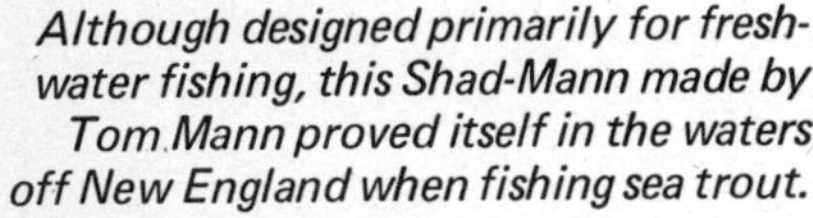

Although designed primarily for fresh-water fishing, this Shad-Mann made by Tom Mann proved itself in the waters off New England when fishing sea trout.

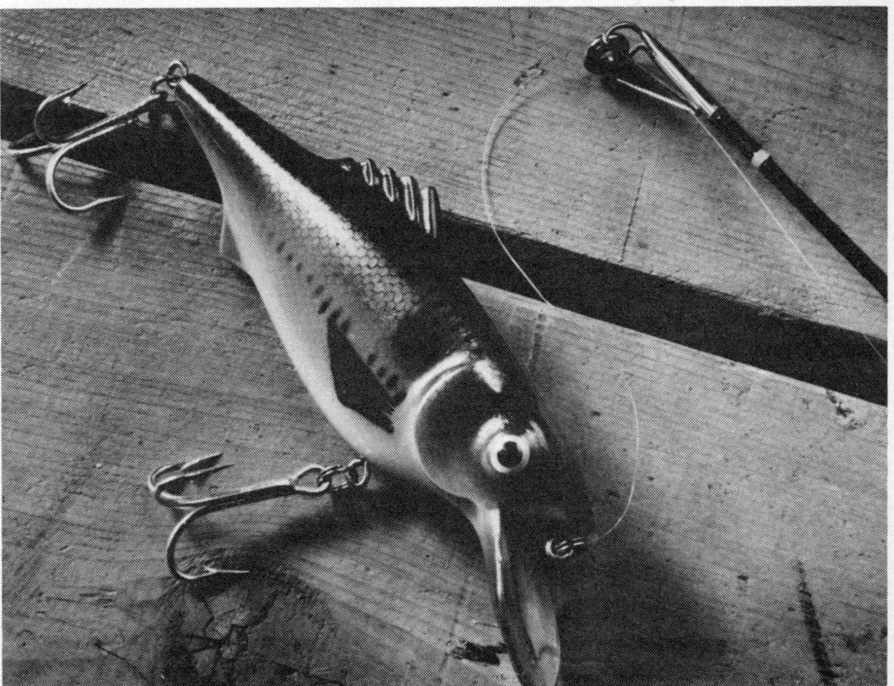

A surface/sub-surface darter cast into the mangroves edging the water proved right for Zwirz to connect with this good-size sea trout in Florida waters.

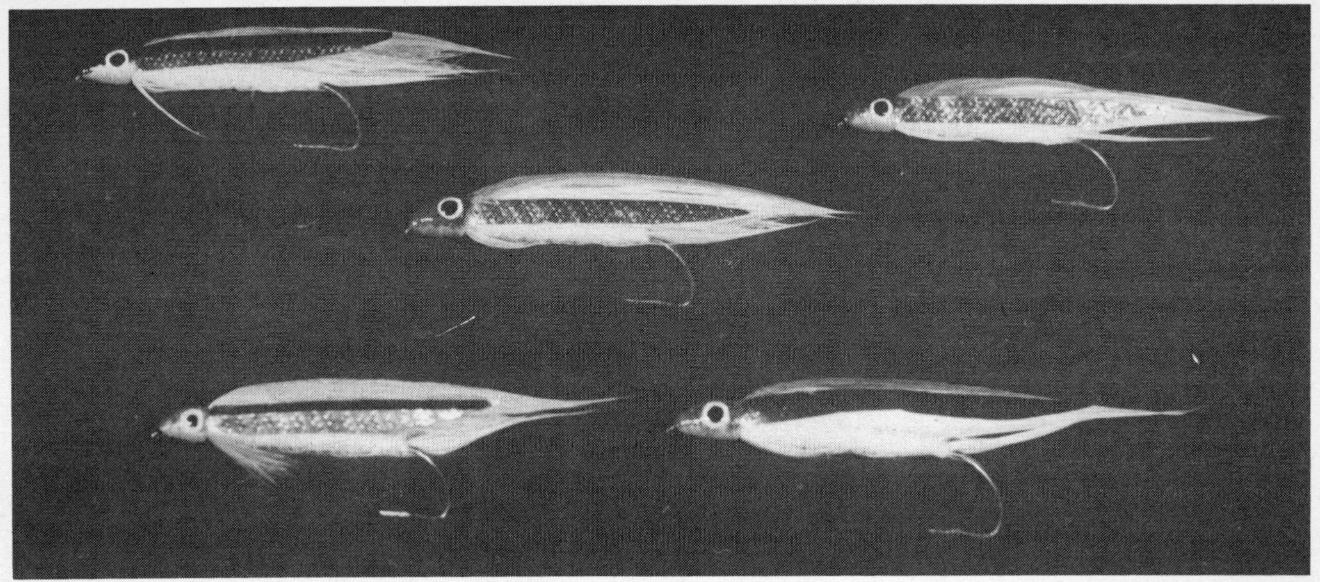

When a bait fish look-alike pattern is needed, Zwirz has found this — his own Miracle Maribou Minnow — will do its share to guarantee proper success.

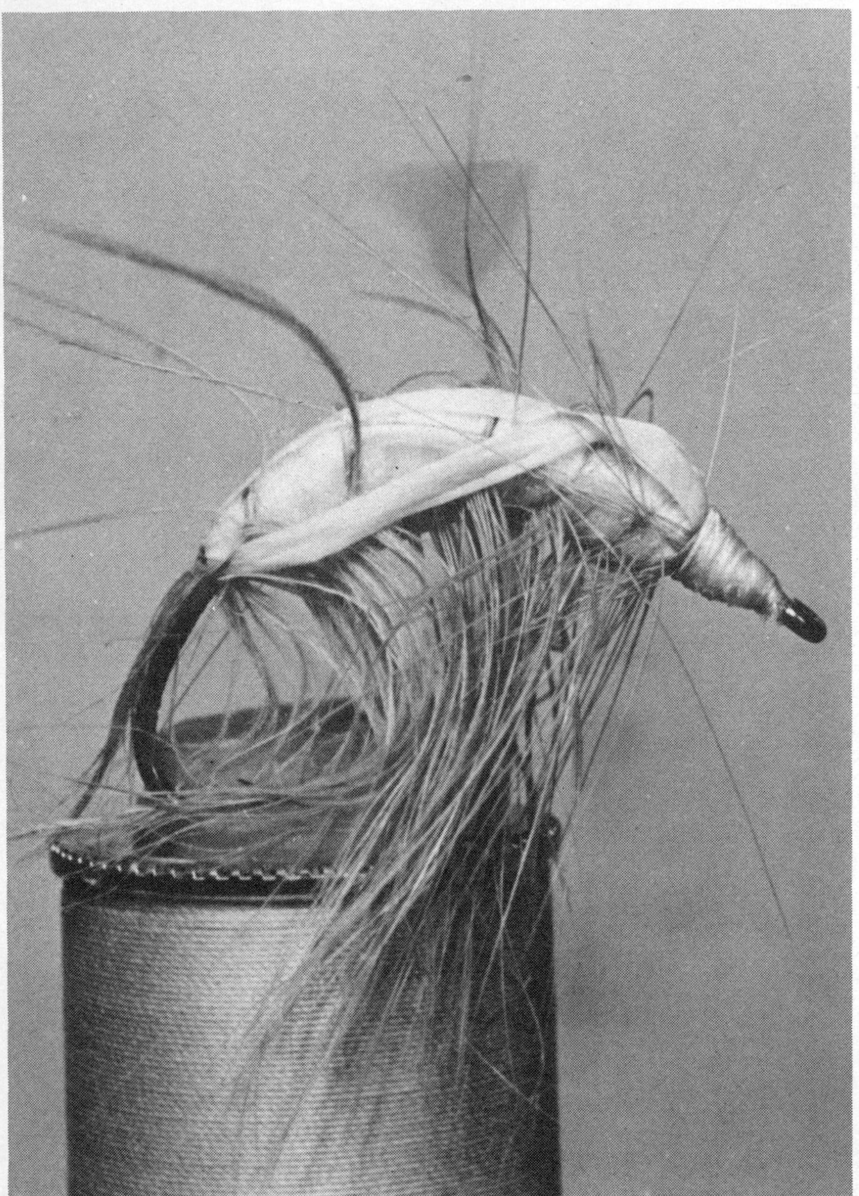

Left: For the fly fisherman seeking sea trout, this artificial pattern tied by Glad Zwirz works well for a fish that loves shrimp on its menu.

Hours of dusk are magic for taking heavy catches of weakfish. Zwirz and three others once boated eighty sea trout, which they found in migration.

open water. Not for situations when they are lurking a whisker away from the mangroves. Summing up this matter of tackle I feel that the best guide lies in your own personal dictates – the rules are simply that flexible.

When asked about the top-producing artificials almost any knowledgeable angler will admit that in addition to the few favorites I've touched upon, a well appointed tackle box should hold such fare as Upperman bucktails, a selection of Mirro-Lures in sizes/actions/colors as proven deadly in the geographical area you will fish, and a "special" offering known as a combination lure. Here we have a surface "attractor" plug with a sub-surface bucktail as a trailer. Most all of your strikes will come on the bucktail.

Just such tactics work as well on a fly rod as with spinning or bait-casting techniques; a cork-bodied bass bug, or one of modern plastic, with a deeper running bucktail or streamer moving under the surface disturber will prove successful the further south you fish from Cape May, New Jersey, to as far south as you wish to venture.

Always stop and try to figure where, based on water temperature/day-night, strata-wise weakfish are apt to be at that point in the season. They're tricky. Believe me when I point out that you are apt to run into them on the top, anywhere between top and bottom, and right on the bottom.

Consider too that a seatrout just loves killies, shrimp, squid, sandworms, bloodworms, plus a number of small fish such as anchovies, butterfish, small eels and even the smaller flounders. Lures should try to imitate both in appearance and the action you strive to impart to them. The fact that I've mentioned specific natural prey of the seatrout should be enough to clue you in to live baits that will serve best.

While speaking of natural baits let me warn you about a common bruhaha that takes place with uneducated anglers who are soaking a bait, become bored, then place rod and reel on the deck – rod tilted against the nearest handy object. Along comes a sea trout, say of seven or eight pounds, and he truly likes your offering. Quite often they forget about teasing the bait and simply smash it like you can't believe a fish of that weight could do; before you drop your cold beer you are part of the buyers market for a new rod, reel and line. It has been my experience that more times than not, a sea trout will strike a bait with such speed and force that, particularly when taking a surface or slightly sub-surface offering, they both take and set the hook by themselves.

Simply to prove nothing is for always, consider that there will be times when this game fish will play with the bait, never actually mouthing it, until you are ready to go over the side with a knife in your teeth. This sea trout approach, where patience and a slack line are a must, reminds me of the brand of practice required when blackfish among the rocks will do no more than nibble at a green crab's legs, yet never seem willing to actually seize the meaty section where the hook lies buried.

Of all said here, consider the geographical areas you will fish, the conditions and local lore established by the old-timers. Then choose your tackle carefully and go look for the action that is there for the wise.

Florida's Gary Bennett displays kind of sea trout one can expect when exploring that southern state's shore waters.

CHECK KENTUCKY FOR ACTION

Manmade Lakes In This Southern State Feature A Broad Span Of Angling Action

FISHERMEN WHO wonder whether there really is a fishing paradise in the United States can stop fretting and begin smiling.

This is the time to plan ahead, oil the fishing outfits, then get ready for a bit of traveling. Such a trip will be well worth it, if you head toward the Midwest/South, ending up close by some of the finest domestic fishing to be found these days. This regional Mecca of angling action features Kentucky Lake, Lake Barkley and Tennessee Valley Authority's Land Between The Lakes as the feature attractions.

Does 3500 miles of shoreline get your attention? Kentucky Lake and Lake Barkley comprise that shoreline mileage and are among the largest impoundments in the

Opposite page: Walleye fishing in Kentucky is a fantastic sport. This river is just one of many holding this popular game fish. In fact, Kentucky has more miles of running water than any state besides Alaska — nearly fourteen times its size! There are 200 species of fish and the yearly bag for good fish only — not coarse fish — is approximately 30 million pounds. Kentuckians are anglers!

A perfect cast near submerged brush of Lake Barkley produced this smashing strike from a largemouth bass.

country. Further, they provide almost unlimited fishing and boating opportunities.

Land Between The Lakes is a green-capped peninsula surrounded almost completely by the twin lakes developed by the TVA as an outdoor recreation and environmental education center. Pocketed with serene, tranquil coves and embayments, the peninsula and two lakes provide fishermen excellent opportunities to land slab crappie and largemouth bass from boat or bank.

Since the mid-1960s Kentucky Lake, bounding the west shore of Land Between The Lakes, has been one of the most consistent producers of crappie and largemouth bass in the Midwest. The largest TVA staircase of impoundments on the Tennessee River, Kentucky Lake's immense size and variety of year-round fishing ranks it near the top of the nation's elite fishing impoundments. More than 2300 miles of shoreline provide the weekend or seasoned fishermen with limitless opportunities to pursue their favorite quarry. I have fished this impoundment twenty-three times and have seen less than an ant's view of its offerings.

Bordering the east bank of Land Between The Lakes is the U.S. Corps of Engineers' Lake Barkley. Completed in 1965, Barkley was formed by impoundment of the Cumberland River. With more than 1000 miles of rugged shoreline, this lake is beginning to rival its sister lake in the production of slab crappie and is considered a hotbed for bass. In fact, I consider it one of the top spots for hog bass in this region of the United States.

A short, open canal near the two dams weds Kentucky and Barkley Lakes, creating the most unique combination of man-made lakes in the United States. Fishermen easily can pass by boat from one lake to the other in three to five minutes, although the canal itself is a popular year-round fishing spot for largemouth bass, crappie and channel catfish. The operating levels of the two lakes cause a slight, but constant, flow of water through the canal, creating an ideal fishing ground.

Kentucky and Barkley Lakes are tops for largemouth

Bass fishing is finest in all of that great water surrounding the Land Between the Lakes.

bass and crappie in spring, early summer and fall. But there's still plenty of action in midsummer and winter for the patient fishermen. Noted for its perennial production of slab crappie and largemouth bass, Kentucky Lake is rivaled by Lake Barkley, a body of water many anglers consider the ideal bass lake.

Long rows of stickups in almost every embayment of Lake Barkley provide natural fish shelters. The result of flooding many of the old fence rows and roadbeds, the shelters were formed when the tops of brush and small trees were left sticking above the surface of the lake.

Lake Barkley, like Kentucky Lake, has thousands of

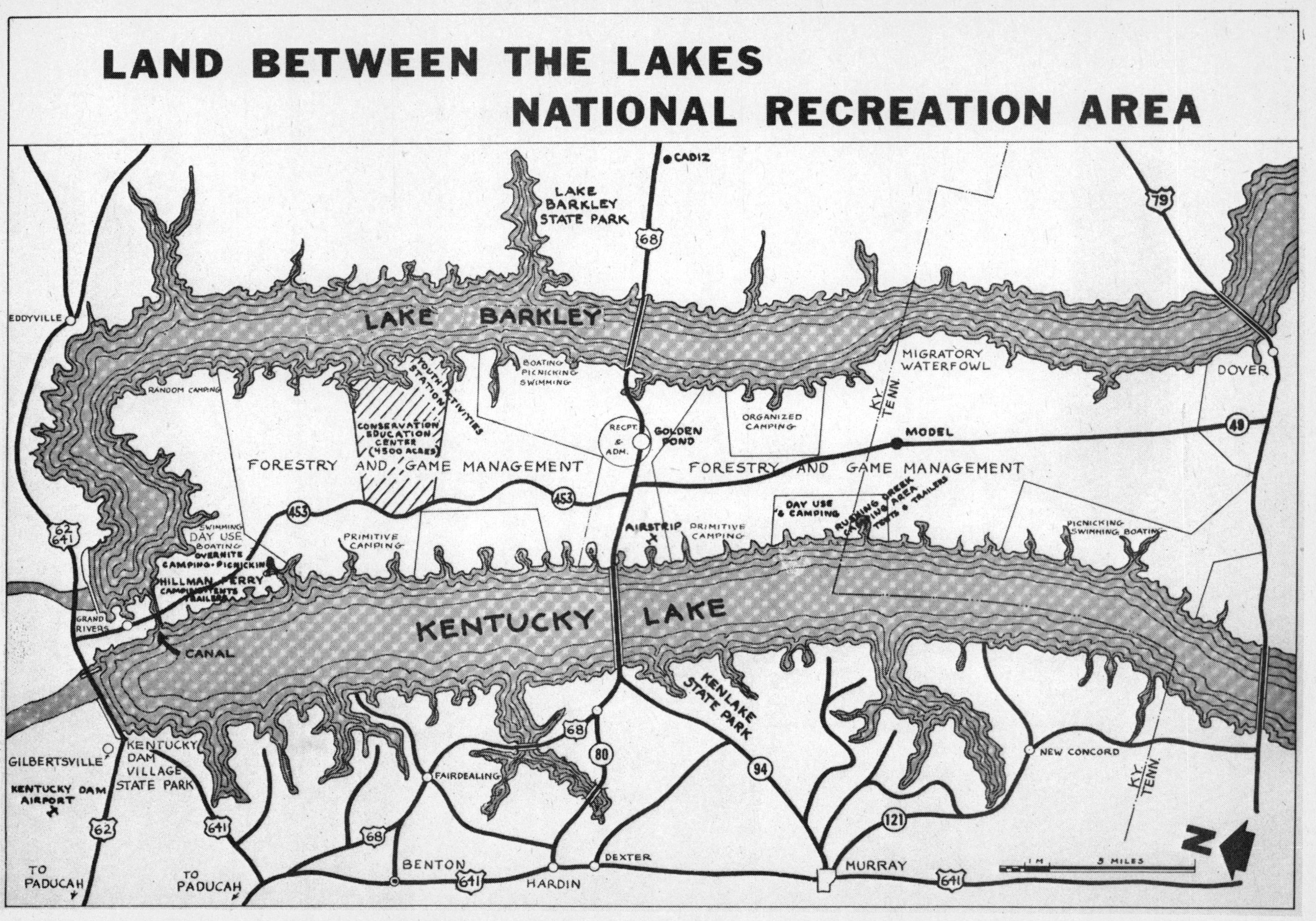
LAND BETWEEN THE LAKES
NATIONAL RECREATION AREA
CADIZ
LAKE BARKLEY STATE PARK
LAKE BARKLEY
EDDYVILLE
DOVER
MIGRATORY WATERFOWL
BOATING PICNICKING SWIMMING
RANDOM CAMPING
YOUTH ACTIVITIES STATION
CONSERVATION EDUCATION CENTER (4500 ACRES)
RECPT. & ADM.
GOLDEN POND
ORGANIZED CAMPING
KY. TENN.
MODEL
FORESTRY AND GAME MANAGEMENT
FORESTRY AND GAME MANAGEMENT
DAY USE & CAMPING
RUNNING CREEK CAMPING AREA TENTS & TRAILERS
SWIMMING DAY USE BOATING OVERNITE CAMPING-PICNICKING
HILLMAN FERRY CAMPING-TENTS TRAILERS
PRIMITIVE CAMPING
AIRSTRIP
PRIMITIVE CAMPING
PICNICKING SWIMMING BOATING
GRAND RIVERS
CANAL
KENTUCKY LAKE
KENLAKE STATE PARK
GILBERTSVILLE
KENTUCKY DAM VILLAGE STATE PARK
KENTUCKY DAM AIRPORT
FAIRDEALING
NEW CONCORD
TO PADUCAH
TO PADUCAH
BENTON
HARDIN
DEXTER
MURRAY
1 M
5 MILES
N

acres of submerged stump beds along old creek and river channel banks that provide ideal cover for crappie and bass. Bass fishing is best April through mid-June and September and November, although a growing number of fishermen are landing big strings of bass and crappie by fishing the deep drop-offs and ledges in midsummer and winter.

Midsummer and winter fishing success is recent on the lakes in the Midwest and South. Armed with contour charts of the lake floors, electronic depth finders or locators and a handful of assorted plastic worms or single spins, thousands of fishermen now are pursuing lunker bass that lie along the deep drop-offs or old stream channel banks.

During the off-season on Barkley and Kentucky Lakes, bass seem to lie in depths from fifteen to twenty-five feet and are best pursued with plastic worms or single spins, fished somewhat slower during the colder season. The time of day doesn't seem to bear on catching largemouth bass, but a thorough knowledge of the lake floor is essential.

From mid-May to mid-June and in October some of the finest surface fishing for bass can be found on the twin lakes. In the spring, chugging or popping lures seem to do the best, while the walking or running lures fare better as the water temperature warms. Fly fishermen also take their share of nice largemouth bass with big popping bugs around button bushes in the coves and along the willow and brush-lined islands that dot the two lakes.

In addition to surface baits, plastic worms and single and dual spinners, the Bomber, Tadpolly and Hellbender-type lures are favorite baits. These diving lures are best used near the mouths of embayments and around deep points and gravel bars.

Slab-size crappie begin their spawning runs during the spring on Kentucky and Barkley Lakes and the resulting fishing is one of the largest harvests of panfish in the Midwest. The major run usually occurs in April and the first part of May when hungry slabs move into the shallow water around button bushes, fallen trees, stumps and other deep cover in the embayments to spawn. Limit strings of sixty crappie are not uncommon and usually can be taken in from one to three feet of water. Average slab weight will

Opposite page: There are 3300 miles of shoreline in the two impoundments comprising Land Between the Lakes National Recreation Area. There's something for any member of the family, not just the angler. But the best months for bass in either Barkley or Kentucky lakes are late April, May, June, and October and November. Above: Crank baits cast to foliage-hung shoreline and deadfall areas provide top action from them ol' hawg basses!

You won't always come off the water with bonanza catches of crappie like these two smug and happy line-wetters, but April and May fishing trips will increase your chances. That's when fish are really hitting.

The justly famous "Mister Twister" plastic worms take their share of trophy-size bass. But a lifelike presentation and your confidence in the bait make crucial difference.

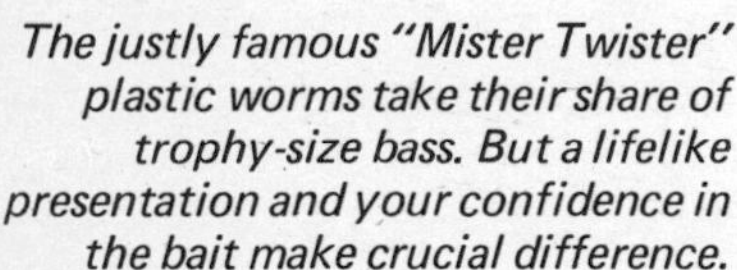

run one to two pounds each.

Some veteran fishermen prefer to fish the deep stumps and brush beds along old creek and river channels where big slabs can be found year-round. Big strings of crappie can be taken in January, February and March at depths from fifteen to twenty feet. Strings ranging from twenty-five to seventy-five fish averaging a pound each are not uncommon during the cooler months. Warm clothing and the touch of a maestro are essential to catch the sluggish crappie during the cooler seasons. Nice size crappie also can be taken off the deep ledges during the hot summer months. Again, patience and a delicate touch are essential for success.

Although crappie riggings vary with the individual fisherman, the favorite rigging around the twin lakes is a cane or fiberglass pole, a double Aberdeen hook rig with a barrel sinker, and shiner minnows – although spin casters using white or yellow jigs of small spinners also take their fair share. Light spin-casting tackle with a small jig is an exciting combination when the crappie are around button bushes and willows.

You don't have to be an expert to take slab crappie on Kentucky or Barkley Lakes! People in western Kentucky are proud of their famous crappie fishing and they will be more than glad to pass along tips, places to fish and local techniques.

Second only to the lakes' famous crappie runs is fishing the jumps for white bass during the summer months. The jumps occur when schools of white bass (stripers) race to the surface to feed on small shad, their favorite food. Best jump conditions occur when the shad reach 1½ to three inches in length and can be seen schooled near the surface on calm days. There's not a scrappier fish in the lake and action is always fast. Stripes often surface for only a minute or two before retreating to the depths for another run to the surface, and those couple of minutes of fishing can provide a thrill of a lifetime.

A fast boat and quick hand on the controls are essential to move with the fish when you see them surface. White or yellow spinners and jigs, bright spoons, white streamers and shad-like artificials are the favorite stripe baits.

You get some perspective of the size of the twin impoundments forming Land Between the Lakes park when you learn that the canal shown connecting the two lakes is 1.6 miles long! Both are man-made lakes and fishing hotspots!

Jump fishing is best in July and continues into the early fall months. Gravel points near the mouths of major embayments and drop-offs around the islands of the main lake are excellent stripe-fishing grounds.

A favorite night-fishing experience can be had during the summer months by shining a lantern light directly over the water, drawing shads and consequently attracting stripes. One of the most popular areas for this peaceful pastime is Eggner's Ferry Bridge area of Kentucky Lake on U.S. Highway 68. On many summer months dozens of boats tie

One of the many campsites in Hillman Ferry Campground on Kentucky Lake. This and others are well-maintained to attract tourists and visitors year after year. There's waterfowling, hiking, bird-watching, swimming...

alongside the bridge abutments and shine lanterns or sealed-beam lights over the water, hoping to attract the stripes.

Rocky points and drop-offs on both lakes also provide ideal night-fishing haunts. Casting and spinning tackle with double-hook line and minnows or small jigs are the standard night-fishing rig. Mayfly hatches also have proven to be excellent bait for stripes.

Big catfish (blue, flathead and channel) are taken year-round below the two huge dams that form Kentucky Lake and Lake Barkley. A variety of game fish including sauger, bass and crappie also congregate below the dams to feed on the bait fish that churn from beneath the giant turbines. From the bank or by boat, it's fishing fun the whole family can enjoy and you never know what your next catch will be.

The sauger, one of the tastiest of all freshwater fish, is especially abundant below Kentucky Dam. A first cousin of the walleye that runs from one to four pounds in size, the sauger thrives on the small shad that congregate below the dam. Some of the best strings of sauger are taken on live shad, but spinners, spoons, and white and yellow jigs also have proved to be acceptable baits. Stripes are best taken on white and yellow jigs below the dams. The numerous slides and fallen stumps on the Tennessee and Cumberland Rivers downstream from the dams provide excellent bass casting opportunities. Jig fish floating produces nice strings of catfish.

Full stringer bring grins to fishermen's faces, and envious green color to onlookers! Knowledge of fish habitat and habits will help you fill your stringer.

One of the most appealing things to many of the sportsmen who fish the twin lakes area is that there are no commercial facilities whatsoever along the east shore of Kentucky Lake or the west shore of Lake Barkley. For a distance of about forty miles Kentucky Lake and Lake Barkley run parallel to each other from six to eight miles apart, creating Land Between The Lakes. TVA is managing Land Between The Lakes for maximum outdoor recreation use including camping, fishing, boating, hunting, hiking and nature study.

Although there are no overnight lodging facilities in Land Between The Lakes, there is a wide variety of vacation accommodations and boat docks along the west shore of Kentucky Lake and east shore of Lake Barkley. There are small and big fishing camps, chain motels, luxurious resorts and state resort parks, lodges and modern family campgrounds.

Most of the embayments on Kentucky Lake and many on Lake Barkley have commercial docks with a full line of boat and motor rentals and fishing tackle available. Lakeside cottages and lodge rooms are available at several locations, and shopping centers and other visitor facilities are nearby. Guide service and lake maps are available at many of the docks along the two lakes and good restaurants are scattered throughout the area.

For additional information write Land Between The Lakes, Tennessee Valley Authority, Golden Pond, Kentucky 42231.

TOP HOT SPOTS FOR THE EIGHTIES

Here's A Current Roundup Of Top Fishing Areas For The Western Hemisphere

COMING UP WITH a Big Ten listing of U.S. freshwater hot spots reflects not only my own experiences, but both Federal and state records, plus carefully kept records amassed by the field representatives who roam far and wide for Evinrude Motors in line of duty. Thus there's a good basis for the choices offered here.

Each year or two, one or another so-called hot spot may cool to a degree, but still represent an area of better-than-average interest to the footloose fisherman. Then, too, almost every year we hear of an impoundment, lake, stream or saltwater area that has blossomed into a fishing Mecca.

For purposes of simplicity, and not necessarily in order of importance, the first group – the Big Ten – are as follows:

Barkley Lake and Kentucky Lake: These two large impoundments parallel each other in the far western portion of Kentucky. Winter or summer, there's a remarkable variety of fighting fish. Springtime marks the beginning of a massive crappie run. Below the Kentucky Dam monster blue catfish are prevalent, with large or smallmouth bass in quantity.

Lake Chautaugua: One of the best muskellunge/pike waters in the nation, the lake covers nearly 13,000 acres in New York's southwest corner near Jamestown. Reports have it that the average take per year is four pounds of muskie per acre.

Lake Erie: Supposedly a dead lake, last year alone over 50,000,000 pounds of walleye were caught. Whether by commercial seine or the rod and reel, there's plenty of large and smallmouth bass, northern pike, white bass, big

Montauk Point, Long Island, New York, is the place to be for stripers, blues and monster sharks. This Zwirz amigo took arm-aching 43-pound striper on plug at night in surf.

Opposite page: Lakes and rivers of Argentina, particularly near Junin de los Andes, hold great trout fishing. Tierra del Fuego is unbeatable for giant sea-run browns like these.

Add the Bahamas to your list of dream spots. It has all of the species you seek, from bonefish to tarpon.

chinook and growing coho salmon – even muskie and rainbow trout. Yellow perch angling is great during the winter.

Lake Michigan: Evinrude's backyard also is the "growingest" sportfishing site in the U.S. Chinook and coho salmon, lake, brown and rainbow trout are the main reasons for Michigan's sudden popularity. Concerted efforts in fish implantment and management by the bordering states have brought new life to an also once-dead lake.

A first-place winner in Field & Stream's *angling contest, this laker set a world record for fly rod that held for more than a year. Zwirz took the lunker at Snowbird Lake, far off in Canada's Northwest Territories. Try your luck!*

Lake Pepin: Actually a bulbous portion of the Mississippi River near Lake City, Minnesota, Lake Pepin offers large and smallmouth bass, muskellunge, walleye, northern pike, white bass, catfish, sturgeon and trout. All types of fishing from fly to plug casting are productive.

Lake Taneycomo: Near the Arkansas/Missouri border in south-central Missouri, this lake offers large and smallmouth bass, white bass and crappie in abundance. Timbered coves and rocky shores make it a productive site.

Pymatuning Reservoir: Over 100,000 acres of terrific bass and muskie fishing is found at Pymatuning, located on the border between northeastern Ohio and northwestern Pennsylvania. Reportedly, summer angling for largemouth bass is good.

Santee-Cooper Reservoir: Large, small and striped or rock bass are abundant. A great all-around water recreational site in South Carolina's southeast, the Santee-Cooper can be productive any time of year.

Toledo Bend Reservoir: Bass fishermen's heaven, the Toledo Bend Reservoir stretches nearly eighty-five miles between the central borders of Texas and Louisiana. It offers the king of fighting freshwater species – the largemouth bass! The reservoir floods over thousands of acres of tall timber, and it is often referred to as the sunken forest. Toledo Bend is the ultimate habitat of old bucketmouth.

Yellowstone Lake: In Wyoming's northwest,

Yellowstone Lake takes up over 100,000 acres of the Yellowstone National Park. It possibly offers the best cutthroat trout fishing in America.

My own all-time favorites include several in the provinces of Canada.

NEW BRUNSWICK

The Restigouche River: One of Canada's top salmon fisheries, it offers 99.4 miles of water. There are private, leased and public sections; a visiting sportsman must be either an invited or paying guest to gain access to the private or leased areas.

Miramichi River: Atlantic salmon.

St. Croix River: With a good population of smallmouth bass, fishing is good all season in the deeper pools and runs, but early summer and early fall are best.

Spednick/Palfrey Lakes: Very good smallmouth bass and landlocked salmon fishing. (Maine/Canada.)

NEWFOUNDLAND/LABRADOR

Conception Bay: With its brackish-water backwaters plus several bays farther north, this area offers a chance to tangle with the sea-run brown trout up to twenty or more pounds.

Pinware River: Pinware Lodge offers excellent Atlantic salmon fishing.

NOVA SCOTIA

More sea-run browns – a really excellent run of them in the Antigonish River. Don't forget giant tuna.

QUEBEC

Labrador Peninsular Area: An extensive area, not overly fished or worked commercially. It promises excellent fishing for a fine variety of game fish.

Mistassini Park: Five hundred miles north of Montreal, the park includes Lake Albanel, Lake Mistassini and the

Zwirz balances adroitly amidships in background while giant tarpon from Nicaragua's famed Rio San Juan does his darnedest to get airborne. Expect more top action from this river that empties into the salty Pacific.

A trophy dorado from deep below the Rio Parana that splits Argentina and Paraguay recalls fond memories for Zwirz.

Rupert and Temiscamie rivers. Top angling for brookies, lake trout, northern pike, walleyes and whitefish. New roads extend one hundred miles north of Chibougamau, opening huge wilderness area. Best time is between June and September.

Lake St. John: Good for big brown trout, the region lies north of Quebec city and is loaded with productive lakes and ponds of all sizes.

La Verendrye Park: Northern pike and walleyes with good trout fishing are immediately nearby.

ONTARIO

Lake Nipigon: Although this general territory receives many sportsmen, it has a sizeable population of lake trout.

Hudson Bay (drainage area): This outstanding water has hardly been touched by fishing pressure due to distance and lack of facilities. It's recommended for experienced canoe campers, who will find northern pike present here in fantastic numbers and size.

Oba River: This country, near the town of Oba in northwestern Ontario, offers top action for northern pike and walleyes.

MANITOBA

Aikens Lake: This water and Lake Sassaginnigak, just to the north, constitute a most beautiful fly-in area offering top trout and walleye fishing.

Cranberry Lake: In Cranberry Portage this lake has excellent fishing for northern pike.

God's Lake: This wilderness region, including God's River to the north, is splendid for trophy brook trout and lake trout.

SASKATCHEWAN

Reindeer Lake (or Cree Lake): Here you will find Arctic grayling and big lake trout in abundance, with magnificent virgin country as a setting.

ALBERTA

Raven River: Containing the Dolly Varden, feeder streams hold both rainbows and whitefish.

Athabasca River: The entire flowage boasts rainbows, grayling and whitefish. This unspoiled area is perfect for experienced backpackers/campers.

You'll find plenty of giant northern pike, walleye and lake trout awaiting your offering in Canada's Ontario province.

BRITISH COLUMBIA

Columbia River System: Cutthroat, rainbows (locally called Kamloops) and Dolly Varden trout abound. The interior areas offer best angling.

Campbell River, Vancouver: For steelhead, salmon.

Glad Zwirz, a private pilot since the early Sixties, prepares tackle and Super Skywagon for a six-passenger fly-in to fish-rich Barkley Lake in state of Kentucky.

NORTHWEST TERRITORIES

Great Bear, Snow Bird Lake: In fly-in areas only, there are excellent lake trout, northern pike, grayling and farther north, Arctic char.

BAJA CALIFORNIA

Out of the town of La Paz, anglers can take their choice of marlin (both striped and black), sailfish, dolphin, chiro (and swordfish at certain times of the year). Bonefish are present in this region for those who can spot likely hot spots.

Lechuguilla Bay (near Las Mochis): This practically virgin bay, coastal and offshore waters are teeming with sea trout, skipjacks, marlin and sailfish.

Mazatlan area: Running southward along this unspoiled coast are great numbers of snook, some close to record sizes. Each lagoon or sheltered cove holds promise of great fishing for the knowledgeable plug caster.

Lake Dominguez (in El Fuerte): Has excellent largemouth bass fishing.

YUCATAN PENINSULA

Campeche and Champaton areas: Wonderful spot for tarpon, sea trout, snook, barracuda and grouper fishing.

BRITISH HONDURAS

Excellent fishing is available in waters off the Truneffe Islands; barracuda are present in great numbers and size.

NICARAGUA

San Juan River: Running south of San Carlos to the sea, this is the author's choice as top light-tackle river in the world for tarpon, snook and freshwater shark fishing.

ARGENTINA

Rio Parana: Separating Argentina from Paraguay, this river is the home of that great fighting fish, the dorado, for top sport!

Chimehuin River or Quilquihue River: Near Junin de Los Andes in the Province of Neuquen, there are mammoth trout; some of the largest brown and rainbow trout caught anywhere in the world are here, willing to do battle.

The Rio Traful: Near Bariloche, it's the top river anywhere for landlocked salmon.

Tierra del Fuego: The Rio Grande cannot be beaten for its population of sea-run brown trout. Size of fish in this land-of-fire is almost unbelievable.

CHILE

Lago Llanquihue (near Puerto Varas): Offers top fishing for landlocked salmon and trout.

VENEZUELA

The area around Caracas is top-drawer for white marlin and other game fish, all within sight of shore and harbor. It is not uncommon for an angler to strike twenty fish in a day.

ALABAMA

Mobile Bay and the Gulf of Mexico, in the Mobile County area, offer tarpon, speckled trout, redfish, sheepshead and bluefish. It is a place made to order for light-tackle fishing in salt, brackish and fresh water. Wheeler Lake and the Tennessee River, in the Decatur region, boast excellent freshwater angling for bass and many other species.

ALASKA

In the southeastern sector of the state, working out of the city of Juneau, there is excellent lake and stream fishing for cutthroat, rainbow and steelhead trout. The better streams and rivers hold great possibilities for the salmon fisherman.

For top grayling and trout fishing, try McKinley National Park. It offers great angling and is classified as under-fished.

ARIZONA

Lake Mead behind Hoover Dam is a watershed nearly 120 miles long; it offers top bass, trout, channel cats and crappie. Lake Mohave is a smaller body of water, formed by Davis Dam; it's almost sixty-five miles long. The same fish are present here as in Mead. All this good fishing is in Mohave County.

ARKANSAS

Lake Conway provides excellent angling. Horseshoe Lake, near Hughes, is producing eight and ten-pound brown trout in addition to record catches of bass and other popular species. The White River has excellent rainbow fishing, larger trout on the average.

CALIFORNIA

The Klamath River, at Regua, furnishes king salmon and steelhead fishing at its best. Try it in late summer or early fall. In the Trinity River, McCloud, and in many nearby

An eye-appealing picture, at both ends of the line! It's difficult to find a bad fishing spot in Florida.

lakes of the region, anglers will find salmon and steelhead. Black bass also are plentiful in the area.

COLORADO

The Rio Grande River offers large trout. I prefer the area near Monte Vista. The entire Gunnison River complex is great. Its tributaries and forks have some of the state's best fishing.

CONNECTICUT

Lake Candlewood, near Danbury, holds good-sized bass, rainbows, browns and white perch. The lake has nearly 106 miles of shoreline and numerous boat liveries. The Housatonic River, in the vicinity of Cornwall Bridge, is well-stocked with rainbows, browns and brookies. Some bass are present. The Farmington River is excellent for trout, while the Niantic area is great for stripers, fluke and flounder. It also is close to the big-game waters where tuna, marlin and swords can be fished.

DELAWARE

Moore's Lake and McCauley's Pond near Frederica, in Kent County, offer above-average freshwater fishing. Griffiths Lake is good for largemouth bass, perch and panfish.

FLORIDA

Shark River is a fine spot for tarpon, snook, snapper and other favorite species; tops for light-tackle casting and trolling.

Ten Thousand Islands and the Gulf area near Monroe County comprise another great stretch of water for snook and tarpon. At Boca Grande, the pass is one of Florida's hotspots for big tarpon; the shallows and beach areas also are great for snook. The Suwannee River is all first-rate bass water and Lake Jackson, at the northern limits of Tallahassee, has been a top bass-producing lake for a number of years.

GEORGIA

The Ogeechee River is a good bet for big bream, black bass and pickerel. Brunswick has good saltwater angling around Sea Island.

HAWAII

Penguin Bank is a shoal area, running heavy with several saltwater species. Several impoundments and estuaries now holding largemouth bass on Maui, Hawaii, Kauai and Oahu.

IDAHO

Lake Pend Orielle is a good choice for bass, trout and big crappie. Bear Lake also has a good supply of bass, and there are rainbow trout in Bear River, near Preston.

ILLINOIS

The Chautaugua Drainage area, in Mason County, boasts a good largemouth bass population, as well as rock bass, crappie and bullheads.

The Illinois River, in the Havana region, plus the lake area, are excellent for big bass. Lake Michigan is excellent for coho and chinook salmon fishing.

INDIANA

Lake Waeasee, in Kasciousko County, provides largemouth bass, pike, rock bass and panfish. Little Elkhart River is good trout fishing.

IOWA

Spirit Lake is the place to go for bass, crappie, pike and bluegills.

KANSAS

Kirwin Reservoir yields bass, walleye, crappie and channel cats. Fall River Reservoir has bass, walleye, white bass and crappie; it's very good.

KENTUCKY

Kentucky Lake, in the Cumberland River area near Eddyville, provides bass and walleye, plus all popular panfish. You'll find very fine angling there. Rough River holds bass, muskie and walleyes.

LOUISIANA

The Lake Charles area offers tarpon, plus deep-sea fishing. The Lake Catherine area, near New Orleans, has a wide variety of fishing, all of it good.

MAINE

Moose River (as well as numerous chains of lakes) near Jackman, is filled with landlocks, togue and trout. This is excellent water.

Spednick Lake is wonderful for smallmouth and landlocked salmon, while Sebago Lake is great for smallmouths, landlocked salmon, white perch and some largemouths. The Dennys, Machias and Marraguagus River have been producing good Atlantic Salmon fishing for the past few years.

Zwirz and his fly rod tame a tarpon that struck a bucktail fly in the Ten Thousand Islands off Florida's West Coast.

Wet and weary author leaves the North Carolina surf after taking this 48-pound channel bass on a bait rig. Hard work!

MARYLAND

Bear Creek or Pine Creek will give you good trout fishing. Severn River is your destination for pickerel and panfish.

MASSACHUSETTS

Deerfield River, near Charlemont, offers good trout fishing, mostly rainbows. Cape Cod's piers, banks and boats are great for weakfish, stripers, cod, blues and small tuna.

MICHIGAN

Black River is a big-fish river, but tough to work. It has rainbows and brookies. The choice is area near Bessemer. Lake Charlevoix is excellent for trout and walleyes.

MINNESOTA

Basswood Lake is great when it comes to walleyes and lake trout.

Rainey River and Lake of the Woods comprise an

excellent fishing area, extending up into Ontario.

MISSISSIPPI

Pass Christian is a fine tarpon spot. Pickwick Dam (TVA) has bass, trout, crappie and panfish.

Bob and Glad Zwirz have been fans of the St. Lawrence River along the New York/Canadian border for a long time, as the truck vintage reveals. They sought bass and big muskies.

MISSOURI

Lake of the Ozarks furnishes bass and other popular species. White River, near Branson, has excellent black bass fishing.

MONTANA

Rock Creek and Rosebud Creek, in the Carbon County area, mean big rainbow water. Madison River, in the Twin Bridges region, is a really great trout hangout. This is one of the author's all-time favorites.

NEBRASKA

Johnson Reservoir holds bass, cats and pike. Blue River, near Seward, has the best catfishing.

NEVADA

Lake Mead is the spot for big largemouth bass. Colorado River, below Boulder Dam, has big water abounding in big trout.

NEW HAMPSHIRE

First and Second Connecticut Lakes, in the Pittsburg region, have fine fishing for landlocks, rainbows, brookies and togue.

Androscoggin River, from Errol to Berlin, is an excellent trout river; this is big water. Lake Winnipesaukee is good for landlocks, smallmouth bass and togue.

NEW JERSEY

From Ocean City to Cape May, there are plenty of surf-stripers, weaks, kingfish, fluke and blues. The

Labrador's famed Pinware River, home to some of the finest Atlantic salmon fishing anywhere, is high on Zwirz' list.

Right: A mess of tuna salad sandwiches goes over the side off the coast of Nova Scotia. You can scale down your expectations somewhat and try for heavy sea-run browns.

The Connecticut River is tops for shad fishing during the too-short time that these silvery-sided fighters make their annual spawning runs. As this angler displays, they can bend your rod in half, especially light ones.

Musconetecong River is strictly a stocked-fishing proposition for trout, but it's very well managed.

NEW MEXICO

Alamogordo Lake features bass, crappie and bream. Elephant Butte Lake has bass, crappie and big cats. A good bet!

NEW YORK

The West Branch of Ausable River is a very good trout stretch and the Salmon River, near the town of Malone, has excellent brown trout. Chautaugua Lake, near Jamestown, is very good for muskie, with Montauk Point, Long Island, offering stripers, blues, tuna, etc.

NORTH CAROLINA

Elk River supplies rainbows, browns and smallmouth bass; this is an excellent area; Lake Hiwassee is good for smallmouth bass. Hatteras has lots of channel bass. This state abounds with excellent saltwater fishes.

NORTH DAKOTA

Heart River gives you pike, channel cats and walleyes. Heart Butte Reservoir, near Elgin area, is abundant in walleyes, black bass, crappies, channel cats and pike. Snake Creek Reservoir holds bass and pike.

OHIO

Piedmont Lake is good for largemouth bass and panfish. Will Creek Reservoir yields muskie and walleyes.

OKLAHOMA

Lake Texoma is a great freshwater area for all popular species. Wichita Mountain Wildlife Refuge includes numerous lakes where bass, channel cats and crappie are found.

OREGON

The Columbia River area has salmon and stripers. Deschutes River provides plenty of trout.

PENNSYLVANIA

Spring Creek in Centre County delivers big rainbows, browns and brookies; Lake Wallenpaupek has bass, walleyes and panfish.

Lake Erie, mouths of tributary streams, and Walnut Creek, Godfrey Run, Trout Run, Elk Creek, west of Erie, all are hot spots for coho, chinook salmon. Sixteen-Mile Creek, Twelve-Mile Creek, and Six-Mile, east of the city.

RHODE ISLAND

Warren River has great fly fishing waters for stripers,

while Bowdish Reservoir, near Glouchester, boasts big bass, pickerel and panfish.

SOUTH CAROLINA

Santee-Cooper Reservoir has both black bass and landlocked striped bass fishing. It's excellent! Edisto River is fine for black bass and panfish.

SOUTH DAKOTA

Andes has bass and walleyes. Redfield Lake has bass, crappie and perch.

The Yucatan Peninsula of Mexico is a hot spot for snook, tarpon, sea trout, barracuda and grouper. Zwirz here keeps a close eye on his rod tip while a snook tries to get away.

TENNESSEE

Norris Reservoir is tops for largemouth bass, walleyes, sauger and smallmouths, while Pickwick Lake holds bass, bluegills, crappie and panfish. Dale Hollow Reservoir has both largemouth and smallmouth bass, walleyes, sauger, cats and crappie. Great!

After ferocious fight, six-foot four-inch Zwirz bested this world record Argentine dorado that was almost the same size! It was taken on bait-casting rig with spoon, wire leader.

TEXAS

Medina Lake takes first place for bass, bream, cats and crappie. Sabine Lake gives you tarpon fishing, plus many other popular inshore saltwater species. Big Cypress Bayou is filled with bass, crappie, bream and cats.

UTAH

Tamarac Lake holds native trout. Strawberry Reservoir features both rainbows and cutthroats. Fish Lake, near Richfield, has good trout.

VERMONT

Lake Memphremagog is the state's best bet for landlocks, togue, brown trout and black bass. Willoughby Lake is good when it comes to trout and landlocks.

VIRGINIA

Moorman's River has rainbow and brook trout. Chickahominy River furnishes good largemouth bass fishing, plus pickerel and striped bass.

WASHINGTON

Lake Chelan is tops for trout fishing. In Olympic National Park, both lakes and streams are tops for fine trout fishing.

WEST VIRGINIA

The South Branch of Potomac River, near Momney, is good for smallmouth bass. Shavers Fork River has good rainbow and brookie waters. The whole area is fine.

WISCONSIN

Lake Owen has plenty of bass and pike. The Manitowish Flowage lakes hold muskie.

WYOMING

North Platte River holds brown and rainbow trout. The Jackson area is great for trout fishing.

GLOSSARY OF FISHING TERMS

ALGAE: Simple plants, most of which live submerged in water.

ANADROMOUS: Refers to fish which spend part of their lives in salt and part in fresh water.

ANCHOR: A weight or hook used to hold a boat in a fixed position when not under way.

ANNEAL: The subjection of metal to intense heat and gradual cooling, in order to increase the strength and reduce its brittleness.

ANTI-REVERSE: A mechanism which allows line to be pulled from a reel while the handle remains set.

AQUATIC INSECTS: The mayflies, stone flies and caddis flies, to name a few. They are hatched in water, leave to mate – then return and deposit eggs. A cycle.

ARTIFACTS: Utensils used by early civilizations, relics.

AUTOMATICS: Reels that utilize a wind-up spring which in turn can be released to take up the fly line.

AWL: A long, needle-shaped instrument.

BACKLASH: A tangle of line caused by overrunning of the reel spool.

BAILER: A utensil for removing water from a boat manually.

BAIT-CASTING: A term used to describe the casting of plugs or lures which imitate baitfish.

BAIT-FISHING: Fishing with bait such as worms, minnows.

BALANCED TACKLE: Tackle that when carefully selected and correctly balanced will perform correctly, i.e., correct relationship between rod, reel and line.

BARBEL: Whisker-like feelers about the heads of some fish.

BARBULES: Tiny barbs which hold the rays of a feather together.

BASS-BUGGING ROD: A fairly stout fly rod of more than usual power to turn over the larger bass-bugs and poppers that are commonly used.

BILGE: The area along the keel inside a boat.

BILGE PUMP: A pump for removing water from the hull of a boat.

BILLFISH: An ocean fish having a long pointed bill.

BOAT NET: A landing net with a long handle for use from small boat or canoe.

BOBBER: A float tied to the line to keep the weighted bait at the correct water depth.

BRACKISH WATER: Fresh water that is mixed with salt water. Where a river joins a bay or ocean.

BUGGING TAPER: A fly line that has a short, heavy section in the forward area to turn over large bass-bugs during the cast.

BUNKER: Menhaden.

CABIN CRUISER: A large powerboat with living facilities for the occupants.

CARRYING RACK: A rack for carrying small boats on an automobile top.

CAUDAL PEDUNCLE: Body of a fish in front of the caudal fin.

CHARTER BOATS: Large, yacht-size boats available for private, day or longer charter fishing.

CHEAP TACKLE: Low-priced junk not worth buying.

CHENILLE: Fluffy, silky material used for bodies of flies.

CHINE STRIPS: Strips of wood at the base of the sides of a flat-bottomed boat to lend rigidity to the structure.

CHLOROPHYLL: The green coloring matter of plants.

CHUB: A baitfish.

CHUM LINES: A slick on the water caused by the dumping of ground-up fish. It is used to attract many school fish in salt water.

CLASPERS: Appendages on ventral side used to join fish during mating act, peculiar to sharks.

CLICK: The sound of the drag mechanism on reels to control line outgo.

CLINKER-BUILT: See Lapstrake.

CLOVE HITCH: A knot made by making two half-hitches around a post, useful for mooring boats.

COMBING: An upright, water-tight rail around a boat's cockpit to prevent spray from washing aboard.

CORK ARBOR: A cork filler to increase the diameter of reel spool.

CRANE FLY: An aquatic insect.

CRAYFISH: A crustacean resembling a small lobster.

CREEL: A willow basket or canvas bag that holds the caught fish.

CRUSTACEANS: Animals with hard exoskeletons.

CUTTYHUNK: Linen line.

DACE: A baitfish.

DEADFALLS: Spots that contain sunken trees, branches and the like. An excellent hideaway for fish.

DIATOMS: Any of a class of microscopic algae.

DINGHY: Usually a short, broad-beamed, round-bottomed boat of light construction, used as a tender on yachts.

DORSAL FIN: The top fin on the back of the fish.

DORY: A rowboat with a high prow, flaring sides and narrow bottom used chiefly for commercial fishing.

DOWNRIGGERS: A device that allows for the fishing of great depths while the unit boasts a quick release system of line and lure when fish strikes.

DRAG (or CLICK): Controls the tension under which a line goes off the reel.

DROP LINE: A handline used without a rod for still fishing.

DROP-OFF AREAS: Where the water suddenly goes from shallow to quite deep. A fast downhill plunge of the shoreline. Fish often lie off these spots and wait for baitfish to show.

DRY FLY: An artificial lure designed to imitate a floating insect.

DUGOUT: A canoe constructed from a single log.

EAGLE CLAW: A type of hook developed by Wright and McGill in which the point bends back toward the shank.

EELSKIN: The skin of an eel used for bait.

EPILIMNION: A thermal stratum in lakes above the thermocline.

FEATHERING: In rowing, bringing the blades of the oars back so that they are parallel with the surface of the water.

FEATHER JIG: A lure used in salt water having a metal head and a body of feathers to imitate a baitfish.
FEMALE FERRULE: The socket part of a ferrule.
FERRULE: A friction joint in a rod to permit it to be disassembled for transportation or storage.
FISHERMAN-SPORTSMAN: A fisherman is a man who fishes to catch fish. A sportsman is a man who fishes for the sport of fishing.
FISH LADDERS: Structures to permit fish to climb over or around dams.
FLASHER: A flashing spoon tied above the bait to attract fish to it.
FLIES, ARTIFICIAL: Those made to represent insects and baitfish on which the gamefish feed.
FLOAT FISHING: Angling while drifting down a stream.
FLUKE: The point of an anchor.
FULCRUM: The point around which a lever turns.
FUSIFORM FISH: A round-bodied fish, tapering toward the ends.

GALLEY: A boat's kitchen.
GAMEFISH: Designated fish species known for their fighting qualities and also those under conservation law protection.
GANG HOOKS: Fish hooks fastened together in series so that they are effective from all directions.
GEAR/TACKLE: Fishing equipment and accessories.
GILLS: Organs by which animals can breathe in water.
GORGE: A sliver of wood, metal or bone hung by its center on a line, forerunner of the fish hook.
GRAPNEL: A hook-shaped anchor with four or more tines.
GUIDES: Eyelets through which line is strung along a rod.
GUNWALE: The upper edge of a boat's side, or a wooden strip used to reinforce the upper side of a boat.

HABITAT: The environment in which fish find conditions satisfactory for existence.
HACKLE: A feather from the back or neck of a cock fowl. Used to simulate legs on flies for fishing.
HELLGRAMMITE: Larva of the dobsonfly.
HERL: Single ray of a feather, used in fly tying.
HORSE (...a fish): To pull in the fish by sheer strength.
HUSHPUPPIES: A Southern dish consisting of batter with chopped onions, dropped in balls in hot deep fat.
HYPOLIMNION: A thermal stratum in lakes below the thermocline.

I.G.F.A.: International Game Fish Association.
IMPOUNDMENT: An artificial body of water.

JIG: An artificial bait for casting or trolling.
JOHN BOAT: A flat-bottomed, square-bowed boat developed for river fishing in the Ozarks.
JOLLY BOAT: A medium-sized boat used for rough work from a sailing vessel.
JUG FISHING: Fishing by tying baited lines to jugs which are allowed to drift on the surface as floats.

KEELSON: A strip of wood fastened along the keel inside a boat.
KEELSTRIP: A plank fastened along the line of the keel in a flat-bottomed boat as reinforcement and protection.
KAYAK: A long, low, canoe-type, one-man boat with a full deck, developed by the Eskimos.

LAMINATED ROD: A rod built by cementing several strips of wood together with the grain parallel.
LAPSTRAKE: A type of construction in which the upper plank overlaps a portion of the lower plank, like clapboards on a house.
LARVA: The early stage through which certain insects pass, usually referring to those that effect a complete change of habits and food in adult life.
LEA: A measure of linen line, usually 300 yards.
LEADER: A strand of gut or nylon used between bait and line to minimize visibility. Also a strand of wire used to prevent fish with sharp teeth from cutting the line.
LEVEL-WIND MECHANISM: The mechanism which winds the line on the reel spool evenly without the aid of the guiding fingers of your hand.
LONGBOAT: A large boat carried by a merchant vessel.
LONG-ROD: Another name for the fly rod.
LUNATE TAIL: Moon-shaped tail.
LURE: A decoy or bait for fish.

MALE FERRULE: The insert part of a ferrule.
MEMBRANE: A thin sheet of tissue separating or supporting living organs.
MILT: In fish, the fluid bearing the sperm of the male.
MONOFILAMENT: Single-strand line.
MOSSBUNKER: A small, oily, saltwater baitfish often used in chum.
MOTHER NATURE: The guiding force and knowledge of creation.
MUMMIES: Mummichogs, saltwater baitfish.

NODE: A leaf scar or joint on a bamboo cane.
NON-MULTIPLYING REEL: Single-action; that is, one revolution of the spool to one of the handle.
NYMPHS: Any of certain insects in immature form.

OARS: Paddle-shaped levers for propelling a rowboat.
OFFSET HANDLE: A rod handle with the reel set offset for better positioning and ease in fishing.
OMNIVOROUS: Having a universal diet.
OUTRIGGER: Long pole used in trolling for big gamefish to carry the line to one side of the boat.

PALMER-TIED: A fly tying technique where the hackle extends the length of the body.
PANFISH: A small fish which is more fun eating than catching.
PARR: A young salmon.
PARTY BOATS: Very large boats, accommodating from twelve to near a hundred anglers in some cases.
PIROGUE: A small dugout canoe developed for swamp and marsh travel in Louisiana.
PLANKED: To cook and serve on a board.
PLANKTON: Minute plants and animals which live in the surface layers of salt or fresh water.
PLEISTOCENE: The epoch or age which followed the Tertiary Age; it preceded the present age.
PLUGS: Wooden or plastic lures designed in different shapes, colors and sizes.
POACH: (1) To fish on private property without the owner's permission. To fish illegally. (2) To cook in boiling water.
PORTAGE: Carrying of a boat or canoe and its duffel by hand, over or around a barrier in the water route.
PRACTICE PLUG: A rubber plug, similar in size and design to a fishing plug without hooks, for practice casting.
PRAM: In the United States, usually a short boat with a square bow used as a tender for a larger boat.
PREDACIOUS: Killing other animals for food.

PULPIT: A protective railing around the bowsprit of a boat or a platform at the bow from which fish may be harpooned.

PUNT: A flat-bottomed boat with square bow and stern built for use in rivers.

QUADRATE: Pertaining to a bony element on each side of the skull of a fish to which the lower jaw is jointed.

QUENELLE: A fish ball, fish chopped fine and highly seasoned.

RIFFLE: A slight disturbance in the surface current of a stream caused by a subsurface obstruction.

RIG: Equipment.

ROILED (water): Muddied or disturbed waters.

ROWLOCKS or OARLOCKS: Accessories fixed on the gunwale of a boat to serve as the fulcrum for an oar and to hold the oar in place.

SAUTE: Fry quickly in hot fat.

SCHOOLS (of fish): Concentrations of fish of the same species.

SCHUSSES: Runs down rapids in a canoe.

SCUTE: Extremely bony or horny plate on a fish.

SEA SKIFF: A rowboat with a narrow, flat bottom, high prow and flaring sides.

SEINES: Nets.

SERRATED: Saw-toothed.

SHINERS: Minnows, baitfish.

SHOAL: A shallow area.

SILT: A fine, earthy sediment carried and deposited by water.

SILURIAN AGE: Pertaining to that part of the Paleozoic period, marked by coral-reef building and the appearance of the great crustaceans.

SINGLE-ACTION REEL: Non-multiplying.

SINKER: Weight for taking bait to deeper water.

SKEG: A small V-shaped strip fixed toward the stern of a rowboat to serve in place of a keel.

SKIFF: A small or medium-size rowboat.

SKITTERING: To draw the hook through or along the surface of the water with a quivering motion.

SNAGLINE: A line fitted with hooks for snagging fish.

SNAP SWIVEL: A swivel with a snap attached to it for attaching leaders, additional terminal tackle or lures.

SOLUNAR: A word coined by John Alden Knight to indicate his theory that living creatures have a tendency to become active during certain periods influenced by the sun and the moon.

SPAWN: The eggs of fish, oysters or other aquatic animals.

SPERRLING: A small saltwater baitfish.

SPINNER: An artificial lure, the blade of which whirls continuously in a circular fashion around the axis of the line of traction.

SPLINE: A thin wooden strip.

SPONSON: A built-in flotation chamber along the gunwales of a canoe.

SPRAY RAILS: Strips along the side of a boat hull to repel spray.

STAR DRAG: A star-shaped adjustment on a reel to increase or decrease the rate at which fish may strip the line.

STEELYARD: A weighing device in which the fish is suspended from the shorter arm of a lever and its weight found by moving a counterweight along the longer arm.

STILL FISHING: Fishing without moving, generally from an anchored boat on a lake or quiet stream. The bait is cast and allowed to stay there awaiting the fish.

STINK BAIT: A malodorous bait formed usually of overripe cheese, chicken viscera and slaughterhouse wastes; used for catfishing.

STONE FLY: An aquatic insect.

STRIKING: A definite or quick tightening of the line in order to sink the barb of the hook into the mouth of the fish.

STRIP LINE: Draw line from the reel for casting (fly-fishing only).

STRIP PLANKED: A type of boat construction in which bottom and side planks are joined together smoothly and tightly. Patented joints usually are used and are sealed with marine glue.

TAGGING: Marking fish by affixing tags to them.

TAPERED LEADERS: Almost transparent leaders attached to the line and the end lure that taper from thick to thin in order to make the cast balance out in the air and float down on the water with a minimum of disturbance (fly-fishing only).

TAPERED LINES: Lines tapered from thick to thin to balance the line in the air for best casting (fly-fishing only).

TERMINAL TACKLE: That which is attached to the end of the line: leaders, spreaders, sinkers, hooks, bobbers, lures.

THERMOCLINE: A thermal stratum in a lake in which temperatures are static.

THOLE PINS: Hardwood pegs used in place of rowlocks.

THROW LINE: A line cast by hand for fishing without a rod.

THUMBING THE REEL: Controlling the outgo of the line by pressing on the spool during the cast (bait-casting only).

THWART: Cross bracing between the gunwales of a boat; the seats in a rowboat.

TIPPET: That section of the leader, nearest the fly, that is normally subject to greatest wear.

TRAILER: A wheeled vehicle towed behind an automobile for transporting boats or dunnage.

TRANSOM: The board forming the end of a square-sterned boat.

TRASH FISH: Fish which have neither game nor high food value.

TROLLING: Fishing by trailing bait and line behind a moving boat.

TROLLING PLATE: Plate fixed to an outboard motor to decrease its speed for trolling.

TROTLINE: Line, stretched across a stream or between buoys, having many baited hooks.

TUMP LINE: A band of soft leather about 2½ inches by eighteen inches to the ends of which are secured leather thongs or ropes about nine feet long; used in portaging.

ULTRA-LIGHT TACKLE: The lightest and sportiest tackle practical for the fishing conditions and fish species.

WET FLY: An artificial lure tied to imitate a drowned insect or the larva of an aquatic insect.

WHALE BOAT: A round-bottomed, double-ended boat developed by the whalers of the Nineteenth Century for harpooning whales.

WOBBLER SPOON: An artificial lure attached to the leader at one end causing it to whip and wobble from side to side as it is drawn through the water.

X DESIGNATION: The diameter and pound test of leader material and monofilament lines for spinning and bait-casting.